My Yesterday,
Your Tomorrow

Also by Lord Boothby

THE NEW ECONOMY
I FIGHT TO LIVE

*The frontispiece portrait of Lord Boothby is by
R. H. Westwater, A.R.S.A., R.P.*

Boothby

LORD BOOTHBY

K.B.E., LL.D.

My Yesterday,
Your Tomorrow

HUTCHINSON OF LONDON

HUTCHINSON & CO. (*Publishers*) LTD
178–202 Great Portland Street, London, W.1

London Melbourne Sydney
Auckland Bombay Toronto
Johannesburg New York

First published 1962

*This book has been set in Bembo type face. It has
been printed in Great Britain by Richard Clay and
Company, Ltd., Bungay, Suffolk, on Antique Wove
paper and bound by them*

To
the students of the
University of St. Andrews

Contents

PART III

The Art of Economics

PART IV

Personal Recollections

Acknowledgements

I am grateful to the Editors of the *Sunday Times*, the *Daily Mail*, the *New Statesman*, the *Spectator*, the *News of the World*, *Punch* and *High Fidelity*, for permission to make free use of material which I have contributed to their columns in recent years; and to Mr. Elkan Allen for suggesting the title of this book.

I am also grateful to Columbia University, New York, and to the Radner Fund, for permission to publish the Radner Lectures; and to the Master of St. Salvator's College, St. Andrews, for permission to reproduce the portrait of myself painted by Mr. R. H. Westwater, A.R.S.A., R.P.

Introduction

WHEN I sat down to write this book I thought it might be a continuation of the first, and autobiographical, part of *I Fight to Live*, which was published in 1947. I soon discovered that this was impossible. Since the war my life has been lived in the full glare of publicity—as a Member of Parliament, as a working journalist, and under the arc lamps of television. In a sense I have had no private life at all. I have, therefore, linked what I hope is an objective consideration of the events which have interested me most, and of the men who played a leading part in them, with the thread of my personal experience in Parliament and the Council of Europe. At least I have had a front seat in the stalls; and the themes I have selected have been chosen with an eye not only on the past but on the future.

Robin Day once asked me, on television, how I accounted for my failure in politics. It has not, I think, been total. But there is a two-fold explanation of the reason why I have never held, or been offered, high office.

The first is that I am what would have been described in the closing years of the last century as a Tory-democrat, and in the opening years of the present century as a Radical. Lord Randolph Churchill and Mr. Lloyd George remain the only political leaders of recent times to whom I could have given unstinted and unswerving support. Unfortunately, I never had the chance to do so. In the early 'twenties it seemed that there might be a revival of genuine Tory-democracy, under the leadership of Stanley Baldwin; and I believe that this is what he himself desired. There was, however, a fatal snag. He never gave the leadership that was required. Since 1930 the Radical has found no place in our public life. But in the long run his views must prevail, because the answer to our problems does not lie in the barren and obsolete dogmas of socialism or of *laissez-faire*.

The second explanation is that I have a pathological and therefore irrational hatred of power, and those who wield it. Some years ago Iain Macleod said to me that I could have had political power if I had been prepared to make the necessary personal sacrifices. This may, or may not, be true—I am by nature, self-indulgent; and power is a goddess who admits no rival in her loves. The fact remains that I have never wanted it, still less the patronage that goes with it. It cannot be wholly fortuitous that my friendship with David Lloyd George began after he had fallen from supreme power; and that my friendship with Winston Churchill ended when he finally achieved it. I count myself lucky to have enjoyed, at one period or another, the friendship of both; for we shall not see their like again.

I am a firm believer in the value of the printed word as it was written or spoken *at the time*. Subsequent events may well detract from its prophetic insight; but it retains a freshness and an impact which can only be blunted by tinkering, however strong the temptation to do so may be. In the political and economic essays which follow, whether taken from lectures, articles or speeches, I have therefore adopted the method used by Lord Keynes in what I regard as his literary masterpiece, *Essays in Persuasion*. This is to omit freely (without special indications in the text) anything which appears to be redundant or unnecessary to the main line of the argument, to be repetitive, or to have lost interest with the passage of time, and to make certain additions for the purpose of clarification; but to alter nothing in the sense of the text that has been retained.

I have included the speeches on economic policy because the subject interests me enormously, and because it affects every one of us more intimately than any other. The pages of *Hansard* during the decade before the last war are bespattered with my protests against monetary deflation, and my pleas for greater capital expenditure on housing, slum clearance, road transport and electricity. Here the continued plea for economic growth and expansion assumes a rather different form: but is, in essence, the same.

I recommend the reader to have a dab at it. Economics was described by the late Lord Birkenhead as a dismal science. In fact it is not a science at all. The great creative economists such as Ricardo, Malthus, Jevons and Keynes, reached the pinnacles of their achievement by means of intuitive genius—in Keynes's own words by spilling their ideas in the form of ephemeral pamphlets, flung to the wind. This is what has made the study of economics so fascinating to me; and I hope that I have managed to convey something of my own interest to others.

To these I have added a few personal pen-portraits outside the field of politics. It has been my good fortune to know, and to know well, some of the leading creative figures of the first half of this century, not in politics alone, but in the literary, musical and theatrical worlds; to have travelled much; and to have touched life at a good many points. H. G. Wells, Arnold Bennett and Compton Mackenzie—still one of my oldest and closest friends—were all extraordinarily good to me when I was a young man. For seven years before the last war I lived in Kent next door to Sir Philip Sassoon, through whom I came to know Shaw and T. E. Lawrence; and Noël Coward, then at the zenith of his remarkable career, lived not more than three miles away.

I have decided to confine myself to brief personal sketches of Churchill, Somerset Maugham and Thomas Beecham, only because I feel that I have a fractional contribution to make of my own. Arnold Bennett, for example, was one of the nicest men I have ever met; and—apart from the management of his domestic affairs—one of the wisest. His concern for my figure, when I began to grow fat, was genuine and great; and one of my most treasured possessions is a book of extraordinary physical jerks, in which he daily indulged, inscribed: 'For Robert Boothby, happily still M.P., from A.B.' But there is really nothing to add to Frank Swinnerton's biography, and to the brilliant *vignette* recently published by Lord Beaverbrook.

Tolerance is the key-note of this book. I have therefore begun it with my Rectorial Address at St. Andrews, and ended with the man who, with Charles James Fox, is perhaps the greatest example of that virtue—Robert Burns.

As Rector of the University of St. Andrews I stood in a line which includes Froude, J. S. Mill, Rosebery, Balfour, Carnegie, Marconi, Haig, Smuts, Nansen, Kipling and Barrie; and to which there is, I think, no parallel in this country. I am not naturally modest, but I know when I'm out of my class! In the circumstances, I have had no option but to follow the example of my predecessors, and of my successor Sir Charles Snow, and publish my Rectorial Address 'neat'.

At the time it caused a bit of an uproar, and was followed by a torrential correspondence in the *Scotsman*. The manses were ablaze, but I had my defenders, and much enjoyed an anonymous post-card from Argyllshire, written in red ink: 'With your love of the flesh-pots, and evident fear of death, you are easy meat for the Roman Catholic Church. I advise you to apply to Rome without delay. They will see you through—for a consideration.' Scotland alone could have produced this.

My plea was for toleration in the widest sense of the term, my protest against dogmatism in any shape or form. That is my faith, by which I stand or fall. The religious wars of the sixteenth and seventeenth centuries, accompanied as they were by secession, destruction, murder, hatred, and almost everything that Jesus condemned and denounced, brought European civilization to the brink of destruction. Their counterpart, the 'ideological' wars of the twentieth century, now threaten the human race with the possibility, if not the probability, of extermination.

I believe myself that the gross misrepresentation which followed my Rectorial Address was caused not by my enjoinder to make the most of life and enjoy it—Barrie himself, in his much lauded Address, had urged the students to be 'not merely courageous, but light-hearted and gay'—but by the criticism I felt impelled to make of the conduct of the Reformation in Scotland, and particularly in St. Andrews. On this I remain utterly unrepentant. Knox was as absolutist, as dogmatic, as brutal and as treacherous as any medieval Pope, or any modern Dictator who has held—as he deemed—the actual verity and secret of the world. And, as Andrew Lang said, in his *History of St. Andrews*, the Cathedral fell with dishonour, and the end came with disgrace. 'It is a fact not sufficiently noted,' writes a chronicler of the times, 'that the period of the Reformation was coincident with the practical extinction of Scotland as an independent nation. All the leading Reformers were venal pensioners of England.'

I feel I owe an apology to my readers for the repeated references to my native land. As Marguerite Steen says of Ellen Terry, in the Preface to *A Pride of Terrys*, I did not wish Scotland to be the heroine of this book; but she proved as irrepressible in history as she has been in my life. Hume, Burns and Stevenson have exercised a dominant influence over me—there is an affinity between them that is essentially Scottish; and to them, and the late Professor Macneile Dixon, I am primarily indebted for the combination of scepticism, tolerance and invincible optimism which is the basis of my philosophy.

Boothby

PART I

The Profession of Politics

TOLERANCE

*The Rectorial Address, delivered at St. Andrews
University, on April 17, 1959*

To be the Rector of the University of St. Andrews is an honour beyond my wildest dreams, and one which I do not deserve. I am not by nature modest or retiring—I am what the psychologists call an 'extrovert', for which small mercy I can only thank Heaven as I face the most formidable ordeal of my life. But I have, I think, a certain sense of proportion. And I know very well that, in the tremendous line in which I now stand, I am out of my class.

Casting around, in some agony of mind, for a subject on which I could presume to address you, I asked my television sparring-partner A. J. P. Taylor, whose academic qualifications to advise me on the matter are beyond dispute, if he had any suggestions to make. 'Barrie did Courage', he replied, 'and did it very well. Why not try Cowardice?' I must confess that, at this moment, it seems to me a most appropriate theme, and I almost wish I had chosen it. I would at least have spoken from the heart. But in the end I decided in favour of Tolerance, for two reasons. First, because I believe that lack of tolerance is the root cause of the troubles which beset the world today—the main reason why our civilization hovers uneasily on the brink of destruction. And second, because I believe it is the only virtue to which I can lay any claim.

Let me begin, therefore, by asking for tolerance from you for myself for a brief period; and by suggesting that I may deserve it not only because of the long association of my family with St.

Andrews, but because I have a personal and emotional link with the most famous Rectorial Address that has been heard in St. Andrews. Barrie would not forgive me if I made no mention of the name of Michael Llewelyn Davies, although he could not bring himself to do it. Michael was one of five small orphan boys, grandsons of George du Maurier, whom he made his wards and brought up; and his beloved son. He was one of my closest friends at Oxford. And it was his tragic death—he was accidentally drowned on a summer afternoon—that drove that strange and wistful little genius whom Barrie called his 'unruly half', M'Connachie, to the peak of his achievement. The fires of a grief to which I know no parallel scorched the dross away, and left us with a message of rare quality that has not yet run its course. And Michael, the student for whom, if the seekers had been kind, the flags of his college would one day have flown, remains 'the lad that will never be old'.

What, then, are the attributes of tolerance? Courage, of course. As Barrie truly said, 'All goes if courage goes'; and Dr. Johnson, 'Unless a man has that virtue he has no security for preserving any other'. Next, compassion. By this I do not mean sloppy sentimentality. I mean the genuine urge to diminish the sum of human suffering, and to help those whose heads are 'bloody and bowed' —Barrie's own transcription of Henley's line—under the bludge-onings of chance. The kind of compassion that has been defined for all time in Lincoln's immortal phrase: 'With malice towards none; with charity for all.' It is rarer than you think.

Next comprehension, which involves not only an understanding of the problems and difficulties of others, but a continuous search for objective truth. And, finally, a sense of humour.

Before I come to deal with these, you will perhaps expect me to touch on the application of tolerance to the political struggle for power that is now taking place in the world. This is, fundamentally, a struggle for the minds of men; and we are in constant danger of losing it because of our failure to grasp that fact. We could indeed defeat the Russians in arms and still lose the world to Communism—if we had not brought it to an abrupt conclusion. The basic strength of the western world lies in individual

freedom, which includes freedom to think, and to propound conclusions and advocate policies arrived at as a result of thought. In
other words, to chase ideas wherever they may lead us. Communism denies this right. It is rooted in an intolerance which is
wholly out of touch with political realities. 'You talk about Marxism and objectivity' says Zhivago: 'I don't know of any teaching
more self-centred and farther from the facts than Marxism ... I
don't like people who are indifferent to the truth.'

Not only the political and economic analysis, but the revolutionary tactics of Marx, who was, despite the massive range of his
intellect, one of the most intolerant men who ever lived, were
based upon the first phase of capitalist accumulation; and those of
Lenin upon the last phase of western colonialism. Today the Communists are everywhere exploiting the reactionary and atavistic
demands of virulent nationalism, which has become an intrinsic
part of the dialectic, for propaganda purposes. In a world crying
out for organic international union, they stand inflexibly for State
sovereignty and power. All these things are out of date; and two
of them have already passed into history. The real danger of Communism, as Barbara Ward has recently pointed out in a brilliant
essay, lies in the widening gap between ideology and fact.

Yet on this point I do not want to be dogmatic, or too pessimistic. I haven't the same sick certainty in the pit of my stomach
as I had in the 1930's that there is going to be another world war.
Many years before the discovery of the atom bomb Freud wrote,
'The fateful question of the human species seems to me to be
whether and to what extent the cultural process developed in it
will succeed in mastering the derangement of communal life
caused by the human instinct of aggression and self-destruction.
In this connection, perhaps, the phase through which we are at the
moment passing deserves special interest. Men have brought their
powers of subduing the forces of nature to such a pitch that by
using them they could very easily exterminate one another to the
last man. They know this—hence arises a great part of their current unrest, their dejection, their mood of apprehension. And now
it may be expected that the other of the two "heavenly forces",
eternal Eros, will put forth his strength so as to maintain himself

alongside his equally immortal adversary.' Freud was no optimist; and the fact that he took the view that, confronted by the stark choice between aggression and annihilation, humanity would probably opt for survival, is itself encouraging.

Let us remember, too, that in human affairs there is perpetual motion. Nothing is fixed or final. As Burns said, 'life is all a variorum.' It seemed in the Middle Ages that Europe must be overwhelmed by the rising tide of Islam in its early militant phase; and in the seventeenth century that she must be torn to pieces by religious strife. In the event, changes which none had deliberately wrought brought solutions that none had foreseen. Similarly today the flood tide of militant Communism has reached the heart of Europe, and laps against us in Asia, the Middle East and Africa. One day the tide will ebb. Meanwhile the answer surely lies in strength, patience and unity of purpose on the part of the western world, accompanied by a tolerant attitude towards everything except violence and cruelty. Despotism, after all, is no new thing; and, as Barbara Ward has pointed out, Khrushchev's recital of Stalin's iniquities was only one more dreary record of the despot's cruelties and crimes. In attempting to combine collective security and economic planning with social justice and personal liberty under the rule of law, the social democrats—in the widest sense of that term—are the real revolutionaries of the twentieth century; and tolerance is, in the long run, the most powerful weapon in their arsenal.

It is time to quit the stage of world politics, and have a look at ourselves. In any consideration of the attributes of tolerance, how do we fare? To courage we can certainly lay claim, unless an invincible reluctance to face unpalatable facts until they are rammed down our throats is held against us. It has proved to be a source of strength in moments of desperate danger; so I think that, on balance, we pass this test.

Compassion? It marches hand in hand with moderation. And here, with an appalling lapse, the Scottish record is not too bad. The lapse, I need hardly remind you, was the Reformation, as it took place in this land and in this town. It brought the Renaissance to an end; and plunged Scotland into a long dark night, from which she was ultimately rescued by Robert Burns. Tolerance disappeared. How could it survive among those who saw life as a narrow path through the fires of hell? And with the disappearance of tolerance came, as was inevitable, the resurgence of dogma and its inseparable companions persecution, cruelty and tyranny.

From this you may deduce that I am not a Knox man. I confess it. And hasten to add that I am not referring to the Principal! The Puritans of those days seem to me to be almost indistinguishable from the Communists of our own, and to have done just about as much harm to the world. If I said what I really thought about them, it would make you sit up. I dare not. John Knox was 'sancti Andreae diocesis authoritate apostolica notarius'; and there is no ghost by which I would be more unwillingly haunted. I therefore take refuge in the quiet irrefutable verdict of John Buchan: 'The Puritan became, by his severe abstraction, a dangerous element in society and the State, since human institutions are built upon compromises. He was pre-eminently a destructive force, for he was without historical sense, and sought less to erect and unite than to pull down and separate.'

You may well ask if there was any alternative, for the abuses inherent in the Roman Catholic Church at the time of the Reformation are not to be denied. There was. It lay in a wise and gentle scholar, who did much of his work in my old College at Oxford, and was tutor to Archbishop Stewart, whom we shall meet, I hope, in the Kate Kennedy procession. If Erasmus, the greatest Christian apostle of toleration and humanism, had been listened to, and had prevailed, we should be living in an easier world today. A world in which the fires of destructive nationalism would long since have been quenched; in which Europe would be united; and in which this ancient Burgh of St. Andrews, instead of being a beautiful ruin, would still be standing in all its medieval splendour.

'There are many kinds of genius', Erasmus wrote in his preface to Hilary: 'each age has its different gifts. Let every man contribute what he can. To the ancients reverence is due, yet they are to be read with discretion. The moderns have a right to fair play. Read them without prejudice, but not without discrimination. In any case let us avoid heated contention, the bane of peace and concord.' Here speaks the authentic voice of the Renaissance. The voice of one whose primary concern was to vindicate the right of every individual to be true to himself; and to help him to develop his own personality by the widest possible dissemination of the civilizing influence of scholarship and knowledge.

With the name of Erasmus I must couple that of his friend Sir Thomas More, the only man who has ever sat in judgment and himself been judged in Westminster Hall; and the only Member of Parliament to be canonized. Gairdner has described him as a true saint, without a touch of austerity save that which he practised on himself in secret, living in the world as one who understood it perfectly, with a breadth of view and an innate cheerfulness which no external terrors could depress. 'His learning was without pedantry, even as his humour was without gall. He loved men, he loved animals, he loved mechanism, and every influence that tended to humanize or advance society.' Is it to be wondered at that the Emperor Charles V declared that he would rather lose the best city in his dominions than such a counsellor?

Moderation is not a thing to be ashamed of. Nor need it be half-hearted. As Buchan wrote of Montrose: 'There is a moderation which is in itself a fire, where enthusiasm burns as fiercely for the whole truth as it commonly does for half-truths, where toleration becomes not a policy but an act of religion.... The moderate man can never become a barren dogmatist.' The practical result of moderation is compromise, which should not be confused with what came to be known, in the dreadful years before the last war, as appeasement. I shall have a word to say about slogans before I sit down; but I often wonder how much harm is done by the auto-intoxication of mere words. In Cyprus, for example, what has been the cost, in terms of human blood, of the words Never, Enosis and Partition? Yet the solution we have reached is a compromise which includes none of them; and for the achievement of which Lord Radcliffe, so happily with us today, deserves much of the credit. Similarly I wonder into how great danger the words Disengagement, Rigidity, Flexibility, Reunification and Confederation are now going to drag us. They can mean anything or nothing; but are all too apt to become symbols around which forces of irrational intransigence gather.

I turn now to comprehension with which, as you may remember, I combined the search for objective truth. It was Whitehead who said that intolerance was the besetting sin of moral fervour. So it is. It is the messianic obsession implicit in Mr. Dulles's dictum that 'our nation was founded by those who felt it their personal mission to help change the world' that causes me most anxiety about American foreign policy. And it applies also to this country. There was a leading article in *The Times* recently which described sin as a transgression against 'morality'; and went on to say that society should not be asked to give its reasons for refusing to tolerate what, in its heart, it feels intolerable. But that is just what society must be made to do. To condemn a belief, or a way of life, as immoral and therefore intolerable, without giving any reasons, is intolerant. To enforce that intolerance in the law courts is tyrannical.

In some respects the English have been, and still are, more intolerant than the Scots; or perhaps I should say narrower in outlook. I am in a good position to judge, because I am myself a mongrel. In so far as their Empire has declined—it has not yet fallen—it is partly due to their failure in personal relationships. In other words, to lack of comprehension. The loss of the American colonies, of Ireland, and of much else, was to a large extent brought about by this intolerance—the 'holier-than-thou' attitude, with its conviction of superior personal rectitude and morality, and a consequent passion not only for governing other people, but imposing upon them alien political systems, and reforming them out of existence, or at least out of the existence they prefer.

It was redeemed, for a time, by the emergence of the radicals at the end of the eighteenth century, under the glowing leadership and inspiration of that tremendous figure Charles James Fox. Here was a man after my own heart, who could lose £16,000 one night, speak in the House of Commons on the Thirty-Nine Articles the following day, sit up drinking for the rest of that night at White's, and win £6,000 before leaving for Newmarket;

and who fiercely resented any interference with his private life. I do not ask you to take him as a model. You will pay too heavy a price if you do. But I would remind you that this was also the man described by Gibbon as 'perfectly exempt from any taint of malevolence' and by Creevey as 'all fire and simplicity and sweet temper', who fought throughout his life for toleration and Catholic emancipation, and abolished the slave trade. We have not since known his equal.

After that came the great era of the English Eccentrics, who inadvertently created Empires in the teeth of Governments, because they understood those with whom they were dealing. The tradition lingered on until the outbreak of the first world war. Then it was snuffed out; and the Civil Service, with its tennis and bridge clubs from which the 'natives' were rigidly excluded, finally came into its own. Gone are the days when the late Aubrey Herbert, half blind and wholly eccentric, could come to Parliament escorted by two Albanian retainers armed with daggers. Eccentricity is no longer tolerated, and even unorthodoxy is frowned upon. I have seen it drained from the House of Commons in my lifetime.

We are all conformists now—or try to be. Why? Can it be that, by methods more subtle than those employed by the Communists, our minds are being conditioned by external forces of which we are scarcely conscious? I have had some experience of television; and I must admit that, from this point of view, it frightens me. The verdict on the United States of one with far greater knowledge than my own has frightened me still more. 'This nation', said Edward Murrow the other day, 'is in competition with malignant forces of evil whose every instrument is being used to empty the minds of their subjects, and then to fill those minds with slogans.' Behind the cameras lurks a new horror—the public relations man, whose sole object is to dilute truth with propaganda. An eminent American professor told me recently that their presidential elections are now conducted almost exclusively by these publicity 'experts' in Madison Avenue; and expert they are, in distorting facts and darkening counsel. For a while the propaganda merchants may well take an objective, if cynical, view of their sales talk; but in the end they come to believe it. The lie on the lips then becomes the lie in the soul.

I am persuaded that this manipulative control over the minds of millions accompanied, as it must be, by the gradual suppression of intellectual independence, is one of the gravest dangers now confronting us; and I am fortified in this conviction by the opinion of one of the most distinguished of my predecessors. Smuts said, in his Rectorial Address to this university, that the disappearance of the sturdy, independent-minded, freedom-loving individual, and his replacement by a servile standardized mass-mentality was the greatest human menace of our time. It could easily put the survival of democracy, as we know it, in jeopardy. I confess that I have no ready-made solution to offer; but I hazard the suggestion that, in this field, competition is less dangerous than monopoly.

There remains humour; and on this subject a few words will suffice. Without a sense of humour we can have no sense of proportion. It is the fourth dimension, from which alone we can contemplate the universe with total objectivity; and, in the words of Somerset Maugham, it is man's only retort to the tragic absurdity of Fate. The Devil himself can't stand up against it. He throve in the sulphurous atmosphere of Geneva (Knox's 'perfect city of Christ'), and in Scotland, when everything except money-making and church-going was forbidden. But as soon as Burns designated him old Hornie, Cloots and Nickie-ben, casually suggested that he might himself repent of his own misdeeds, and finally sent him away with the exciseman, he shrank from the lightning challenge of the poet's hilarity. A humorous outlook on life is the greatest gift the gods have to offer. It is the one infallible solvent of mental tension; and, in the present struggle for the souls of mankind, it operates on our side. Lord Brabazon is a living exemplar of its power for good.

To sum up. Tolerance is not a negative quality. It is the antithesis of dogmatism and fanaticism; and, it seems to me, an essential condition of all that is valuable in human life, without which any real comprehension of nature or of mankind is impossible. Do not let us pitch our claims too high. 'Man is not born to solve the problems of the universe', said Goethe, 'but to find out where the problems apply, and then to restrain himself within the limits of the comprehensible. His faculties are not sufficient to measure the actions of the universe; and an attempt to explain the outer world by reason is, with his narrow view, vain. The reason of man and the reason of the Deity are two very different things.' The purpose of the universe, if there be one, we cannot tell. The purpose of life, as I conceive it, is simply the enjoyment of it. And too few people are permitted to do that. I do not always, or indeed often, agree with Richard Crossman. In his book *The Charm of Politics* he refers to 'that astonishing amalgam of high principle in general and scepticism in particular; of obedience to authority and personal initiative; of shrewd practical conclusions buttressed with shaky metaphysics, which is the essence of the British philosophical tradition.' The Principal and the Master of St. Salvator's, not to mention Sir Maurice Bowra, to whom we have just done well-deserved honour, may have mental reservations about this. But from his conclusion there can, I think, be no dissent. 'There is no better contribution which the British universities and churches could make to this world of conflicting dogma and intolerant power politics than to revive the tradition of toleration and devotion to the pursuit of human happiness, which is Britain's unique contribution to western civilization.' If you ask me what constitutes happiness, I cannot tell you. You must find that out for yourselves.

Why can't we accept life as the process of Becoming, which most assuredly it is; admit that we know nothing of its origin or purpose; and find our own solutions by giving free rein to the creative impulse, or will-to-live, which is its essence? I believe that it is the mystical, artistic, creative intelligence of the individual that alone can make more of the experience of human life than a mere sequence of events; and at this very moment there has come, from the other side of the Iron Curtain, as remarkable an affirmation of the value of the individual, in and against history, as any that we have ourselves produced. 'When I hear people speak of reshaping life it makes me lose my self-control, and I fall into despair. Reshaping life! People who say that, they have never understood a thing about life—they have never felt its breath, its heart—however much they have seen or done. They look on it as a lump of raw material which needs to be processed by them, to be ennobled by their touch. But life is never a material, a substance to be moulded. If you want to know, life is the principle of self-renewal, it is constantly renewing and remaking and changing and transfiguring itself, it is infinitely beyond your or my theories about it.' If Boris Pasternak can write this out of the depths of his experience over the past forty years, then things are on the move in Russia—as indeed one would expect them to be—and there is more reason for hope than for despair.

My advice to you today, for what it is worth, is to make the most of life. It won't last long. As Robert Louis Stevenson said, we sail in leaky bottoms on great and perilous waters, we have heard the mermaidens singing, and know that we shall never see dry land again. 'Old and young, we are all on our last cruise. If there is a fill of tobacco among the crew, for God's sake pass it round, and let us have a pipe before we go!' Therefore I say to you, enjoy yourselves, and be gay. By so doing you will obey the will-to-live, and fulfil the only divine orders we know of. Beware of those who talk of salvation rather than happiness. What kind of a God is he that creates a world from which we have to be saved? Above all, beware of those who spend their time nosing out the alleged sins of other people, in order to punish them. They are mad, bad and dangerous to know.

This does not mean that you should confuse tolerance with licence. In a remarkable speech last week Lord Templewood reminded us that the advent of the Welfare State, coming rapidly after the tremendous revolutions of two world wars, and accompanied by the most incredible inventions and discoveries of science, has swept the world off its feet. The old landmarks have gone; the old conventions have been abolished; and the general impression has grown up that there are no particular rules in the game of life. It can hardly be doubted that this is one of the causes of the wave of criminal violence by which we are now beset.

I have already said that compassion is an integral part of toleration; and between compassion and cruelty there can be no compromise. The only answer to the nihilism which, in the wake of nuclear physics, threatens the world is a revived belief in individual creation. 'Nothing is great,' said Disraeli, 'but the personal.' When all is said and done, one over-riding fact emerges in life from a welter of fantasy, mirage and illusion—the existence of individual human personality, which is diverse and complicated and inconsistent; but of absorbing interest and paramount importance.

I thank you for your patience and your kindness. If this address has done no more than kindle your interest in the human situation, and induce you to give some thought to it, it will have served its purpose. In conclusion I turn, as I so often do, to the Gifford lectures of the late Professor Macneile Dixon. For I agree with him that the most astonishing thing about the human being is the range of his vision; his gaze into the infinite distance; his lonely passion for ideas and ideals for which he will endure suffering, privation and death, in the profound conviction that, if nothing is worth dying for, nothing is worth living for.

'The inner truth is that every man is himself a creator, by birth and nature, an artist, an architect and fashioner of worlds. If this be madness—and if the universe be the machine some think it, a very ecstasy of madness it most manifestly is—none the less it is the lunacy in which consists the romance of life, in which lies our chief glory and our only hope.'

THE BRITISH PARLIAMENT

*The first Radner Lecture, delivered at Columbia
University, New York, on November 28, 1960*

How can I follow President Truman's brilliant performance last year with any hope of success? It is an impossible
task. Why, then, have I chosen to attempt it? Why have
I accepted your most flattering invitation? I will give you the
answer in a single word—vanity. It has always been my besetting
sin; and on several occasions has led me into situations of personal
disaster. I have a notion that this may be the most disastrous
of all.

The lectures I am about to deliver fall naturally into the two
parts suggested by their title. Clearly Parliament is going to be the
duller of the two. And yet I feel that it is the more important. If
you want to understand the British Parliament, you must know
something about its history, its development, and the ideas and
ideals by which it is animated. It is, I fear, unavoidable. I am reminded of a concert which I once attended, conducted by Sir
Thomas Beecham. The first, and the longer, part was devoted
to the works of Richard Wagner. At the end of it, as was his
custom, he addressed the audience. 'This,' he said, 'has been
pretty heavy slogging. A bit Germanic. Now we'll have some
lollipops.'

I wish to give you fair warning that tonight's lecture is
going to be pretty heavy slogging. And, if any of you can't
take it, and decide to leave, I shall be the last to complain.
To those who do, I would say: 'Don't despair. Come
back. Tomorrow you shall have some lollipops.' So now to

work. The sooner we get down to it, the sooner it will be over.

Britain has never had a written constitution. Our parliamentary democracy has developed, from precedent to precedent, by means of what the lawyers call Case Law. Such pronouncements as have been recorded, from Magna Carta to the Statute of Westminster, have been *declaratory*; and bear the character of milestones on the road that our constitutional life has gone, rather than direction posts for the future.

The British Constitution, if such it can be called, has followed the laws of its own growth rather than any preconceived intellectual plan. This is what makes it at once the toughest and most elastic in the world. Instead of working to a set of political rules, we have complied with a code of political ethics based on two fundamental principles. These are the supremacy of the Common Law, and of the central Government. The first dates from Saxon times; and has survived—except in Scotland—the influence of Roman Law. The second was imposed by William the Conqueror, who laid the foundations of a strong centralized government which had no parallel in medieval Europe, and continues to this day.

As L. S. Amery pointed out in his *Thoughts on the Constitution*, the key to our constitutional evolution is to be found in the inter-action between the Crown, as the central governing initiating element in the national life; and the nation in its various estates, as the guardian of its written and unwritten laws and customs. From this continuous 'parley' between the central Government and the nation, all our existing political institutions, including Parliament and the Privy Council, have sprung. It is possible to trace the development of the Privy Council, which still formally transacts a great deal of public business in the presence of the Sovereign, from the small and highly centralized body which governed England a thousand years ago; and the evolution of Parliament from the need of the Crown to obtain not only the finance but the assent of the nation, through its representatives, in order to carry on government.

When King John attempted to exercise tyrannical powers, the Parliament of the day, consisting of barons and other notables, presented him with an ultimatum at Runnymede, which he accepted.

The Tudors, who governed strongly, were careful not to do it in the teeth of Parliament. When Charles I proclaimed and practised the Divine Right of Kings, Parliament fought him and killed him. When Cromwell's puritan fanaticism resulted in a dictatorship, in the name of democracy, the restoration immediately and inevitably followed; because fanatical beliefs of any kind produce despotic absolutism, and render democratic institutions impotent.

The political ferment in England during the half century between 1610 and 1660 is, indeed, without parallel in history. Every conceivable theory of government, from Platonism to a kind of embryonic Marxism, was canvassed, debated and fought over.

The result was the political settlement of 1688—a classic example of the English love of, and genius for, compromise. Under this arrangement the basic relationship between Crown, Church and Parliament was firmly established; but on conditions which allowed for the continuous adaptation which has taken place ever since. For us civil wars—unless you count the pathetic attempts at rebellion of the Stuart Pretenders—were a thing of the past.

The appearance upon the scene of George I, who could not speak a word of English, gave rise to the system of Cabinet government which gradually strengthened the power of the administration, not only against the Monarchy but against Parliament itself. But the party system, as we know it today, did not begin to emerge until the end of the eighteenth century.

Walpole's Parliament was predominantly a Parliament of place-men. In his monumental work *The Structure of Politics at the Accession of George III*, which has revolutionized historical method, the late Professor Sir Lewis Namier—who was, incidentally, my tutor at Oxford, and but for whom I should have acquired neither knowledge of what I am now talking about nor a degree—drew from a mass of detailed evidence the undeniable conclusion that the politicians of those days were more interested in offices (and the perks that went with them) than principles; that the King himself exercised a greater influence over policy than we had been led by previous historians to suppose; and that the inter-action of personal relationships and intrigues was what then made Parliament tick.

At that time there was, I regret to say, an ancestress of mine, a certain Mrs. Boothby, who was most importunate in seeking a job for her son. Namier showed me one of her letters, in high delight. It indicated, in no uncertain terms that if the son was given the job he would do whatever might be required by his particular benefactor, and vote as he was told. I asked him to suppress it, for the sake of the family reputation. But he printed it, as a footnote.

Mind you, the basic relationship between Crown, Church and Parliament had, as I have already said, been established by the Act of Settlement. If that had been seriously challenged there would have been fierce resistance, based on principle, to the point—if necessary—of renewed civil war. But it was never seriously challenged.

The challenge to the British parliamentary oligarchy of the eighteenth century came from abroad. From the revolt of the American colonists, and the doctrines enunciated by Jean Jacques Rousseau, which culminated in the French Revolution.

It is no part of my duty or business tonight to comment on the Declaration of Independence. I will therefore content myself by saying that I share the views of all the most enlightened British statesmen at the time—that you were right, and we were wrong.

But the challenge of revolutionary totalitarianism is of immediate relevance and importance because, when it was originally made by Rousseau, it was met and defeated by the counter-revolution of the Founding Fathers in the United States, and the radical conservatives, headed by Burke, in England. And we are still fighting it, side by side, at this very moment, in its twentieth century form.

In a book called *The Future of Industrial Man*, Dr. Peter Drucker made a penetrating analysis of this challenge, which has had such a profound effect upon the constitutional development both of the United States and of the United Kingdom; and I shall be heavily in his debt during the next passage of this Address. He pointed out that there never was any pretence that Rousseau's 'General will' was rationally ascertainable or realizable. It was an 'irrational absolute', which enabled him to throw overboard the rationalism of the Enlightenment, while retaining a belief in human perfectibility, and thus to deny human freedom, and light the fuse of a revolutionary totalitarian blaze which continues to this day.

Similarly, in the nineteenth century, Marx threw overboard the rationalism of the Liberals, and proclaimed instead another 'irrational absolute'—the determination of all human action by the class situation of the individual.

From Rousseau and Marx, the theorists, to Robespierre and Lenin, the men of action, who discovered that totalitarian theory could only be translated into action by the exercise of absolute despotic power, was a logical historical process. The challenge of totalitarianism was met in the eighteenth century, and can be met again in the twentieth, only if its intellectual basis is understood and attacked: the belief in man-made absolute reason, the belief that a select élite possesses it, and the conviction that whoever is the possessor of absolute reason has the right and duty to enforce it.

Absolutism is the eternal enemy. We have, therefore, to reassert our disbelief in human omniscience; to accept the fact of human imperfection; and to deny the justification or the right to inflict one iota of additional or avoidable suffering upon humanity in the cause of any creed or dogma.

I am not concerned tonight to dwell on the differences between the Founding Fathers and the British political thinkers of the eighteenth century—the substitution in the United States of the individual citizen for an evolving constitutional monarchy as the initiator of the political process; and the written constitution, with its lack of flexibility, and somewhat artificial distinction between executive and legislative functions which are necessarily interdependent.

I am primarily concerned with the basic principles on which they were agreed. For it is these great men—Jefferson, Madison, Burke, Hamilton, and I must add Charles James Fox—who gave us the system of democracy, and therefore the freedom, which we now enjoy.

They were in agreement about the supremacy of the Rule of Law, and the independence of the judicial function. They were in agreement about the supremacy throughout the whole country of the central Government, for which principle Lincoln was subsequently prepared to fight a civil war. They were in agreement that any monist basis of power must become absolute. And, finally, they were agreed in principle about the method of checks and balances which should be used to develop a free and functioning society, and prevent abuses.

Restoration was never their intention. Traditions and precedents were ruthlessly discarded when they no longer worked. Dogmatism was eschewed. The existing political and social reality, rather than a theoretically ideal society, was taken as the basis for political action. Religious Man, Economic Man and Intellectual Man were rejected because they were based on the doctrine of determinism which, in itself, denied the possibility of achieving the ultimate objective of their political faith—Free Man. Hence they became, in a very real sense, conservatives of the present and future, rather than of the past.

Now let us see how this worked out in Britain during the nineteenth century.

The Reform Act of 1832 has been followed by successive extensions of the franchise. When the House of Lords ceased to represent territorial and ecclesiastical estates of the realm of sufficient magnitude and importance to justify its existence as a separate, independent and powerful Chamber, capable of challenging the Commons on the annual Budget, its powers were reduced by the Parliament Act of 1911. And the recent establishment of Life Peerages has now tilted it in a new direction, which could transform its constitution within a few decades, and make of it a Senate which will embody not only the experience of the British nation, but exemplify some of its most typical characteristics—independence, tolerance, and dislike of fanaticism in any form.

During the reign of Queen Victoria the governing authority of the Crown, in theory still enormous, fell gradually into the hands of the Prime Minister of the day. Now the transfer is complete.

Theoretically the Queen can still choose her own Prime Minister, and grant or refuse a dissolution of Parliament at his request. In practice she does not do so. Her sole remaining political function is to warn, to encourage and to advise her Ministers; and to confer certain honours. But this is more important than many people realize.

Meanwhile control over the Executive by Parliament in the fields of expenditure and administration has steadily diminished. Today—and this may startle you—the Prime Minister wields greater executive power within the United Kingdom than the President within the United States; and the power of the Congress is greater than that of the House of Commons.

The point I want to make is that none of these revolutionary changes was written into a formal constitution. Indeed it is hard to find a single reference to the Prime Minister or the Cabinet in any statute, although they constitute the Government of the country.

Now I must make it clear that, in Britain, Parliament does not govern, or attempt to do so. The Administration does that, under the symbolic authority of the Crown, and subject to the support of a majority in Parliament. Thus the balance between government initiative and parliamentary control is struck although, under the pressure of events, the scales are becoming too heavily weighted in favour of the Executive.

It would be quite wrong for you to regard political power in Britain as a delegation from the individual citizen through the legislature to an Executive dependent on that legislature. On the contrary, it is established constitutional doctrine, authoritatively laid down by Burke, and generally accepted since his time, that a Member of Parliament is not a delegate. He is the representative of his constituency as a whole; and votes, or should vote, in accordance with the dictates of his own convictions. Sometimes his obligations to his party, or to the Government of the day, or to both, clash with those of his conscience, giving rise to interna conflict. It has happened to me on four occasions—over Munich, over the crisis which resulted in the fall of the Chamberlain Government, over the payment of members, and over the Suez crisis; and on two of them, Munich and Suez, I had difficult meetings with my party Association in my own constituency, with which I will be dealing tomorrow night.

All I want to emphasize now is that the primary task of Parliament is to secure full discussion and ventilation of grievances and of other matters, legislative or administrative, as a condition of giving its assent to Bills or its support to Ministers; and that the House of Commons remains the ultimate repository of political power in Britain not because it legislates or governs, but because it can sustain or dismiss governments on behalf of the nation as a whole. As L. S. Amery truly said, the combination of responsible leadership by government with responsible criticism in Parliament is the essence of our unwritten constitution. The system can best be described as democracy by consent—government of the people, for the people, with the people, but not by the people. Leadership thus becomes not the enemy of self-government, but the means by which it can be made to work.

I must now make a passing reference to the constitutional development of the British Empire, which has proceeded on parallel lines.

The Balfour Committee which drafted the Report upon which the Statute of Westminster was subsequently based was of the opinion that nothing would be gained by a written constitution for the British Empire. Federalism was rejected. Voluntary co-operation was preferred. The position of the self-governing Dominions was defined as follows: 'They are autonomous communities within the British Empire, equal in status, in no way subordinate to each other in any aspect of their domestic or external affairs, although united by a common allegiance to the Crown, and freely associated as members of the British Commonwealth of Nations.'

Since then there have been further developments. The word Empire has, by tacit consent, been displaced by the resounding title of Commonwealth, which goes back to a period long before the Lord Protector. The right of secession has been recognized. And republican forms of government have been established within the Commonwealth.

Grave difficulties still confront us in parts of the African continent. But it now looks as if the transformation of a great Empire into an association of free and independent multi-racial states is going successfully to be accomplished. It will be the first time in history that this has happened.

This 'system to have no system' is almost incomprehensible to any logical Latin mind. Nevertheless, as one shrewd continental observer remarked, it worked so well in 1940 that the Commonwealth, which to the Roman-minded appeared to be little more than a Victorian myth, saved mankind. True, the Dominions were then faced with the dilemma that they must either confirm a policy which they had had only a partial share in framing, or break up the Commonwealth; and that this dilemma still potentially exists. In the event they chose the former, conforming to the British pragmatic tradition; and, if more adequate consultative machinery can be devised, the probability is that, in similar circumstances, they will choose it again.

Sir Winston Churchill well summarized the British attitude when he told the Council of Europe, in 1950, that they were not making a machine but growing a living plant. This conception of constitutional growth is basic in Anglo-Saxon thought, which has its origins in ancient Greece. But Sir Winston's continental audience, apart from the Scandinavians, would have none of it.

They wanted to 'make' Europe, not to grow it; and to their eyes this involved a written 'supra-national' constitution, with an elected European Parliament, which would delegate power to an International Executive dependent upon it.

To the British this meant nothing but a paper Europe, destined to fall to pieces at the first impact of reality. For them the European plant had scarcely begun to grow; and they were reluctant even to give it a name until they found out first whether it could be grown at all, and then what kind of a plant it turned out to be.

I have been associated with the European Movement since its inception; and, if you want to know the reason why the objective of a united Europe has not yet been achieved, here it is.

The conflict between Anglo-Saxon and Roman thought is deep. British pragmatism is derived from ancient Greece—from Democritus and Aristotle. The Romans feared the future, and sought always to provide against it. The Aristotelian pursued the inductive method, and reached his conclusions by the observation of phenomena. He was composed in the face of new discoveries, and never afraid to change his mind in the light of them. The question he asked was not, 'What is true?' but, 'What will work?' Reaffirming the doctrine of Heraclitus that 'all flows away, nothing will stay', the Athenians feared theoretical systems which might bind them to a future which they regarded as unknown and unpredictable; and therefore rejected Plato's ideal, and totalitarian, Republic.

In order to comprehend the mysteries of British parliamentary democracy you have to realize that, whereas the French approach to politics is rational and juridical, and the German authoritarian, the British approach is always empirical and practical.

We have solved our political crises by talking them over, drinking them over, sleeping them over, and finally calling them off. And we put nothing down on paper, if we can possibly avoid it. The Germans have solved theirs by hurling political power into the hands of a leader. And the French have solved theirs by going to a tennis-court, not (as we should) to play tennis, but to draft a written constitution that doesn't work. This lack of unity of thought and purpose is one of the reasons why the West has at present no convincing democratic answer to the Communist challenge; and has achieved no political unity worthy of the name. But I detect a gleam of hope. General de Gaulle is not an easy man to deal with. He has, however, devised a political system which confides effective executive power to the Government, under the authority of the President, subject to the right of the French nation to express its 'sovereign decision' in elections—the moment of truth in any democracy.

This pattern may be reproduced in other European countries;

and can ultimately be reconciled with both the British and American systems, of which it is a blend.

General de Gaulle has further put forward the idea of an 'imposing confederation' of nations which would retain rather than submerge their own national characteristics. And this may yet prove to be the starting point, in Western Europe and in the North Atlantic Treaty Organization, for the regional groups of freely consentient nations which I believe to be an essential preliminary stage in the process of evolution towards some kind of world order. Call them United States, Confederations, Commonwealths—what you will. They should be something less than a single federal sovereign State with a written 'supra-national' constitution; and something much more than a League of independent sovereign States.

We have covered a lot of ground, and I thank you for your indulgence. The British parliamentary system is not an easy thing to comprehend. It is the product of centuries of growth; and it is based on a homogeneous society, and a sense of political responsibility on the part of Government, Opposition and electorate. It seemed to me essential that, before I came to recount my personal experience of it during the past thirty-five years, you should get the general hang of it. And I only hope that I have succeeded in giving you that.

Let me say this, in conclusion. It is not suitable for general export; and I think we have made a grave mistake in attempting, as we have done, to impose it in its entirety upon communities in which conditions are wholly different, and the paramount need for strong and stable government is not sufficiently recognized.

A few years ago I was a member of a small British parliamentary delegation which visited Malaya, Singapore, Borneo, Hong Kong and Ceylon. As we moved from one legislative council or assembly to another, and watched the Speaker in his grey wig, the clerks, the mace, the copy of Erskine May's Rules of Procedure upon the table, and members of the Opposition moving amendments and putting questions to Ministers who asked for further notice—in short, the whole British works—I could not help feeling a trifle uneasy; and, at one point, I was impelled to seize one of my parliamentary colleagues by the shoulder, and say, in all too audible tones, 'I hope to God we're right!'

It is easy and justifiable to criticize Dr. Nkrumah for authoritarianism. But the transition from tribal rule to full parliamentary democracy cannot be achieved overnight; and I think that in failing to have worked out alternative systems which could be adapted to conditions differing so greatly from our own, and at the same time preserve the basic character of our constitution, we shall be found blameworthy before history.

Don't forget that the Communists are offering to vast territories, and millions of people in Asia and in Africa who are impoverished and highly discontented with their lot, dictatorships using technicians; and that in countries which are under-developed, illiterate, and which possess only a handful of fully educated men and trained civil servants, their methods are much easier to apply than those of parliamentary democracy and the free enterprise system. Choices such as those between Senator Kennedy and Mr. Nixon, or between General Motors and Ford, or between United Steel and Bethlehem, are at present too complicated for the natives of darkest Africa.

With the best will in the world I cannot recommend any slavish imitation of British institutions which have been built on a long tradition. What I can and do recommend is that countries which have decided to come down on the democratic side of the fence should take a good hard look at the balance between the initiative exercised by the Government and the control exercised by Parliament which we have succeeded in establishing; and then find the methods best suited to themselves of reconciling the necessity for strong and stable government with popular consent.

The need to accept strong leadership as an essential and organic part of the democratic process is vital. As Alexander Hamilton wrote, the way to preserve freedom is not to enfeeble the Executive but to strengthen the residual power of the people against it.

What is the alternative? A hopeless diffusion of decision and purpose, followed by dictatorship flowing into power like air into a vacuum. It is failure to come to terms with the problem of leadership that has forced the French Republic, in Raymond Aron's words, 'to have recourse, from time to time, to saviours.' And this, of course, applies with redoubled force to Germany.

The dynamics of effective democratic leadership, as we have seen during this century in the cases of Theodore and Franklin Roosevelt, Wilson, Asquith, Lloyd George and Churchill, lie not in the manipulation, still less the forcible seizure of political power; but in effective persuasion.

Finally, I would commend to your earnest attention the philosophy of democratic empiricism, which is the product of the great truths of eighteenth century rationalism and nineteenth century liberalism; and upon which, with few lapses, our system of parliamentary government has been nurtured and is now firmly based. Dogma breeds authoritarianism, intolerance, persecution and terror; and the vehement opposition of Hume, Locke and Burke to dogmatism, which has now become an intrinsic part of our political life, is Britain's greatest contribution to the democratic faith we share.

Well, there you are. The foundation has been laid, and I feel as if I were covered in cement. I hope you don't feel the same.

Tomorrow night I will try to tell you something of the events and personalities I have seen, against the background of Parliament. I shall indicate certain dangers which, it seems to me, confront our parliamentary system and the profession of politics in Britain; and suggest certain reforms which I think ought now to be carried out. This will be much more fun for all of us.

POLITICIANS IN ACTION

*The second Radner Lecture, delivered at Columbia
University, New York, on November 29, 1960*

I DON'T know why I went into politics so young. From an
early age I was interested in public affairs. And I always liked
the sound of my own voice. I think, perhaps, that the decisive
factor was my father. He was a very gifted man. Prominent and
popular in what seemed to me the bleak worlds of insurance and
banking; a fine shot; a natural golfer, born and bred in the classic
school of St. Andrews of whose Royal and Ancient Club he became Captain; and a writer and composer of songs, one of which
has already found its way into our Scottish folklore. He was the
happy possessor of infinite charm, and a great sense of humour.
For years he tried in vain to let me better him at some sport, or
beat him at some game. I therefore began to look for some
field in which his effortless superiority would be less apparent.
And, inevitably, chose politics, in which he took no interest
whatsoever.

I got off to a quick start. My maiden speech was not very good,
but a lot of people said it was. It was about economics. And it
must have sounded clever, because I read it the other day and
couldn't understand a word of it. Then, when I was twenty-six,
Churchill appointed me his Parliamentary Private Secretary. No
wonder I got swelled head. Only one voice was raised against
this—that of Sir Oswald Mosley, then the rising star of the Labour
Party. 'He will demand,' he said, 'a personal allegiance which you
are incapable of giving; and, when you try to break away, as you
will, he will regard it as disloyalty. Keep your independence.' This

at least I managed to do, mainly by taking to heart a wise maxim
of the late Sir Alfred Hopkinson:

'I would give a word of advice to all Members entering the
House of Commons, and that is—never hope to get on. Never
have a career. If you do, you will always be miserable. The only
way to have a happy life in the House of Commons is to have no
ambition for office whatever; then you are not torn by jealousy as
other people get office, and can keep a single-minded desire to
serve your constituents.'

It is difficult, now, to recapture what I may call the spirit of the
'twenties. When I went up to Oxford in 1919 we had emerged
victorious from the war that was to end all wars. We were still a
Great Power. Our Prime Minister, Lloyd George, dominated the
continent of Europe. For the majority, this was a period of tremendous psychological and emotional release. All dogma was
suspect, and all inhibitions discouraged. You could go where you
liked, say what you liked, and do pretty well anything you liked,
without fear of public opinion or censure. Self-realization was the
avowed aim. We thought that personal relationships and personal
enjoyment—in a word, ourselves—were more important than
anything else; and this was largely due to an underlying sense of
personal security. Every morning I used to say to myself, while
shaving: '*Make the most of this enjoyment. It can't last.*' It didn't. But,
in that fleeting moment, and for the last time, we held in our
hands a future that looked assured, and really good. So good, indeed, that we were mildly scandalized by Churchill's evident
desire to strangle Communism at birth, when it would have been
easy to do so. To us, the Russian revolution was simply another
interesting experiment in human relationships. We were anxious
to see how it worked out in practice.

Looking back, the fall of Lloyd George, which took place just
before I entered the House of Commons, was the central political
event of the 'twenties. Churchill has described him as the greatest
mover of men and of events whom he has encountered in politics.

His resignation deprived Great Britain of one of the most formidable instruments of government we have ever possessed; and it is
interesting, at this distance of time, to recall its immediate cause.
The Irish settlement, although accepted as inevitable, had aroused
deep resentment in an influential section of the Tory Party. But
the political crisis which led to the fateful vote at the Carlton Club
in the autumn of 1922 arose directly from the decision of the British Cabinet to resist the invasion of Europe by Mustapha Kemal's
triumphant army, fresh from its victory over the Greeks in Asia
Minor, if necessary by force, if necessary alone. Kemal disposed of
sixty or seventy thousand men, against whom we had only a few
battalions—and the Mediterranean Fleet. But, in Churchill's own
words: 'I found myself in this business with a small group of
resolute men: the Prime Minister, Lord Balfour, Mr. Austen
Chamberlain, Lord Birkenhead, Sir Laming Worthington-Evans.
We made common cause. The Government might break up and
we might be relieved of our burden. The nation might not support us; they could find others to advise them. The Press might
howl, the Allies might bolt. We intended to force the Turk to a
negotiated peace before he should set foot in Europe. The aim was
modest, but the forces were small.' The aim was achieved, as a result of British determination and the political sagacity of Kemal
himself. But the event was fatal to the Prime Minister. Powerful
forces in the Conservative Party, headed by Mr. Baldwin, were
convinced that we had been driven too near to the edge of war.
Mr. Baldwin knew his 'twenties. He knew the average elector,
upon whom his gaze was constantly fixed, was not prepared even
to think in terms of war. This was the last occasion upon which
a British Government stood up to a potential aggressor until
1939.

A decade which struck down greatness wherever and whenever
it raised its head; which enthroned political mediocrity; which
tolerated isolationism, prohibition, gangsterism and racketeering
in the United States—and massive unemployment in Western
Europe; which preferred Poincaré to Clemenceau and Stalin to
Trotsky; which overthrew Wilson and Lloyd George, and assassinated Rathenau; which dissolved the Grand Alliance that might

have preserved the peace of the world; which paid lip-service to the principle of collective security, but rejected Briand's protocol for Europe; which refused to listen to Keynes on economics; which attempted to return to complete *laissez-faire*, and culminated in the greatest economic disaster known to history, can hardly be acclaimed. Still it was fun—for some of us—while it lasted.

When I first became a Member of Parliament I found a substantial number of back-benchers who enjoyed national reputations in their own right, and whose words commanded widespread public attention. There were Sir Alfred Mond, Sir Robert Horne and Mr. Walter Runciman, to voice the opinions of Big Business. The Clyde group, under the leadership of John Wheatley and James Maxton, to call our attention to the tragic plight of the slum-dwellers and the unemployed, and sometimes to prick our consciences into action. There was Lloyd George, still at the height of his powers, and a law unto himself. And to these were added University Members of the calibre of John Buchan; Alan Herbert, who later carried through a major reform of our divorce laws; and Eleanor Rathbone, the pioneer of the system of family allowances which we now enjoy.

Last, but not least, there was a degree of independence and toleration which no longer exists. When Wheatley or Maxton made speeches they did not ask Ramsay MacDonald what they should say. They said it. Lord Henry Bentinck called himself a Tory, but the views he expressed were always radical, sometimes socialist. Even our own little group, which was dubbed the 'Y.M.C.A.', and of which the present Prime Minister was a member, kept the flag of independence flying. We had little influence on the course of events: but we did our best—and no one asked us to leave the Conservative Party.

As time went on the House of Commons became perceptibly duller. This was because Baldwin, with solid support from the British middle-classes, decided to make politics dull; and succeeded beyond his most sanguine expectations. In private life the

31

most delightful of companions, he contrived almost miraculously to invest himself in the eyes of the public with all the attributes of dullness, which soon became synonymous with respectability. Subtle, sensitive, the great 'maestro' of political tactics, he set himself the task of lowering the temperature of political life to zero. For a year or two Churchill and Birkenhead lingered uneasily on the fringe of the Establishment, dining surreptitiously with Lloyd George when the boredom of their colleagues overwhelmed them. Then Baldwin found the perfect instrument for his purpose in Ramsay MacDonald; and, with the formation of the so-called 'National' Government in 1931, the decade of the political pygmies began.

The alleged purpose of the 'National' Government was to save the pound, and keep us on the gold standard, to which we had returned in 1925 at the wrong parity of exchange. Within a month they had been driven off it, greatly to our advantage; and whatever purpose they were supposed to have ceased to exist. They had given an explicit pledge that the Government had been formed solely to deal with the national economic emergency, and would not appeal to the electorate. They broke it; and, unable to agree among themselves about anything, asked for and received what was euphemistically called 'a doctor's mandate'. Why did they do it? Why did MacDonald desert his party to cling to office, and Baldwin refuse to accept his responsibilities as Leader of the Opposition, and form an alternative administration? Could it have been that, with Lloyd George ill in bed and Churchill in self-imposed political exile, the chance to exclude from office—permanently it was hoped—the only two men of authentic genius in our public life was too great to be resisted? I must tell you that I suspected it at the time; and am now convinced that this is the true explanation. When the herd suspects the presence of two rogue-elephants they are apt to cling together in self-defence.

What happened is beyond dispute. We got the most futile and feckless administration Britain has ever experienced, with the possible exception of Lord North's. A Government without conviction, theme, leadership or courage which, within a decade, brought a great Empire from a position of world power and absolute security to the brink of total destruction. It took the Roman Empire two centuries of enjoyable decadence to achieve the same result.

Those of us who opposed the policy of appeasement and the Munich Agreement had a pretty rough time. But we survived. Churchill once said to me, 'It took Armageddon to make me Prime Minister.' The answer is, 'Armageddon and the House of Commons.' For, in May, 1940, the House of Commons at last faced up to its responsibilities, and dismissed the Chamberlain Government, after a tense and dramatic debate.

This was the single decisive vote I cast during my thirty-four years as a Member of Parliament. I was one of thirty-three Conservatives who voted against the Government we had been elected to support. Others abstained. And the result was that, although the Government obtained a majority, it was not of sufficient size to command public confidence in the greatest crisis of our history. Mr. Chamberlain resigned. A new Government was formed, at the request of the King, by Winston Churchill, which was in effective control of our affairs the same evening. The nation accepted the verdict of its representatives in Parliament, and the choice of the Sovereign. And the war was carried to a successful conclusion without a dissolution. You will forgive me for saying that it could not have happened in this country.

Here was a classic example of the British Constitution working at its best. You will remember that I said last night that the House of Commons was the ultimate repository of political power, because it could sustain or dismiss an administration. Churchill himself has always maintained that a Government should accept dismissal only at the hands of the House of Commons or the electorate.

I believe that he is right. The Asquith Government fell from power in 1916 as the result of a brilliantly conducted palace revolution. Lloyd George fell as a result of a vote taken not in Parliament but at a private meeting of the Conservative Party. The Labour Government of 1929 was brought down because the Prime Minister and two of his principal colleagues deserted to the enemy. Churchill alone was given power by the Commons, dismissed by the electorate, and restored to power by the electorate. And this is as it should be.

I come, in conclusion, to certain developments in the British parliamentary system during the past forty years which seem to me to give cause for anxiety.

Politics are about power. And the balance of power has shifted from the legislature not merely to the Executive but to the Prime Minister himself. Professor Max Beloff has gone so far as to suggest that we are in a process of evolution to what is virtually a Presidential system; and it may well be so.

The House of Commons has at times abused the powers it still possesses by excessive and even ludicrous claims for privilege; and by means of tribunal or select committee procedure applied to questions of personal responsibility. Some years ago Reginald Paget, Q.C., M.P. wrote, in a letter to *The Times*: 'The fault in tribunal procedure is an ancient fault, the fault of the Inquisition. It confuses investigation with trial, and that I believe inevitably results in injustice.'

At the same time the power that really matters—the control which Parliament ought to exercise over the Executive in the fields of expenditure and administration—has, as I said last night, diminished to an alarming extent.

There are several reasons for this.

First, the House of Commons ceded to the Treasury and the Bank of England the right to issue money in the emergency of 1914; and, at the end of the first world war, unfettered control over monetary and credit policy.

The Governor of the Bank, Montagu Norman, was a characteristic figure of the inter-war years. Ostensibly eschewing publicity, he moved in a perpetual limelight of *alibis*; but wielded the real economic power. His object was to restore the supremacy of the City of London, and with it the political independence of the mercantile society. Technically responsible to no one but his self-chosen Court of Directors, he was never called upon to justify or even explain his policy, which was one of continuous deflation.

The effect of this was to relegate taxation power to the rôle of secondary importance which it still plays in relation to monetary policy, which remains outside the control of Parliament.

Another reason is that the parliamentary machine is badly over-loaded; and the procedure of the House of Commons has not been adapted to meet twentieth-century conditions. The procedure of the Lords is, by comparison, up to date.

I myself believe, as a result of long parliamentary experience, that the remedy lies in the transfer of the committee stage of all legislation except the Finance Bill to standing committees of the House of Commons; and in the development of functional committees, either of the House of Commons or of both Houses, of members interested in the work of particular departments, with power to send for 'persons and papers'.

Any British Member of Parliament who has seen the Senate Foreign Affairs or Banking and Finance Committees at work in Washington cannot fail to have been enormously impressed; and to have realized, with something of a shock, the very real power exercised by the Congress over the Executive in this country, despite the fact that members of Congress are not themselves part of it.

The functional parliamentary committees I have in mind would do much to restore the balance of political power between the Prime Minister and the legislature, because, as in the case of 'standing' committees, they would reflect in their composition the majority upon which his authority must rest; and therefore reproduce in miniature his basic relationship, and that of his Ministers, with Parliament as a whole.

If we had had a Finance Committee before the last war, with power to summon the Governor of the Bank of England to appear before them, we might have had a very much better economic policy. If we had had a Foreign Affairs Committee after the war, in close touch with the Foreign Secretary, not giving him orders, but hearing reports from him, asking questions, and showing continuous and well-informed interest, neither the Palestine crisis of 1947 nor the Suez crisis of 1956 could have arisen in the form they did.

It is objected in some quarters that such a system of functional committees would lead to 'specialization'. Why not? We live in an age of specialization. And back-bench Members of Parliament who try to know something about everything end up by knowing nothing about anything. Hence their sense of impotence and frustration. All that is at present required of them, as Mr. David Price has ruefully pointed out, is faithful and compliant attendance at the House, while acting as public relations officers to their parties in the constituencies.

I do not think that the process of concentrating political power in the hands of the Prime Minister can now be reversed, or even that it should be. He can appoint or change his Ministers without regard to the wishes or views of Parliament at any given moment; and these appointments are not subject to parliamentary approval. The Cabinet office is fast becoming, if it has not already become, the Prime Minister's office. But, in face of such overwhelming personal power, there must be safeguards. The ultimate right of the House of Commons to dismiss the Government is one. The question hour—one of the chief glories of our parliamentary system, because it is an example of free democracy in full action—is another. The functional committees which I have suggested could be a third.

There remains for brief consideration the growing power of the party machines or caucuses; and a disturbing trend towards authoritarianism, especially on the part of the Labour Party.

The treatment of dissident M.P.'s on both sides of the House after the Suez crisis was really shocking—with, I must add, the exception of myself. Attempts were made by party constituency associations to enforce their immediate resignations. And in one or two cases they succeeded.

These associations are a small minority of the electorate, usually self-appointed; and therefore any claim on their part to dictate to Members of Parliament on political issues is an arrogant usurpation of the rights of the electorate as a whole. If they don't like their Member, or his views, they have one remedy—and only one. They needn't adopt him as a candidate at the next General Election.

The trend towards authoritarianism in the Labour Party is, I think, more serious. They have decided that members of the Parliamentary Party must be bound by votes taken at party meetings held in private, with an 'escape clause' in respect of conscience. As a result, most of the vital discussions within the Parliamentary Labour Party take place in rooms upstairs, from which the Press is excluded. This seems to me to be the negation of democracy, the essence of which is that debates of importance should take place on the floor of the House. Conservative Members hold private meetings upstairs, at which discussion is often vehement. But they do not vote. I think this is right. Votes in Parliament should never be taken in secret, always in public.

Aneurin Bevan, who narrowly escaped expulsion in 1955, said afterwards: 'We get into a Party meeting upstairs. Then we come down to the floor of the House of Commons. We make speeches, and if they do not accord with what has just been decided in private upstairs, we are threatened with expulsion. Is that democracy? It is conspiracy. ... The caucus is getting more powerful than the electorate itself.' And Sydney Silverman, M.P., summarized the whole matter in two sentences: 'The right to dissent in debate is no adequate compensation for being compelled to vote in conformity. The function of Parliament then becomes one of giving public assent to decisions arrived at secretly elsewhere.'

The Conservatives are more tolerant, and far wiser. Perhaps that is why they are almost perpetually in power. I know that, if I had been a member of the Labour Party, and had behaved as I did for thirty-four years, I should have been expelled at least six times. But what did the Conservatives do? They made me a Lord.

For my part I would like to see a reversion in Britain to two main political parties, for which our present electoral system and the structure of our Houses of Parliament were devised—both radical in outlook, but one leaning towards the Right, the other towards the Left; and both, in their strength, tolerating great individual independence within their ranks.

I think this may well come about. As you know, there is at

present a deep cleavage in the Labour Party on the subject of nuclear disarmament. If, as I expect, Mr. Gaitskell wins this battle, I see no reason why there should not be a small Independent Labour Party of the Left, separated from the official Labour Party on this issue, but on many other questions in alliance with it. There was exactly such a party when I first entered Parliament. And it did not prevent either electoral arrangements in various constituencies, or Mr. Wheatley from taking Cabinet office in the Mac-Donald Government of 1924.

When you come to think of it, Governments of the Left have nearly always been coalitions of one kind or another. From 1910 to 1914 the Liberal Government was maintained in office by the Irish nationalists. There was nothing secret about this. And nothing undemocratic.

After over thirty-five years in Parliament—the House of Lords is still part of Parliament—I can look back on astonishingly few concrete achievements. I have been a great one for espousing lost causes. I was against the policy of deflation, the policy of disarmament, the policy of appeasement and the Munich Agreement to which it led, before the war. I was against the Bretton Woods Agreement after it, because I did not think it provided adequate liquid reserves for the Free World; and the American loan of 1945, because I thought the terms were too harsh, and could not be carried out. For ten years I advocated a united Europe, when we could have had the leadership of Western Europe on our own terms, and deliberately threw it away. Finally, I was against the Suez escapade.

The fact that I was always right, and 'they' were always wrong, is inadequate consolation for such continuous failure.

Oddly enough, the roughest treatment I ever got from the Tory Party was when I advocated an increase in the salaries of Members of Parliament, in the interest of the future service of the House of Commons. There was a moment when I hardly dared face the party Committee, and addressed it with my hand on the door, in case immediate escape became necessary. However, two years later they did it.

I think I can justifiably claim that I was the prime mover in getting the Wolfenden Committee on homosexuality and prostitution, and the Radcliffe Committee on monetary and credit policy, set up. At least I was the first publicly to suggest them. The results which will ultimately flow from the reports of these committees, on two such widely differing subjects, may be far-reaching; but imponderable and incalculable. On the whole I believe that the best that can be got out of political life is the satisfaction to be derived from public service, provided it is not smug; and from the belief that the game itself is good provided, in Leo Amery's words, that one plays one's best for one's own chosen goals, and by one's own rules.

The West is at present conducting a global struggle against the forces of totalitarian Communism without any central organs of political decision, without effective strategic or economic direction, and without any policies worked out in common. That is why, on balance, we have been losing it for the past five years. We have not even achieved an integrated deterrent power for the West, as the Communists have for the East; although in practice, and despite what some politicians tell us, it exists between the American Strategic Air Command and British Bomber Command, which constitute—in fact if not in theory—a single and inseparable force, under our joint control.

I remain an invincible optimist. I reckon that, if the balance of nuclear world power is maintained, at some level, the odds are in favour of peace; and, as I said in my Rectorial Address at St. Andrews, I am fortified in this belief by the opinion of that dark pessimist, Sigmund Freud, that, confronted by the stark choice between aggression at the cost of annihilation and survival, humanity will probably opt for survival.

Finally I believe that, in the long run, democracy will prevail against totalitarianism; and that, sooner rather than later, we shall find the means by which to achieve that basic unity of thought and action which is essential for this purpose.

INADVERTENT LEGISLATION

*It ought to be done by legislation directed to the point,
and not by a side wind in a different Bill*—Viscount
Kilmuir, in another context.

L ET me start with a sweeping assertion, which I claim cannot
be denied. Homosexuality is far more prevalent in this
country than is generally admitted. It is increasing steadily,
and it is by no means confined to the metropolis. There is, in fact,
a homosexual 'underground' in most of our large provincial cities
of disturbing dimensions, which is a continuous menace to youth.
We have reached a situation in which no man with any regard for
his reputation will dare to enter a public urinal after dark; and in
which the number of male prostitutes parading our streets is a by-
word in every other country, and a disgrace to our own.

For this the innate hypocrisy of the British people on all matters
concerning sex is largely responsible. It is a hang-over from the
Victorian Age. Unless and until it is forced upon our attention by
the activities of the police, we shut our eyes to the existence of the
problem.

Those who are most revolted by the whole subject are the
worst offenders. Instead of facing up to it they shroud it in a veil
of secrecy, silence and shame. As for the police, their sporadic
campaigns against homosexuality, which are often accompanied
by methods of great dubiety, do nothing towards its eradication.
On the contrary they intensify the squalor by which it is surrounded, and widen the areas in which the underground flourishes.

The law still enshrines not only the ecclesiastical doctrines of the
Middle Ages, but many of our most archaic moral prejudices.
These are derived directly from the Israelites, with the inevitable

emphasis of a race struggling against overwhelming odds for survival, upon reproduction. Solomon could have a thousand wives; but homosexuality was punished by death. So it continued in this country, where the ecclesiastical tradition long prevailed. Death in the Ecclesiastical Courts until the reign of Henry VIII; death again by a statute of 1533 which was repealed in 1547 and 1553, but re-enacted in 1548 and 1562. And, until well into the nineteenth century, attempted homosexuality was punished by the pillory—a fate which at one period was almost worse than death. It is, however, significant that no laws, however savage, have succeeded in stamping out homosexuality. Indeed it is arguable that heavy penalties have added an extra kick to the pursuit of homosexual practices, and also to the sensationalism and exhibitionism by which they are so often characterized.

Kenneth Walker, in his book *The Physiology of Sex*, says:

'In France during the old Monarchy when a homosexual, as the law then stood, was liable to be burnt at the stake, inversion was both fashionable and conspicuous; whereas in modern France, under the Napoleonic Code, homosexuality is looked down upon and very little in evidence. The mere fact that there are harsh laws against an activity may lead to a glorification of it.'

The present laws governing the treatment of homosexual offences in this country are sections 61 and 62 of the Offences against the Person Act of 1861, and section 11 of the Criminal Law Amendment Act of 1886. Both were passed long before the discoveries of modern psychology; and, in my submission, they are no deterrent to the practice of homosexuality. My objection to sections 61 and 62 of the Offences against the Person Act is simply that the prescribed penalties of imprisonment for life, or ten years, are so severe that judges and juries are reluctant to impose them. This tends to bring the law into disrepute.

My objection to section 11 of the Criminal Law Amendment Act of 1886 is much stronger. Here I base myself on the observations of Sir Travers Humphreys in his Foreword to *The Trials of Oscar Wilde*, which seems to me to be sufficiently important to deserve quotation in full:

'Until that Act came into force, on January 1st, 1886, the criminal law was not concerned with alleged indecencies between grown-up men committed in private. Everyone knew that such things took place, but the law only punished acts against public decency and conduct tending to the corruption of youth. The Bill in question, entitled "A Bill to make further provision for the protection of women and girls, the suppression of brothels and other purposes", was introduced and passed by the House of Lords without any reference to indecency between males. In the Commons, after a second reading without comment, it was referred to a committee of the whole House. In committee Mr Labouchère moved to insert in the Bill the clause which ultimately became section 11 of the Act, creating the new offence of indecency between male persons in public or *private*. Such conduct in public was, and always has been, punishable at common law. There was no discussion except that one member asked the Speaker whether it was in order to introduce at that stage a clause dealing with a totally different class of offence to that against which the Bill was directed. The Speaker having ruled that anything could be introduced by leave of the House, the clause was agreed to without further discussion, the only amendment moved being one by Sir Henry James with the object of increasing the maximum punishment from 12 to 24 months, which was also agreed to without discussion.

'It is doubtful whether the House fully appreciated that the words "in public or private" in the new clause had completely altered the law; but as soon as the Royal Assent had been given and the Act was published, there began a spate of correspondence in the newspapers, both legal and lay, and references to the subject on various public platforms, which were duly reported. A learned Recorder dubbed it "The Blackmailer's Charter", and an eminent Q.C. prophesied that juries would refuse to convict where the alleged acts were in private and not visible to any member of the public. On the other hand those interested in the welfare of girls welcomed the Act as a whole so warmly (and indeed it was an excellent Act apart from section 11), and it was so clearly impossible to do anything except let the law take its course, that after a few weeks the clamour died down and the public interest became centred upon some more savoury topic.'

It is this section that has introduced the horrifying elements of tainted evidence and blackmail into a situation which was already sufficiently dark and difficult; and the sooner it is repealed the better. In cases involving alleged acts of indecency committed in private, where there is no injured party, the witnesses are almost invariably accomplices, actuated by motives of hatred, avarice, jealousy or fear. These emotions lie at the root of all evil, and have made the field of homosexuality a happy hunting-ground for the blackmailer.

What has modern psychology got to teach us? (1) That mature forms of sexuality are a composite product in the formation of which primitive infantile elements, hereditary factors, upbringing and environment have all played their part; (2) that sub-conscious bi-sexuality is a component part of all of us, and that a majority of males pass through a homosexual period at one period of their lives; (3) that congenital homosexuals are seldom happy, but often endowed with creative or artistic gifts which can—within limits and in favourable circumstances—be diverted into fruitful channels; (4) that homosexuality should be regarded as a physical and mental disability which may sometimes be cured,[1] and not as a crime which must always be punished. It is, in short, a biological and pathological condition for which the victim is only to a small degree responsible.

I conclude from this that the existing laws dealing with the matter are outmoded—and indeed medieval. By attaching so fearful a stigma to homosexuality as such, they put a large number of otherwise law-abiding and useful citizens on the wrong side of the fence which divides the good citizen from the bad. By making them feel that, instead of being unfortunates they are social 'pariahs', they drive them into ineffable squalor—perhaps even into crime; and produce that underground movement which it is

1. The Home Secretary stated, on March 16, 1954, that the number of prisoners convicted of offences of a sexual nature who were under regular treatment by a visiting psychotherapist for a period exceeding six months in the year 1951, 1952 and 1953 was only 25, 26 and 27 respectively.

so clearly in the public interest to eradicate. Since the homosexual finds that an important part of the moral code is unworkable so far as he is concerned, he tends to question and reject other parts of that code; and to challenge both society and the State in other fields as well.

There is a sharp distinction to be drawn between conduct which may be held to be sinful and that which is criminal. The duty of the State, as I see it, is to protect youth from corruption and the public from indecency or nuisance. What consenting adults do in privacy may be a moral issue between them and their Maker: but is certainly not a legal issue between them and the State. Where does this lead us? It leads straight to a revision of the law on the lines of the 'Code Napoleon'. The law must provide for the appropriate punishment of those who are guilty of the seduction or attempted seduction of youth; of violence in any shape or form; of importuning; or of acts of indecency committed in public. And there the law should stop.

Infanto-homosexuals, like other homosexuals, may be cured by institutional treatment provided their active co-operation is obtained. Unless and until they are cured, they must clearly be segregated, as must all those who commit offences against children of either sex. At the same time it should be borne in mind that the prolonged repression of homosexual tendencies results not infrequently in their ultimate diversion towards young children. In his book *Society and the Homosexual*, which is the best short analysis of the problem that I have read, Mr. Gordon Westwood points out that practically all the cases where a cultivated and socially-minded man has had a lapse in later life concern the seduction of young children. 'Surely it is better,' he adds, 'that two like-minded men should indulge together than that one man should give way to a sudden impulse and seduce one of our children.'

To send confirmed adult homosexuals to our ordinary prisons is—to coin a phrase made famous in another connection—'midsummer madness'. I have a letter from an ex-prison official with twenty years' experience in which he says: 'I feel convinced that prison is a most unsuitable place for the detention of such cases, especially under the present-day overcrowded conditions. In my opinion such persons are not criminals in the same sense as many others who receive far less severe sentences. Moreover, owing to the small proportion of prison staff available, it is impossible for prison officials to give the proper supervision necessary for this particular type of case. If the problem is not one for medical attention, it is certainly not one which will be solved by the prison authorities.' This view is endorsed by Dr. Stanley-Jones, who wrote in the *British Medical Journal* of February, 1946 that to commit a cultured invert to the soul-crushing experience of imprisonment was as futile from the point of view of treatment as to hope to rehabilitate a chronic alcoholic by giving him occupational therapy in a brewery.

In his introduction to Mr. Westwood's book, Dr. Edward Glover says: 'The greatest obstacle to an objective understanding of sex problems lies in the moral prejudice, either conscious or unconscious, of the observer. Whether it manifests itself in the obtuseness of the scientist, in gales of music-hall laughter, in the harsh disapproval of the sexually inhibited "hearty", or the more pious reprobation of the moral philistine, the common prejudice regarding homosexuality can be traced to a common cause, namely, the tendency of the average man to castigate in others the impulses that lie hidden in his own subconscious mind.' In short, the greater the hysteria, the stronger the subconscious impulses—so you'd all better keep calm tonight!

I am well aware that this is not a popular cause. The inhibitions on the part of the public and of Parliament are indeed daunting to anyone who espouses it. Nevertheless I believe that the magnitude of the problem, and the amount of avoidable suffering that is now being caused, demand that it should be faced. That is why I am asking for the appointment of a Royal Commission, or some similar authoritative Enquiry, to furnish Parliament with the expert knowledge and guidance which are necessary for appropriate legislative and administrative action.[1]

1. This speech to the Hardwicke Society, delivered in February, 1954, led to a correspondence between the author and the Home Secretary (Sir David Maxwell-Fyfe) which resulted in the appointment of the Wolfenden Committee.

POSTSCRIPT

As the politician who was mainly responsible for getting the Wolfenden Committee set up, I welcome Mr. E. M. Forster's verdict that its report is a living document which will be constantly discussed and will gradually influence public opinion. That was the object of the exercise.

The British people have never accepted Nietzsche's excellent advice to distrust all those in whom the impulse to punish is strong. On the contrary, they have tolerated, for 400 years, criminal laws and methods of punishment, which, by any standards, have been a disgrace to a country claiming to be civilized; and which have rightly been regarded with horror by our Latin neighbours on the continent of Europe.

They accepted without protest the savage use of the death penalty—long after it had been abandoned elsewhere—for petty theft and vagrancy in the seventeenth century, for witchcraft in the eighteenth, and for sodomy in the nineteenth. The 'hanging judge' as exemplified by Jeffreys in England and Braxfield in Scotland, and immortalized by Robert Louis Stevenson in *Weir of Hermiston*, is an authentic figure; and the tradition is dying hard. Less than forty years ago Edith Thompson was executed, in fact if not in name, for adultery.

Why have these things been allowed to happen? The English are not a cruel people. They are hypocritical; but, by nature, they are gentle and tolerant. I think that George Orwell found the answer when he wrote, in one of his essays, that the savage sentences handed out by some gouty old bully with his mind rooted in the past are accepted because they are part of 'the law', which is assumed to be unalterable. Remarks like, 'They can't run me in; I haven't done anything wrong,' or, 'They can't do that; it's against the law,' are part of the atmosphere of England. Nevertheless, I now detect a sea change; and believe that, not for the first time, public opinion is ahead of the House of Commons.

Let me tell Mr. Forster what I think is going to happen.

There will be, as he says, much animated discussion of the Wolfenden Report; and in the meantime the more disgraceful methods which have hitherto been used by the police against homosexuals will be—shall we say?—greatly modified. This, in itself, will be a tremendous gain.

After a time the argument will die down, but the climate of opinion will have been altered. Then some private Member of Parliament or, better still, some private Lord will introduce a measure which will, I suppose, be carefully designated a *Bill for the Further Protection of Young Girls*. Into this Bill a clause will be inserted to delete the Labouchère amendment to the similar Bill of 1886, which made acts of 'gross indecency', committed in public *or private* by consenting male adults, a criminal offence. It will be passed, as the Labouchère amendment was passed, in an empty House on a hot August night, without discussion and without a division. And the job will have been done.

THE PAYMENT OF MEMBERS OF PARLIAMENT

I WANT to deal briefly, and at the beginning of my speech, with three major objections which have been made to the proposals for a straight increase in Members' allowances. It is said, first of all, that there is no mandate for such a proposal. With all respect, I want to suggest that in this there is an element of humbug. It is really an evasion, as *The Times* said this morning. There was no mandate for the original allowances or for either of the subsequent increases. How could there be? Does anyone seriously suggest that this question should be made the principal issue at the next General Election? If it is not so made, how can the electorate express an opinion one way or the other, unless one has recourse to a referendum? That would be contrary to the custom and political tradition of this country. It would be a very marked innovation, and not altogether a desirable one. Our mandate is the unanimous report of the Select Committee which, on this sort of issue, I suggest is well qualified to pronounce judgment.

The second objection to which I wish to refer was summarized in the *Observer* yesterday when it said: 'It would be scandalous for Members to relieve their own distress without doing the same for old-age pensioners and others struggling with poverty.' I want to grapple with this point right away, by saying that this House has been engaged for the past fifty years in legislating for social reforms which have completely transformed our society, and which have now culminated in the establishment of the Welfare State.

Adjustments to pensions have been, and still are, continuous. We raised one group of pensions only recently. I want to say quite frankly that if a further adjustment is now necessary in the case of old-age pensions, then it is the plain duty of this House, on the recommendation of the Chancellor of the Exchequer, to make it. But what has this got to do with the salaries of hon. Members? The argument, in my submission, is entirely irrelevant. This question has nothing to do with legislation, or any other administrative action which we may think it right to take.

The third point was made in *The Times* leading article this morning when it said that an increase of Members' allowances by £500 was insupportable because it was direct compensation for the rise in the cost of living for which, it went on to say, this House was entirely responsible. I do not think the Chancellor would entirely concur with that view. Certainly I do not. *The Times* went on to say: 'It is the Member's expenses as a Member which must be met.'

Again, I submit that this argument is false. We are concerned today not with the cost of living, but with the radical change which has taken place in the conditions of parliamentary service. We have to consider not merely the expenses, but the continued existence of Members of this House in modern conditions. Take £600 as the average figure of expenses. I am not taking £750, which the Select Committee indicated; I am taking £600 which I think is, perhaps, fairer for my argument, at any rate, as the average figure of expenses.

I ask hon. Members, can a Member who has no other source of income maintain a wife and family on the remaining £400 a year? Manifestly he cannot. If we continue, therefore, as we are now doing, the conclusion is inescapable. It is that membership of this House will shortly be confined to those who have private incomes of their own. In other words, to a privileged minority which exists on both sides, although the nature of the privilege differs.

I want to take a very brief glance at the past. When I first entered this House, in 1924, it was possible to live quite comfortably on one's Parliamentary salary. Happy days those were. It was also possible to work in another profession, and many Members did. I should say the majority did, and this was of great value to the House and to the country. In those days it was quite a thing to be a Member of Parliament. One had prestige and social *cachet*. The doors of a society which no longer exists, were open to one; and if one was so minded, one could eat and drink and spend one's holidays entirely at other people's expense. They were delighted and honoured to have you, and you were delighted and honoured to consume their food and drink.

Ministers were, of course, tremendous swells, occupying Olympian heights almost beyond the ken of ordinary mortals; and even Parliamentary Private Secretaries cut quite a dash. I was a Parliamentary Private Secretary to the Chancellor of the Exchequer, before the present Chancellor of the Exchequer entered this House. Just think of that, Mr. Speaker! Instead of being derided, as so many Parliamentary Private Secretaries are derided today, I was hailed and welcomed as a future Prime Minister. Moreover, despite the fact that the present Prime Minister was my chief, my work was by no means excessive, and I had quite a lot of spare time.

Today, conditions have completely changed. I say without fear of contradiction that as against the 'twenties, the work of the ordinary Member of Parliament has at least doubled. We are all now welfare officers, discharging in that capacity an essential function of the Welfare State. At innumerable points we touch the lives of our constituents who seek our assistance and guidance, and expect us to know the answers. Only the other day I had a letter from a constituent asking me whether I was aware that the birthrate of Peterhead was falling rapidly, and what action I proposed to take. (Hon. Members: 'Answer.') I must have further notice of that question.

Last but not least, the complexities of the modern State have enormously increased the burden of our parliamentary work. Membership of this House is now a full-time job, in the sense that it is almost impossible to combine it with full and active membership of any other profession except journalism. This has brought no addition to the dignity or status enjoyed by Members of Parliament. On the contrary, they are subject to a sustained volume of public criticism, some of it reckless, which has greatly increased in recent years. As for Ministers, most of them now work themselves to death in comparative obscurity, until they are guilty of an error of judgment, or one of their officials makes a mistake. They are then flayed alive in the Press. That is the life of a Minister these days.

In these conditions I maintain, as I have said before, that the terms of public life in this country are rapidly becoming unendurable, or very nearly so; and that the effect upon our democratic system is wholly evil. Good young Members are unobtrusively but steadily leaving this House, and this has been going on for a number of years. Any hon. Member who searches his recollection can remember one or two young Members on both sides of the House who have recently left it, and who will be sadly missed. But, worse still, good young men and women are not coming in, or thinking of coming in.

I have been talking recently in some of our universities. In the old days, in the 'twenties, any student or undergraduate of outstanding promise was at once considered as a potential candidate for this House, perhaps not in the immediate future but in the near future; and it was natural that he should consider entering public life, and be encouraged to do so by his tutors and by the heads of colleges and universities. I am assured that nowadays the question of public life simply does not enter in, in any of our universities. No young man, however brilliant or promising who contemplates marriage and bringing up a family, even begins to think in terms of entering this House. Why? Because there is no security of any kind. I cannot help thinking that that is a great tragedy from the point of view of our democracy.

We are suffering today from the loss of what is called the missing generation—the generation that was killed between 1914 and 1918. It has left a terrific gap; nobody denies that. Are we certain that we are not now making sure of another missing generation in twenty or thirty years' time? That is what worries me. In fact, what worries me most is that we are gradually reaching a stage when membership of this House will be confined to company directors, trade union officials, journalists, and the rapidly diminishing number of those who have inherited wealth. That is about all it will come to.

Now, I come very briefly to the question of methods, which was dealt with extremely well by the hon. Member for Cardiff, West (Mr. George Thomas). First, there is the case of retired Members. I think it is generally agreed that the pensions proposals of the Select Committee are not acceptable in their present form. As I criticized *The Times* in the earlier part of my speech, perhaps I may quote with approval from another passage of their leader this morning, in which they say:

'The question of retired members' privations may now be passed to the trustees of the members' fund. They are the right people to consider it. The fund needs to be increased. As has been suggested before, there is no fiscal, humanitarian or constitutional reason why the Treasury should not come generously to its aid.'

I was delighted to hear the Chancellor of the Exchequer say in his speech the other day that although he did not think we had found a solution, he would come into the question and discuss it further if it was thought that his services could be of any use. I am quite sure that his services will be of infinite use. That is all we are asking; that this question should now be referred to the trustees of the fund and that they, in turn, should have consultations with the Chancellor of the Exchequer.

If I may make a personal suggestion, it is that a proportion of salaries which should be substantially increased should be earmarked as an obligatory contribution to a fund which would be repayable, with interest, as a capital sum when Members of Parliament retire or lose their seats. This would at least give to the young ones the chance to start again in some other profession, and to the old ones the chance to buy an annuity; and at the same time avoid a means test which was described in evidence to the Select Committee as 'harrowing' to those who have to conduct it.[1]

Then there is the question of Ministers. I think we all feel that Ministers should not be penalized simply because they are Ministers. I should have thought that the simple solution would be to treat all Ministers as Members of Parliament who are, in fact,

1. This particular suggestion was given specific form in a subsequent article.

Members of Parliament—just like that. It may involve, as the Select Committee pointed out, some reconsideration of Ministerial salaries, but surely that is the simple answer to this question. Ministers do not cease to be Members of Parliament, with responsibilities to their constituents, simply on account of the fact that they are Ministers.

Now I come to the question of whether it should be a direct increase in the allowance—and let me make it quite clear that the allowance is, of course, the salary—or some kind of an expenses scheme. I read with great care the Chancellor's speech the other day and I thought that, with the best will in the world, he was getting into deepish water at the end of it. It seems to me quite impracticable to differentiate between, for example, telegrams and secretarial assistance, or between London Members and the rest. I do not think we can fiddle about with all these things. It would give rise to great suspicion, and would be susceptible to abuse at the same time.

As for a lump sum allowance for expenses, the danger of this is that it might well be thought to differentiate between Members and other taxpayers so far as taxation is concerned; and the Select Committee came down very heavily, and, in my opinion, quite rightly, against this. At present, expenses necessarily incurred by hon. Members are claimed and allowed for tax relief against their Parliamentary salary. This puts us on an equal footing with the public we serve. I do not believe that this system can be bettered, and I therefore think it should continue.

When it comes to the straight increase in salary, I am not one of those hon. Members who regards the *Economist* as their bible; but last week it did come out with a paragraph upon which I base myself so far as this question is concerned:

'The most important point is that the method chosen should not merely be a means of pulling wool over the electorate's eyes. As Mr. Butler pointed out, a lump sum expense allowance would not be very different from a salary increase; and any expense allowance, particularly a subsistence allowance, would have the advantage that it would direct the extra money to where it is most needed. The Chancellor might have added that to tax-paying M.P.s such proposals could also be more profitable. The Government should reconsider whether these advantages really outweigh the disadvantages of departing from the stark simplicity of a straight salary increase.'

I sympathize with the point of view, although I do not agree with it, of those who say we should do nothing. But if something has to be done, I have no doubt that a straight increase of £500 a year is the best way to do it. It makes no attempt to fudge the issue, no attempt to deceive the public. Everybody knows exactly where we stand; and if we think it right, we ought to have the guts to do it.

Why £500? Not, as *The Times* said, because it represents the increase in the cost of living, but, so far as I am concerned, because I believe it to be the bare minimum. It would at least avert some impending personal tragedies; but it will not in itself—let us have no delusion on this point—solve the basic problem of future recruitment for this House, for which other remedies will, sooner or later, have to be sought and found.

I am one of the lucky ones. I earn my living by journalism and broadcasting. I must admit that the party machines have done their level best to put a stop to the latter. Nevertheless, I do quite well. I have no need for this increase myself, nor do I expect to get much out of it; the Chancellor of the Exchequer will take very good care of that. Incidentally, I would remind hon. Members, as my hon. Friend the Member of Hexham (Mr. Speir) pointed out the other day, that there is no obligation upon any hon. Member to accept the extra £500 if he does not need it. A brief note to Mr. Moyes, in the Fees Office, is all that is required from anybody who conscientiously feels bound to forgo this addition.

In conclusion, I say that at present, the public are imposing on their servants, largely through ignorance, which has been in no way dispelled by a far from impoverished Press. As a result, the public are losing good servants, and if this continues they will not find it easy to replace them. This is one of the reasons, although not the most compelling, which has led me to support the Motion.

The most compelling reason is that, like the Leader of the Opposition, I have seen hon. Members dying on their feet in this House because they could not afford to leave it. I know that some Members today, on both sides of the House, are so hard pressed that they are never free from financial anxiety. That does not enable them to do their job as it should be done. I am sure that it is not good for democracy, and I do not think it can be right.

For my part, I am quite prepared to tell my constituents that if they do not think I am worth £1,500, a year they can find somebody else to represent them. I do not think they will, but I am willing to tell them. But it is not with individual Members, or even the hardest cases, that I am chiefly concerned today. What matters most in this debate—and here I echo the words of Quintin Hogg in the debate of 1946—is the service of this House of Commons, now and in the future. That is what we have to think of more than anything else, because nothing else is of comparable importance.

May 1954.

SUEZ IN RETROSPECT

B Y comparison with Munich the Suez crisis was *Opéra Bouffe*. The real tragedy lay not in Port Said but in Budapest, about which we could do nothing, having deliberately deprived ourselves, at that particular moment, of any claim to moral authority.

What led up to it? To some extent personal failure and frustration on the part of Anthony Eden, whose tenure of office as Foreign Secretary during the previous five years had, with one notable exception, been wholly lacking in concrete achievement. For this Dulles and Churchill were largely responsible. Dulles on account of his bull-headed 'brinkmanship'; Churchill because he realized that the ephemeral political power which came to him, too late, in 1951, bore little relationship to his permanent historical fame, and was understandably anxious to do nothing that might jeopardize the latter. In consequence nothing was done, or allowed to be done, in London, beyond a transient pursuit of the *mirage* of 'Summitry'.

Our European policy, or lack of it, was the basic cause of all the troubles which subsequently befell us, including Suez. Churchill had launched the campaign for European unity at Zürich after the war, and pursued it with eloquence and vigour. Bevin opposed it. Churchill's return to power was therefore hailed with enthusiasm and high expectation on the Continent. The countries of Western Europe would, at that time, have accepted British leadership on any terms.

They never got it. They therefore felt themselves the victims of a colossal betrayal, as in fact they were. At Strasbourg the

British delegates to the Consultative Assembly of the Council of Europe, of whom I was one, had a ghastly time. We saw Europe falling apart, and turning in bitterness against the United Kingdom. We could do nothing. Our protests to the Government were not even acknowledged. Eden, with strong support from the Foreign Office, was determined to keep us out of Europe. And Churchill was unwilling or unable to stop him. The inevitable result was the division of Western Europe. And we are not yet through with the consequences of this.

If Eden had been brought right into the European Movement from the beginning there might have been a different story to tell. He attended the Congress of The Hague in 1948. He was the predestined Foreign Secretary in a future Conservative administration. But he was not encouraged to take any further part in the formulation of plans and policies for closer European integration, and did not come to Strasbourg as a delegate. I thought at the time that this was an enormous mistake. The European Movement, encouraged by Churchill and dominated by Duncan Sandys, charged ahead—to the delight of the 'continentals'. If Eden had played his part we might not have gone so fast, or accepted so many commitments. But the Europeans would never have been able to say, as they subsequently did with every justification, that they had been led up the garden path. In the event Eden, feeling himself to be right out of the European swim, and disliking the whole conception of Strasbourg, hardened against a 'European' policy with every month that passed.

However, a singular and unexpected diplomatic triumph came his way, and one which remains without parallel in these post-war years.

In 1954, after the French defeats in Indo-China, Dulles wanted to intervene in South-East Asia with atomic weapons in order to prevent the fall of Dien Bien Phu. He flew to Geneva. So did Eden. There was a confrontation. Eden said No. Dulles flew back to Washington in a rage. The film of his departure from the airport ran for several weeks, as a 'comic', in the Swiss cinemas. Bidault, then in charge of the French delegation, was about to fall, and powerless. Eden was left alone to face Molotov and Chou-enlai. He did not flinch. Mendès-France, the new French Prime Minister, arrived in time to put his signature to the agreement. But the terms of the settlement which hauled the French out of an impossible situation, and prevented a Communist victory throughout South-East Asia, were negotiated by Eden. I was in Geneva myself, as a journalist. I have never seen more political courage and patience, accompanied by greater diplomatic skill than he then displayed. For once glittering personal success, which had so often eluded him, was Eden's portion. This was his finest hour.

Dulles never forgave him. And indeed there was a mutual antipathy between these two men that led ultimately to Eden's downfall. I have known Anthony Eden, not very well, since we were at Oxford together forty years ago. He has a habit, when he is talking to you, of calling you 'My dear'. Although sometimes not entirely convincing, I have always found it engaging, because it denotes at least a friendly intention. Many years ago Churchill described a certain Member of Parliament, in a letter written to me, as 'sour for the sour purpose of being sourer to others.' I can think of several to whom this description still applies. Too many people nowadays are cold—and even rude. But Dulles never found this habit of Eden's engaging. That stark, single-minded, high-principled puritan from New England had little time for the pleasantries of social intercourse. He wanted to get on with the job in hand, as he saw it. And he didn't want to be anyone's 'dear'.

Having turned his back on Europe, Eden had to find a foreign policy when he became Prime Minister in 1955. He looked around. Churchill's attempt at 'Summitry' had failed; and, if he could not succeed with the Russians, who else could expect to do so? Eden's gaze settled, not unnaturally, upon the Middle East. Here our prestige was at a low ebb. In Palestine Bevin had abandoned all our responsibilities, thrown up the Mandate, and gone on to back the losers. The State of Israel had been established not with our assistance, but in our teeth, against odds of ten to one. The refugee problem was only one, although by far the worst, of the legacies of this cowardly retreat. We were out of Suez, with nothing to show for it; and the Arabs, apart from Nuri, regarded us with increasing suspicion. As Churchill rightly said, we had been led through one humiliation after another to the fomenting of injurious hatreds.

Eden, who had read Oriental languages at Oxford, was by nature and temperament an Arabophil. His first major speech as Prime Minister was at the Lord Mayor's banquet, when he took as his main theme the necessity for a 'revision' of the frontiers of Israel. The clear implication was that we should revert to the partition proposals of the United Nations in 1947. Impossible! Far too much water, carrying Jewish refugees from all over the world, had flowed under the bridges since then. Eden's proposal would have meant the dismemberment and destruction of the State of Israel; although I dare say he did not consciously admit this, even to himself. I watched him on television with mounting indignation, but without dismay. If he thought Ben-Gurion would stand for this, he had another thought coming.

In January 1956 the Prime Minister, accompanied by his Foreign Secretary, Selwyn Lloyd, went to Washington to confer with President Eisenhower and Dulles about Middle-Eastern policy. They agreed about nothing; and every journalist there knew it. Nevertheless, at the end of the conference, the President and the Prime Minister issued a 'Joint Declaration', which contained only one sentence that meant anything at all—'We shall never initiate violence.' And ended thus:

'We shall help ourselves and others to peace, freedom and social progress, maintaining human rights where they are already secure, defending them when they are in peril and peacefully restoring them where they have been temporarily lost. While resolutely pursuing these aims, which are the products of our faith in God and in the peoples of the earth, we shall eagerly grasp any genuine opportunity to free mankind of the pall of fear and insecurity which now obscures what can and should be a glorious future.'

Not to put too fine a point on it, this declaration was, in intention and fact, a narcotic as well as a compound of clichés. There was no concrete policy of Anglo-American co-operation. On the contrary, the Tripartite Declaration of 1950, which committed us to action in the event of hostilities between Israel and her Arab neighbours, had been whittled down. 'And why,' demanded Randolph Churchill of an outraged Canadian television audience, 'drag God into it?' Why indeed!

Eden returned to London committed only to the Baghdad Pact, which thenceforward became the focal point of his Middle-Eastern policy. This was an invention of Dulles, based on his conception of a 'Northern tier'. But Dulles himself refused to join it! Here was the point at which Eden should have insisted on effective Anglo-American co-operation in the form of an agreed and publicly declared policy for the Middle East as a whole. Without American participation the Baghdad Pact was useless. And even with it, it would have been of dubious value because, as I wrote at the time: 'It is a mistake to demand military alliances as the price of economic aid in the Middle East or in Asia. They act as a value-less irritant; and the Russians have been clever enough to avoid it.'

The bitter fruits of the growing friction between Dulles and Eden were soon to be gathered. In March Glubb was summarily dismissed from the command of the Arab Legion in Jordan, while Selwyn Lloyd was actually in Cairo. Thereafter the Communists vaulted the 'Northern tier' with ease; and Communist arms began to flow, in steadily increasing quantities, into Egypt.

What was our answer to this? To go on giving arms to Nasser ourselves, and deny them to Israel.

All through the summer the situation deteriorated, while Dulles sat in glum silence in Washington. In the House of Commons I besought the Government at least to strike a balance by giving sufficient arms to Israel to deter an attack upon her with jet bombers, MiG fighters and Stalin tanks supplied to Egypt by Russia through Czechoslovakia. I also suggested that we should enter into negotiations for a defensive alliance with Israel, accompanied by a guarantee to the Arab countries against aggression; and that this might include the establishment of a British base at Haifa which, from a military point of view, would be far better than Cyprus.

Nothing happened until Dulles, suddenly and without warning, withdrew the offer of an American loan for the construction of the Aswan Dam, the British Government tamely followed suit, and Nasser thereupon nationalized the Suez Canal.

Upon this I asked my final question about the supply of arms to Israel—at the beginning of August. The reply of the Foreign Office was a classic of its kind; and, as such, deserves to be recorded:

Sir R. Boothby asked the Secretary of State for Foreign Affairs whether, in view of the aggressive action taken by the Egyptian Government in respect of the Suez Canal, Her Majesty's Government will reconsider their decision not to allow the Government of Israel to purchase such arms as they consider necessary for the effective defence of Israel.

Lord John Hope: 'Her Majesty's Government's policy with regard to arms supplies to Middle East countries is based on the Tripartite Declaration of 1950 which relates to the Arab-Israel dispute. *The nationalization of the Suez Canal is not related to that dispute. Her Majesty's Government, therefore, see no reason to change their policy as regards the supply of arms to the Middle East as a whole.'* [1]

Sir R. Boothby: 'Does my noble Friend really mean to tell us that, in the light of the present situation, Her Majesty's Government are going to make no change in their policy of refusing certain classes of modern arms to Israel, at Israel's own request—that they do not recognize any difference in the situation which has arisen in the last few days?'

Lord John Hope: 'I have tried to tell my hon. Friend what the Government's policy is with regard to the Arab-Israel dispute, and upon that we stand at present.'

In September came the first of the great series of Suez debates. I spoke last on the first day, and began by saying:

'The Nasser story would be incredible if it were not true. He was put there by the American Ambassador in Cairo. His ban on Israeli ships was acquiesced in by all, despite the order of the Security Council of the United Nations Organization. Arms were given to him and denied to Israel. And all this time he was working against us in the Sudan, Saudi Arabia, the Persian Gulf, Jordan

1. My italics—B.

61

and Syria; and beaming anti-British propaganda at every part of Africa and Arabia within range. He then buys Communist arms and is rewarded with the offer of a loan for the Aswan Dam. The offer is then precipitately withdrawn; whereupon he seizes the Suez Canal. I am content to recite these bare facts.

'It seems to me that there are two basic lessons to be drawn from these startling events. The first is that it is really the absence of effective Anglo-American co-operation which has been, and is, the primary cause of the present decline of the West; and the crumbling of the Western defence system, not only in the Middle East but in south Asia and the eastern Mediterranean. Instead of acting together in advance of events, we have reacted separately as events have caught up on us. . . .

'The second lesson, I believe, is even more fundamental. It is that the nationalism which has been developing in this century is a bad and not a good thing. The hon. Member for Gorton (Mr. Zilliacus) came very near to admitting that in his speech. I believe that the rabid nationalism which is now developing is reactionary and atavistic—a revolt against the demands of the modern world and of life itself, and is used by the Communists for their own purposes, to the point at which it has become an intrinsic part of the Communist dialectic.

'I share the views of the hon. Member for Coventry, North (Mr. Edelman) expressed in an admirable letter which he wrote to *The Times* two or three days ago. I believe that the insistence on absolute State sovereignty is a primary cause of the evils which now confront us all, and that the only solution lies in a merging or pooling of national sovereignty.'

I ended my speech by saying, in unequivocal terms, that, although Nasser was a dictator, I thought it would be possible to negotiate with him under certain conditions which might well come about; that we must be prepared to give him the ownership of the Canal; that the matter could not be finally settled without reference to the Security Council of the United Nations; that we must stand absolutely firm on the principles laid down by the Prime Minister; and that shameless appeasement did not really pay.

Next morning Eden rang up to thank me for this speech. He sounded resolute, and cool. But certain newspapers attributed to it a 'jingoistic' attitude which I had not intended. I therefore immediately wrote an article in which I said: 'What matters more than anything else is first, that Britain should not put herself in the wrong by using force unless it is used against her; and by failing to take the case to the United Nations if Nasser continues to be obdurate. And second, that Britain should stand firm by her principles, which are that the rule of law rather than the rule of the jungle should be applied to the conduct of international affairs.'

A few days later the 'Yale and Towne Company' of the United States held their annual European Conference at Brighton, and invited me to be the guest of honour at the dinner. I thought it best to be blunt. 'What we want from the United States,' I said, 'at this eleventh hour is not a loan, is not your oil. We want your hand for effective political co-operation and, above all, a joint policy resolutely pursued throughout the Middle East. If we had had a common policy the present Suez crisis would never have arisen. Nasser was put into power by you, and sustained by the promise of water for the people of Egypt by means of a loan for the Aswan Dam. In the words of your own columnist, Joseph Alsop, Mr. Dulles then "kicked him in the teeth", without warning or explanation, by withdrawing the offer of the loan; and he struck back at Suez. This is the immediate cause of the crisis. I cannot believe there was any co-operation here. What I do believe is that Nasser thinks we are still not working together; and that this accounts more than anything for his intransigent attitude. If he thought we were really working together, I believe he would negotiate.' This went down surprisingly well with my American audience.

Meanwhile Dulles had produced, out of a hat, a scheme for a 'Canal Users' Association'. It very soon became clear that he had no more intention of using it than he had had of using the Baghdad Pact. Dulles himself, and Dulles alone, had precipitated the Suez crisis. And I sustained the impression that he was now gradually driving Eden round the bend.

I therefore wrote a letter to the Prime Minister on September

26, of which a copy was sent to the Foreign Secretary. I said that, in view of the fact that our principal allies, the United States and France, were widely divided in the sense that France would like to settle the matter by force, and the United States were prepared to go to almost any lengths to avoid the use of force, the primary responsibility for the conduct of Western policy now clearly devolved upon us. In my submission our immediate objective should be to bring Nasser to negotiation, and to obtain sufficient support from the United Nations Organization to compel him openly to flout world opinion if he still refused to negotiate.

I went on to suggest that Nasser could no longer accept international operation of the Canal without a loss of personal prestige which would seem to him intolerable. But, I asked, was international operation essential from our point of view? I doubted it. Our case was that the free and efficient use of the Canal should be guaranteed; and since it was in Egypt and—unless we put a garrison there—within the military power of Egypt, neither a private nor a public international operating company could effectively guarantee this.

'It may be argued,' I continued, 'that, in accepting such a basis for negotiation, we should to some extent be saving Nasser's face. My answer is that it is necessary to save it to this extent if he is to be brought to negotiation of any kind; and that our present objective should not be the overthrow of Nasser himself, but the establishment of certain basic principles in accordance with the accepted doctrines of international law. *In the final analysis the rights and interests of the users can only be guaranteed by their own power and influence, and this must be related to the amount of unity between them, and the amount of support they are able to obtain from other countries.*'

I went on to say that the alternative, an ultimatum, was pretty dire. If it became necessary (which it never did) I would support it; but there was an invincible reluctance in Britain to do anything that might smack of an attempt to pull French chestnuts in Algiers out of the fire.

I concluded by saying: '*I therefore come back to negotiation. Make him negotiate, if you possibly can. If you succeed in doing this, I believe you can win a substantial victory. At Geneva you faced an apparently impossible task when they all ran out on you, and achieved it. Let's have a repetition!'*

On October 2 the Prime Minister replied to my letter. He said he agreed with much of what I had to say, but that it would be disastrous if the result of negotiation was a settlement which strengthened Nasser's position and increased his prestige. We should then all be finished in Asia and Africa, and in no long time either. It seemed to him that we stood a chance of achieving our objective by negotiation only if we showed the greatest firmness and resolution—but it was not more than a chance. In the last re-sort force might be all that was left to us. He added that he had found the French vigorous and firm. They were young by our standards, and he had felt a *doyen*.

This was a disturbing letter. It dramatized the situation to the point of absurdity, and revealed no calm or steady view. By comparison, Selwyn Lloyd's reply, from New York, was sensible, brief and clear. 'We certainly aim to bring Nasser to the conference table,' he wrote: 'That is what I am now trying to do here.'

In October I went to the Persian Gulf, with three parliamentary colleagues, as the guest of the British Petroleum Company. The situation was quite different from what we expected. Dr. Ardalan, the Foreign Minister of Iran, told us that he was convinced that a settlement of the Suez Canal could be achieved by negotiation. When we got back I wrote:

'Wherever we went—in Iran, in Kuwait, in Beirut—we found a good deal of genuine bewilderment over British policy in the Middle East; and I'm bound to say that it was not easy to explain precisely why we had helped Nasser to power, sustained him there by our unconditional evacuation of the Canal Zone and supplies of arms, offered him a loan for the construction of the Aswan Dam despite his purchases of Communist arms, and then precipitately withdrawn that offer.

'On one point, however, opinion was unanimous. Force, or the serious threat of force, could have been used only as an immediate act of retaliation against the seizure of the Canal. Now we had no alternative but to "sweat it out"—which did not mean total surrender to Nasser. In the circumstances it was madness to talk about him in the way we were doing.

'Every time we described him as the greatest menace to the West since Hitler we were building up his prestige among the Arabs to quite unwarranted heights, and adding fuel to the fires of the Pan-Arab movement. Another six weeks of this, and we would have turned him into what we said he was!... But I have returned from the Middle East in a far more optimistic frame of mind than when I set out. What matters to us is oil. I now believe that, if we pursue a constructive policy with wisdom, coolness and determination, it is secure; for we have many more friends in the oil-producing areas than I had imagined.'

On the day of the sudden invasion of Sinai by Israel I lunched with my friends Mr. and Mrs. John Tilney. Mr. Levin, a leading member of the Knesset, was present. I asked him what he thought we ought to do. He said: 'Leave us alone. We want to clear out the armour which we know exists in the Sinai desert, and which is a serious threat to us. It will take us four or five days to do it. Then the whole position will be easier.' As we were ourselves largely responsible for the threat, this seemed a reasonable request.

Afterwards I ran into Walter Elliot at the House of Commons. 'I have always thought that Jehovah was on our side,' he joyfully remarked, 'and now I know it. We have only to sit tight and then, as Nuri has been saying in daily telegrams, one side or the other— and probably both—will ask us to mediate, and settle the business.' Wrong over Munich, he was unquestionably right about this.

Alas, it soon became apparent that the Prime Minister took a very different view. Two days later, when we were up to the neck in the Suez Canal, I met him in the lobby, and he said: 'You have been very patient, and we might have played it your way; but I think this is better.' He then gave an explanation of what he was trying to do which left me completely bewildered; and John Strachey, who happened to be with me, equally so. All that was clear was that his mind was closed.

While my own sympathy for the Israeli cause has been well known for many years, and continues unabated, I have little doubt that the campaign against Egypt was in fact planned by the Governments of Mr. Ben-Gurion and M. Guy Mollet; and that, at some point, Eden was informed of it. But, if you are going in for Machiavellian tactics, in itself a doubtful expedient, you really must have the guts to see it through. Having given the green light to the Israelis, the only possible thing to do was to let them finish the job. And from this Eden flinched.

I still can't imagine what the devil they thought they were up to. The objectives adduced by various Ministers, which included the defence of British lives (unthreatened), the cessation of 'hostilities' (*sic*), the 'separation' of the combatants, and the salvation of Israel from extermination at the hands of Nasser (after a campaign of almost unparalleled brilliance in which he had been decisively beaten), didn't begin to add up. In a final and farcical speech, after our withdrawal from Port Said, Peter Thorneycroft lumped a number of flatly contradictory excuses together, and almost reached the point of asking, 'How do you like this one?'

His speech afforded considerable justification for Angus Maude's bitter quotation from Burke: 'They never had any kind of system, right or wrong, but only invented some miserable tale for the day, in order meanly to sneak out of the difficulties into which they had so proudly strutted.' It was the cause of my own abstention from voting. As the curtain had already fallen, amid general boos and groans, upon the *Opéra Bouffe*, this seems in retrospect to have been pointless. The truth is that I never gave much thought to it, one way or the other, but went to the smoking room for a badly needed drink. There was the hell of a row in my constituency Association, which I had not foreseen. And for several weeks the whole country was in a state bordering on hysteria.

Fortunately I was on the record; and able to say to the House of Commons that our right course, when Israel invaded Egypt, was to go straight to the Security Council, and refuse to brand Israel as an aggressor because she had been provoked beyond endurance—largely as a result of our own policy, and that of the

United States. If we were going in for 'ultimatums' they should have been addressed neither to Egypt nor Israel, but to the Security Council itself. In a dispatch to the *Observer* from Beirut, Mr. Philby, perhaps the greatest living authority on Arabia, confirmed this. 'If the Israelis had reached the Canal on their own,' he wrote, 'Nasser's prestige would have suffered a blow from which it could not have recovered. But the Anglo-French invasion afforded him the *alibi* of the stab-in-the-back variety which Cairo Radio is busily exploiting.'

The sad thing is that the Israelis *did* reach the Canal on their own. Two years later a young and extremely intelligent member of the Israeli Foreign Service said to me, in Tel-Aviv: 'You'll never guess where I was when you landed at Port Said. Sitting quietly in the sunshine on a little hill above the town of Ismailia, your ultimate military objective. And what did you do? You sent us an ultimatum ordering us to go back into the Sinai desert.'

Thus we saved Nasser. But we are not yet 'finished' in Asia or in Africa, as Eden foretold. Nor are we likely to be.

What are the lessons to be learned?

First, that you cannot 'play' at war. The late Lord Fisher, who knew something about it, coined two aphorisms which have come down to us: 'The essence of war is surprise,' and 'Moderation in war is imbecility'. Eden disregarded both. It took him six days to reach Port Said with troops which he was reluctant to commit to serious action. If you are not prepared to accept casualties, it is really better not to go to war at all.

Second, that Anglo-American co-operation is essential to any Western enterprise of any kind in any part of the world. It was the sudden and final realization of this fact—that we are no longer a Great Power, in the nineteenth century sense of the term, and can never 'go it alone' again—that made so many people in Britain so angry at the time of Suez. They will have to learn, and are in fact learning, to take this. In the event, when it came to a crunch, neither Britain nor France were able to defend what they then conceived to be their vital interests in the Middle East, either by diplomacy or by force. If Eden finally took leave of his senses, Dulles was primarily responsible for the lack of Anglo-American co-operation. Never at any moment did he extend a hand of friendship or of confidence—not even to the point of implementing his own ill-starred conceptions of the Baghdad Pact and the Canal Users' Association. When the full story of the Suez fiasco comes to be written he will, I think, be more harshly judged than Eden.

Thirdly, that the long love affair between the English and the Arabs is at an end. The Scots never had any part in it. They have always confined their emotions to Robert Burns. But the Arabs are the only race whom the English have ever genuinely loved. This is to some extent due to the extraordinary influence exercised by a group of remarkable men (Burton, Doughty, Lawrence, Philby, Clayton, Arnold Wilson, Glubb) and women (Gertrude Bell, Freya Stark) who found personal redemption with the Bedouins in the desert. I have listened, bored, to many Englishmen expatiating on the nights they have spent, and the camel rides they have taken, in the Arabian desert. But the Bedouins are no longer thinking of camels. They are thinking of Cadillacs. The day of the technician has arrived; and, for a long time now, the love affair has been one-sided. It is therefore no bad thing that the English have had to rid themselves of what Richard Crossman once described as an attitude which adds up to 'news from nowhere'—boyish (and I emphasize that word), romantic, in some aspects genuinely idealistic; but no longer relevant either to Anglo-Arab relationships or to the political and economic emancipation of the Arab peoples.

1960.

WESTERN UNION

TWICE in this century the Western Powers have won a world war and lost the peace. Why? Mainly, I think, because of their continuous refusal to acknowledge political realities, without attempting to alter them; and because of their failure to comprehend the nature of the twentieth century revolution. As E. H. Carr pointed out in his *Conditions of Peace*, they continued to preach, and in part to apply, the once valid but now disruptive ideals of the sovereign rights of nations and *laissez-faire* capitalism; while their enemies were striving to build up the world into larger units, under centralized planning and control.

Despite the terrible warning of the inter-war years, the Western democracies clung, at San Francisco in 1945, to the out-dated Wilsonian principle of 'self-determination', which in practice meant secession and isolation; and covered it up with the smoke-screen of a high-sounding but impotent international super-structure. Despite the rise of two highly protected economies of continental scope and limitless potential power, to the East of them and to the West, the little countries of Western Europe made yet another attempt to return, on an independent national basis, to the multilateral system of the nineteenth century. While they chattered about sovereign rights, and 'united' nations which did not exist, the Russians acted; and filled, almost overnight, the vacuum created in Central Europe by the collapse of Hitler's Empire.

I have some claim to be heard on this matter now because I attended the San Francisco Conference as a newspaper man, and I then summarized and published my conclusions as follows:

'The United States have completed the regional organization and defence of the American Continent, and Stalin is bringing a similar process in Central and Eastern Europe to a rapid conclusion. If the Western European democracies do not get together fairly soon, nothing is more certain than that the entire Continent will be brought within the Russian orbit. It is becoming increasingly clear that neither the Americans nor the British had worked out sufficiently precise plans to deal with the situation arising out of the total collapse of Germany. Here lies the root of the trouble. Molotov had a clear-cut policy and was tough. That policy was to deploy existing Russian power in such a way as to get as much as possible while the going was good. There is only one way out of the present *impasse*, and that is for Great Britain and the United States to formulate clear-cut policies, and carry them out with resolution. We have now to decide where we must stand, and there stand. So far as Europe is concerned the Western democracies, including Scandinavia, constitute for us an essential minimum; and our continuing failure to form a regional group is greatly to be deplored. It is my firm conviction that the foundations of a new world order can best be laid on regional groups of nations which have strategic, political and economic interests in common. And, so far as Western Europe is concerned, the lead must be given by Great Britain.

'To suppose that the Charter of the United Nations now provides any kind of collective security is to be the victim of a dangerous illusion. No World Authority consisting of separate sovereign States will keep the peace unless those sovereign States are prepared to submit unconditionally to its basic decisions, and to place their armed forces unreservedly at its disposal. At present they are not so prepared. The objective of any realistic democratic foreign policy must therefore be to achieve a combination or combinations of democratic sovereign States, held together by a realization of their common principles and interests, which can be depended upon, if challenged, to act together.'

In the event, the total military victory of the Allies in 1945 was accompanied by the heavy political defeat of the Western Powers.

And the reasons are not far to seek. They stem from failure to decide and state, during the war, the political objectives for which we were fighting, other than the 'unconditional surrender' of Germany. If the rapidly developing political situation and problems had been considered at a much earlier stage by a Supreme Allied Council, for which I vainly pleaded in a letter to *The Times* in 1943, there might have been a different story to tell. De Gaulle raised the question of Anglo-French unity with Churchill in 1944, but met with no positive response. The emigré Governments assembled in London were never called together to discuss the future of Europe—and, particularly, of Western Europe.

As a result, when the Russian and American armies met at Torgau in April, 1945, amidst the total collapse of the European system of 1919–39, the Western Allies found themselves without settled convictions or positive policies of any kind; and saddled with a zoning system for Germany the authors of which, although apparently unknown, should be certified as insane if they are still at large. Thereafter international politics became a game of animal grab, at which the Russians proved themselves incomparably superior, and from which they emerged triumphant winners.

At Yalta whole nations had been handed around like plums, without any regard to their own wishes. 'All right, old boy,' they said, over the caviar, vodka and cigars, 'we'll give you Bulgaria and Rumania, if you give us Greece.' To this Stalin agreed with alacrity; and after that it was easy enough for him to collect ten countries in Central and Eastern Europe, and for Molotov to run through the broken ranks of the Western democracies and kick goal after goal.

I watched him doing it. After he had casually told Eden and Stettinius at San Francisco that the Polish democratic leaders who had gone to Warsaw at their request were in prison, Jan Masaryk, the Czechoslovak Foreign Minister, received instructions from Prague to propose that the puppet Communist 'Lublin' Government should be invited to the Conference. He was an old friend of mine, and we dined alone together that night, off aspirin and champagne. I besought him to refuse, and to resign. But by midnight I saw that his mind was made up. 'I cannot run away from my country,' he said; and went back to his death.

There was not really much excuse for our failure in 1945. We were in the process of defeating an enemy with whom a negotiated peace was impossible, by the side of an ally whose ultimate objective was the destruction of our political and economic systems, and the triumph of Communism. 'The fact,' wrote Professor Varga, the acknowledged mouthpiece of the Kremlin at the time, 'that the Soviet Union and the highly developed capitalistic States were in the same camp against Hitlerite aggression meant that the struggle of the two systems inside the democratic camp was relaxed and temporarily stopped. It did not mean that the struggle was ended.' It should surely have been clear to us that the war could only end with the disintegration of Germany, and the division of Europe by a line with the Red Army on one side and the armies of the Western democracies on the other. This line, subsequently described by Churchill as the Iron Curtain, was decided not by political or ethnic considerations, but by military operations which brought the Russians to the Elbe, and left half Europe in their grip.

This was the moment when Britain could, and should, have taken the undisputed leadership of a united Western Europe. We were the only country which had not been defeated and occupied, our prestige was as high as it has ever been, and we could have had it on our own terms. We did nothing. The death of Roosevelt and the subsequent defeat of Churchill at the General Election left the West bereft of leadership for a critical year, and Stalin took full advantage of it. The Potsdam Agreement set the seal on the Russian *fait accompli*.

A year later Churchill, although out of power, again took a hand in the game with the famous speech at Zürich in which he advocated a united Europe. He was careful not to give any precise definition of Britain's rôle; but shortly afterwards he said that we were 'geographically and historically a part of Europe, with a full part to play as a member of the European family.'

I think that, at this point, I must give a very brief account of my relationship with Churchill, which has been so extraordinary that in retrospect I can hardly bring myself to believe that any part of it is true.

In the 'twenties I was his protégé; and for several years lived almost as a member of the family. In the 'thirties I was behind him in opposition to the policy of appeasement; and on November 28, 1934, he invited me to be one of six signatories to an amendment to the Address in the House of Commons, which read as follows: 'But humbly represent to Your Majesty that in the present circumstances of the world, the strength of our national defences, and especially of our air defence, is no longer adequate to secure the peace, safety and freedom of Your Majesty's faithful subjects.'

In May 1940, he gave me office, as Parliamentary Secretary to the Ministry of Food; and, within a matter of days, the old intimate friendship had gone, never to return. It was largely my own fault. The irrational power 'complex', from which I have always suffered, was soon at work; and, at the height of the crisis which accompanied the fall of France, I wrote him a long letter telling him how to run the war, which now seems merely ridiculous, but which infuriated him at the time. Then someone told him that I was involved in an intrigue to make Lloyd George Prime Minister. As I had been one of the thirty-three Conservatives who had voted him into power, and Lloyd George was beginning to fail, and knew it, the idea was quite fantastic. Many years afterwards Frances, Countess Lloyd George, wrote to me: 'I was tremendously interested in what you said (last night) about your being accused of intriguing with L.G. I can certainly endorse your statement that you did no such thing. There were many reasons why L.G. refused to join the Churchill Government, but I think the chief was that he was too old for such a terrific strain.' Nevertheless, I have reason to suppose that Churchill believed this story. Perhaps he wanted to believe it.

Finally, through thoughtlessness, not guilt, I got into parliamentary difficulties, and joined the Royal Air Force. Churchill held out no helping hand in this time of trouble, and I began to feel that he wanted to do me in. Sometimes I woke up in the night trembling. I could not understand why this mighty Titan, then at the zenith of his power, and carrying the main burden, whom I had known so well, and served for so long to the best of my capacity, should harbour such resentment against anyone as completely unimportant as myself. But on the day of the censure debate which followed the fall of Tobruk in 1942, he sent for me. I could see at once that he was anxious. He asked me whether I 'still supported the Government'; and, if so, whether I was prepared to speak. The answer to both questions being an emphatic affirmative, he led me to the Speaker, and said that he wished me to be called early in the debate. In *The Second World War* he was good enough to write that I made 'a powerful and helpful speech'. Such praise is far too high. What I did manage to do was to lower the temperature and the tension, and put the House in better humour; and this was useful at that moment. Later he took me to the smoking-room, ordered two whiskies, and drank a toast to 'the Pegasus wings of my oratory'. And, after that, he never spoke to me again until the end of the war!

This time I thought it must be the finish. Not at all. In 1946 he picked me up again, and made me a member of the Committee of his Council for United Europe. We launched our campaign under highly respectable auspices at the Albert Hall, with the Archbishop of Canterbury in the chair. Up to a point, it caught on. It was followed, in May 1948, by the Congress of The Hague, held under the auspices of the international European Movement, of which Duncan Sandys and the late Joseph Retinger were moving spirits. From this much flowed, including the Council of Europe.

I must now ask the reader to take time off in order to read some extracts from speeches which I made over ten years ago; because, between them, they constitute the theme song of this chapter.

The first, from a speech which I made to the House of Commons on the eve of the Hague Congress—the actual date being May 5, 1948:

'In my submission war is inherent and endemic in a world of completely independent sovereign States.

'I remember fifteen years ago taking a long walk with Philip

Lothian at Sandwich; and he then expounded to me, with great force and passion, his belief that the principle of the sovereign equality of nations was false and wrong; that it had no basis of reality; and could only lead to war. He told me that his underlying idea during the peace conference of 1919, in which he played a great part—he was Secretary to Mr. Lloyd George at the time—was that the United States, France, and Britain should collectively discharge the function which Britain alone performed during the nineteenth century through the exercise—invisible but unchallenged—of universal sea power. He said that the breakdown was caused by the fact the United States contracted out and turned towards isolation; and that we ourselves withdrew from Europe following the abortive French occupation of the Ruhr in 1923.

'The result could only mean anarchy; and anarchy was what we got. For twenty years the disarmed, disunified and isolated democracies of Europe writhed in the rigid structure of separate sovereign States evolved in the eighteenth and nineteenth centuries, until distrust, poverty and unemployment gave way to hatred, dictatorship and the new combination of Fascist aggressor States which led to yet another attempt to impose integration upon the continent of Europe by force. Isolation in the modern world is a terrible thing. The dream of every potential aggressor is to isolate his opponents one by one. As Burke said: "When bad men combine, the good must associate; else they will fall, one by one, an unpitied sacrifice in a contemptible struggle."

'It seems to me that the supreme object of our policy should surely be to build a democratic world order so strong that no State or combination of States will dare to challenge it. I realize that, for this, we shall have to make sacrifices. But adequate deterrent power is essential. As Admiral Mahan truly said, "The function of force is to give time for moral ideas to take root."

'Such a democratic world order can only be built up by the creation of a United States of Western Europe, in some form or other, in close association with the British Commonwealth, and with the United States of America, upon whose material strength the entire structure must in the first phase depend.

'The process must be one of spiritual growth, as well as of material progress; and the end must be a series of organic acts of union. I see no other way. The choice that confronts us is fundamental. I do not think it is obscure. It is the choice between international anarchy and the rule of law; between the rebirth or the doom of our Western civilization.'

The second quotation is from the speech I made to the meeting of the Consultative Assembly of the Council of Europe, at Strasbourg, in August 1949. Churchill had appointed me a member of the Conservative delegation of five, of which he was himself the leader, in the teeth of considerable opposition; and did me the honour of listening to it:

'The trouble with Western Europe is that, while the ideal of the rule of law based on reason, custom and morality, has been applied within the nation-States, it has been accepted but never applied as between nation-States. We must now face the fact that, so long as each nation-State recognizes no authority above itself and no duty except to itself, wars will continue.

'Sovereignty, in the sense of the exercise of absolute political power, is the supreme source of law. Whenever it resides in groups or individuals within a society, and not in the society itself, there is internal anarchy. Whenever it resides in nation-States, and not in a society of nations, there is international anarchy. For my part I am convinced that the doctrine of the sovereign equality of nations is not only nonsense, but a mathematical formula for war. I share the belief of my friend, the late Lord Lothian, that insistence on absolute state sovereignty is one of the principal causes of the evils of our modern world; and hold the view that the only solution of this problem lies in some merging or pooling of national sovereignty.

'I feel most strongly that in this Assembly, and in the Committee of Ministers, we have the instruments with which an organic European union can be forged. We live in a rapidly shrinking world. Yet we have continued since the war the fatuous struggle to maintain complete national political independence, and to achieve complete economic independence. With what result? We cannot trade freely with each other. We cannot even visit each other!

'How can we get rid of the present formidable obstacles to European unity? Let me give three examples. In order to free our exchanges for current transactions, we shall have to co-ordinate our monetary and fiscal policies. In order to increase our productivity we shall have to plan investment in our basic industries on a European scale, and to encourage specialization. In order to increase our trade with one another we shall have to negotiate reciprocal trade and payment agreements, and adopt a preferential system.

'All this will require the establishment of a number of permanent functional European authorities. It will also require frequent and major decisions of policy. For instance, the doctrine of non-discrimination, accepted in principle at Bretton Woods and Havana, but seldom applied in practice, will have to be reconsidered in the light of entirely new conditions. Unless we establish, at the same time, an executive international political Authority, the functional authorities will be powerless; because somebody has to decide policy, and somebody has to give the orders. When you come to think of it, this political Authority can only be the Committee of Ministers. What other body has the necessary power? Who else can decide policy on behalf of the participating Governments?

'What I have in mind is a number of functional committees working under the general direction and supervision of the Committee of Ministers which should itself meet at frequent intervals, and have a permanent secretariat of its own, manned by a European Civil Service. It follows from this that the Assembly, which in my opinion should meet at least twice a year, should have the right to put forward any proposals it may wish to make for consideration by the Committee; that the Committee should be required to make periodical Reports to the Assembly, and to answer any questions which we may put to it; and that the Governments should, in turn, furnish the Committee with adequate information and powers. Here, then, is the constructive proposal which I wish to put forward. After much reflection during the past two years, I am convinced that it is by far the most hopeful line of advance.

'In his opening address, M. Herriot reminded us that there were some good German philosophers before Fichte introduced, and Treitschke developed, the accursed doctrine of power. He mentioned Goethe and Kant. Let me conclude by quoting one sentence of Humboldt which I think we should all keep on our writing tables: "The State is merely a means to which man, the true end, must never be sacrificed."'

At this meeting a resolution was passed by the Assembly enjoining the Committee of Ministers to develop a European political authority 'with limited functions but real powers'. All the Conservative members of the British delegation voted in favour of it; but when, soon afterwards, the Schuman Plan for a Coal and Steel Community was put forward, the Labour Government rejected it out of hand, refusing even to take part in the discussions on the ground that any such invasion of national sovereignty was quite unacceptable to them.

Then came a bombshell. In August 1950, Churchill demanded, in the Consultative Assembly at Strasbourg, the immediate creation of a European Army, under a unified command with a single Defence Minister, 'in which we should all bear a worthy and honourable part.' He added: 'Those who serve supreme causes must not consider what they can get but what they can give.'

This had an electrifying effect, and was immediately followed by two mistakes which seem in retrospect to have been even more disastrous than they did—to me—at the time. These were, first, the refusal of the British Government to participate in the discussions about the form which the European Army should take; and secondly, American insistence on German rearmament before we had made peace with Western Germany—indeed while we were still dismantling her factories and blowing up her shipyards. This led to French insistence upon an elaborate 'supra-national' structure for the proposed European Defence Community, to which I shall hereafter refer as the E.D.C., under what became known as the Pleven Plan.

I was oppressed by the folly of putting so many carts before so many horses—of the attempt to rearm the Germans before we had peace with them, to create an international European Army without British participation, and to embark on either of these ventures without first defining political relationships.

On November 13, 1950, I said to the House of Commons:

'The other day I read a very interesting little book prepared by a Chatham House group called *Defence in the Cold War*. It said: "The Western nations cannot put off their plans for integrated balanced forces and joint financing of war production until they have decided what form of political association they will accept."

'With all respect I do not find myself in agreement with that view. I should like to compare it with a recent statement by Field-Marshal Lord Montgomery, who in my experience of his writings and actions is apt to get to the heart of the matter. Lord Montgomery said: "The strategic centre of the battle for world peace today is Western Europe. We must be able to hold the position there. The task before the nations of the West is primarily political. Economic fusion and military strength will not be obtained until the political association between the group of nations concerned has first been defined."

'I believe that Lord Montgomery is right; and that, in considering Germany from a political point of view, German public opinion can no longer be disregarded. That opinion, at the moment, is overwhelmingly pacifist. We cannot force any nation to arm unless we are ourselves a totalitarian State. We can arm a willing ally, if they ask for arms; but we cannot arm an unwilling ex-enemy.

'I therefore submit that our first objective must be to make of Western Germany an ally and a friend. Until that is done, the Germans will bear no part of the burden of Western defence, and they will be right. I think the time has come to make peace with Western Germany, and to assure her of an honourable place, if she wishes to take it, in the Western world; to restore her national status and responsibility; and to accept her as a full partner both in the Western European Union and in the Atlantic Pact. Then, and only then, will she find, if she wishes, the necessary means to resist the Communist technique of disruption and aggression.

'Nationalism has brought neither security, prosperity nor peace to the peoples of continental Europe. In a sense, the tragedy of Beneš is the tragedy of them all. He was the arch-nationalist; and the man who lived to see the little nation-State he did so much to create conquered, first by Hitler's Germany, and then by Stalin's Russia.

'But if the United States of Europe are to come into existence, as I fervently hope that in some form they will, I believe it can only be as an integral part of an Atlantic Union with which the United States is closely associated in political, military and economic terms. A European union by itself we might have had. I think that the time for that has passed, and that we must go straight for the larger goal. I was very interested in a document written not long ago by Mr. Edward Dickinson, Jr., of the State Department in Washington, in which he concluded: "We will have to redefine our relationship to Western Europe in terms which make us no longer an outsider. This can probably best be done by a clear statement of the longer-term objective, emphasizing that a Western European Union within a looser Atlantic Union are, in our eyes, two parts of the same policy; and that we do not ask for the first without a whole-hearted commitment to the second."'

I followed this up with a speech to the Consultative Assembly of the Council of Europe on November 22, in which I said:

'The time has arrived when we should consider very seriously our relationship to the Atlantic Union. This does not mean that we should not make a united Europe. On the contrary. A few years ago the conception of a "Third Force" rose like a phoenix, only to subside. Since then we have been losing the global war against Communism, and it has become clear that the Western democracies cannot succeed or survive unless they act together.

'The truth is that the United States alone can now give vitality to any association of democratic nations; and that action restricted to the executive level of Governments acting independently no longer meets the minimum requirements of our situation. Its inadequacies have been painfully illustrated in the Far East in the last few months; and were implicit in the dilemma which confronted the British Commonwealth in 1914, and again in 1939, when the Dominions, although exercising undisputed national sovereignty, were obliged to choose between belligerency and neutrality in wars which had resulted from foreign policies which they themselves had played no part in framing.

'In any vague or unformulated association between greater and lesser Powers, the strongest is bound to make the vital decisions imposed by the dynamic of events; and it is time that we realized that we can retain a far greater control over our own destinies by advancing our views and claims in a Council which ultimately decides policy, than by keeping up the pretence of total national sovereignty.

'Let me summarize my suggestions as follows: the negotiation of a formal Pact of Western European Union for mutual defence and economic co-operation, the gradual development of the Committee of Ministers into an executive political Authority with limited functions but defined powers; the subordination of all functional European organizations to the ultimate authority of the Council of Europe; the integration of the United States of Europe into the wider Western Union of the Atlantic Community; the reorganization of the Committees set up under the Brussels Pact and the North Atlantic Treaty Organization into a single military council charged with the creation of an integrated defence force for the Western world; and, finally, the establishment of a Supreme Council, including representatives of Western Europe, the United States and Canada, to direct the foreign policy, the military strategy and the economic development of Western Union as a whole.

'I am well aware that these proposals will be decried as over-ambitious and Utopian; and that I shall be told that it is no part of our business to make suggestions to the United States. The fact remains that they represent our minimum requirements now; and that the United States, who have strongly pressed for the unification of Europe, cannot dissociate themselves from a "grand design", if only for the reason that the Elbe today is the frontier not only of the Atlantic Community but of free democracy everywhere. There is now loose in the world a mighty force dedicated to the proposition that we shall never again enjoy peace, security or prosperity. Since 1945 this force has conquered half the world; and the other half must needs bestir itself if it is to escape total destruction.'

In the autumn of 1951 there was a change of Government in the United Kingdom, following a General Election, as a result of which Sir Winston Churchill again became Prime Minister, with Sir Anthony Eden as Foreign Secretary. This brought fresh hope to the Council of Europe.

In November a debate was held at Strasbourg between representatives of the Consultative Assembly and of the Congress of the United States. Once again in the teeth of considerable opposition, Churchill invited me to represent the Conservative Party, and by implication the British Government, in this debate; and, under friendly but strong pressure from Senators Wiley and McMahon, I agreed that our attitude towards the projected Coal and Steel Community and the European Army would be the acid test of our sincerity.

One week later the Home Secretary, then Sir David Maxwell-Fyfe, came out to a plenary session of the Consultative Assembly and gave the following pledge, on the subject of the European Army, on behalf of His Majesty's Government:

'I cannot promise full and unconditional participation, but I can assure you of our determination that no genuine method shall fail for lack of thorough examination which one gives to the needs of trusted friends.... There is no refusal on the part of Britain.'

That same night Eden announced at a Press conference in Rome the refusal of the United Kingdom to participate in a European Army on any terms whatsoever. The effect of this announcement upon the Council of Europe was catastrophic. Every delegation thought we had betrayed Europe, as indeed we had. I have never seen a more demoralized Assembly. The British Conservative delegates, of whom I was one, were themselves so disturbed that on December 3 they sent a formal protest to the Prime Minister, signed by the lot, the concluding paragraph of which ran:

'We venture to appeal to you to take some positive action designed to restore British prestige in the Consultative Assembly, and to show that His Majesty's Government mean to play their part in the military defence and economic development of a united Europe.'

To this there was no reply. M. Spaak resigned the Presidency of the Consultative Assembly in order to lead the campaign for a 'Little Federation of the Six', without Britain; and the European Movement, against my passionate but solitary protest, decided to give it full support. These were formidable events.

There followed the long and exhausting struggle over the European Defence Community. We now have it on the authority of Mr. Anthony Nutting, at the time Minister of State in the Foreign Office, that Eden reacted to his suggestion, and that of Sir Gladwyn Jebb, in Paris, that we should at least guarantee to leave a certain number of divisions on the Continent of Europe for the duration of the proposed Treaty 'like a kicking mule'. He, at any rate, was determined to get out, and stay out.

I expressed my own anxieties at a comparatively early stage, in a speech to the House of Commons on November 6, 1952.

'At the moment, we are passing through a phase of difficulty and even of confusion in European affairs, for which we bear some responsibility ourselves; but I believe it is only a temporary phase, or need only be a temporary phase. It is always intolerable to quote oneself, but I should like to recall some words of mine written in 1951: "The approach of the Western Powers to the problem of Germany could hardly have been more unfortunate. It was a mistake to try and re-arm what amounted to an enemy-occupied country before making peace. We should have negotiated a political settlement first."

'What should we do in this situation? We have now to go back to first principles, always advisable in politics, and perhaps most advisable in the conduct of foreign affairs. I have never wavered in my belief that we ought long ago to have taken the lead in uniting Western Europe on a confederal or commonwealth basis, and to have used the Council of Europe as the instrument of our policy. I hold that belief just as strongly today as I ever did. I think we ought to have joined in the discussions which led to the creation of the Coal and Steel Community, and to the proposed European Defence Community; and participated in both. I believe there is only one solution to this problem, and that is a merger of E.D.C. with N.A.T.O. on terms which will ultimately permit of equal French and German status within the ambit of the larger organization; but the French will never agree to this unless and until we are ourselves part of the European Defence Community.'

No attention was paid to this. On the contrary, the pressure on France steadily increased. 'If,' I wrote, 'the Government really feel that the E.D.C. offers the best solution to the problem of European defence, there is only one thing for them to do—join it.' And again, in a letter to *The Times* on July 12, 1954: 'What are the alternatives? The outright rejection of the E.D.C. treaty by the French Assembly, or a shot-gun wedding between a resurgent Germany and a fear-ridden France. Neither of these would increase the security of the West. The truth is that Franco-German reconciliation, which seemed within reach three years ago, is more important than any preconceived military scheme. It is the necessary prelude to the establishment of any genuine partnership in the common defence of Western civilization; and it has been put in jeopardy first by the attempt to make the restoration of sovereignty to Federal Germany conditional on German rearmament, and secondly by the attempt to force the French to enter a European army and a political union which we are not prepared to join ourselves. Sooner or later we must face the fact that there can be no hope of European unity, or of European defence, except on the basis of British participation.'

To all such arguments the American and British Governments

alike remained impervious. The E.D.C. treaty became to the Foreign Office what the groundnuts scheme had been to the Ministry of Food. Absorbed in their own wishful thinking, they were deaf to all warnings; and when the French Assembly finally threw it out they received the news with dazed amazement and dismay. This, it must be added, was followed by galvanic diplomatic activity on the part of Eden, which resulted in our putting British troops on the Continent after all.

The sands were now running out. But, in 1952, there came, for us, yet another chance. What became known as the 'Strasbourg Plan' was designed to harness the industrial resources of Western Europe to the raw material resources of its associated territories overseas, with the object of expanding the production and trade of the whole. It recommended the utilization of the resources of the member States of the Council of Europe, under a comprehensive preferential system, for the economic development of these countries; a close association between the European Payments Union and the Sterling Area; the co-ordination of monetary policies and investment plans; international commodity schemes for stabilizing the prices of basic products; the establishment of a Central European Bank; and the automatic provision of credit for countries in temporary balance-of-payment difficulties.

As Vice-Chairman of the Committee on Economic Affairs, I attended all the discussions; and can testify that some of the finest economic minds in Europe gave much time and thought to the Plan. We got it passed, unanimously, by the Consultative Assembly; and forwarded to the British Government with a request that it should be considered by the Conference of Commonwealth Prime Ministers. What happened? It was pole-axed overnight by the Treasury; and, instead of being participants, we became envious spectators of the subsequent economic upsurge of 'The Six'.

The Council of Europe, together with a subsidiary and quite unnecessary Council of Western Europe, collapsed into total impotence; and was speedily driven to the desperate expedient of passing scores of hastily drafted resolutions, based on inadequate statistical information, to which no attention was ever paid. As Mr. Herbert Luthy truly said, in his interesting book on *The State of France*; 'The Foreign Ministers of Western Europe, like actors on a revolving stage which had got out of control, kept reappearing every few days against a different backcloth, always playing a never-completed first act. True, their numbers, grouping and function changed; they appeared as representative of the sixteen or eighteen Powers of O.E.E.C., or of the five Powers of the Brussels Pact, or of the ten, twelve, and eventually fifteen Powers of the Council of Europe, or, with their American partners, as the select inner group of three Powers of N.A.T.O., or as the twelve Powers representing all the members of N.A.T.O. Each of these organizations set up its own permanent organization, exchanged delegations and accredited representatives with the others, and co-ordinating committees were set up, the number of which grew in geometrical progression with the foundation of each new organization. Their functions overlapped to such an extent that a special bureaucracy was set up for the sole purpose of exchanging and filing their statistics, plans and resolutions; a sham world of "supra-national" organizations tirelessly organizing their own activity in the void.'

Meanwhile the Common Market went ahead. We refused to take it seriously. We sent no Minister to their Conference at Messina, and only a junior official to their Conference at Brussels as an 'observer', who took no part in the discussions, and was politely shown the door. Having drugged ourselves into the belief that it was a fantasy, we suddenly woke up to the fact that it was a reality—a mighty union of nearly 200 million people, in which we had elected to have no part.

What did we do then? Immediately we panicked, and rushed into the creation of a 'Free Trade Area' which consolidated rather than healed the fatal division of Western Europe. By this time I had quitted the Council of Europe, in total despair. I felt that the choice before us was one of full participation in the Common Market, or active estrangement; and that we had chosen the latter. Not at all. We have since chosen to apply for membership and, whatever the immediate difficulties, it is in the stars. Which just goes to show that you should never, *never* give up. There is only one infallible rule; and that is that you should not allow yourself to be beaten by life. All the frustrations and miseries of Strasbourg had not, after all, been in vain.

I do not suppose that the advent of the United Kingdom to the Common Market will solve all the problems; but it is bound to lessen the danger of war. For centuries the continent of Europe has been the main battleground of the world, from which we have never been absent. Isolationist voices have been raised recently— Lord Hinchingbrooke, for instance, has talked about a return to the 'small ship' philosophy which, in his opinion, accounted for Britain's past greatness. Has he forgotten Blenheim, Ramillies, Malplaquet? The Peninsula, Corunna, Waterloo? Loos, Neuve Chapelle, the Somme and Passchendaele, where the flower of an entire generation was destroyed? There were not many small ships there. The fields of Northern France and Flanders are drenched in British blood; and all because Europe could not, or would not, unite.

European Union must also bring to an end the insane policy of 'independent national nuclear deterrents', not only because they would make nonsense of the whole affair, but because the conception of a wider and looser Atlantic Union, in which Western Europe would participate as such, is already on the march. On this subject Herr Strauss, the Federal German Minister of Defence, made some extremely pertinent observations not long ago. He said that France and Germany composed a single strategic unit; that the choice for Western Germany was either to go Communist or to join the West for good; that he was a convinced enemy of any German hegemony in Europe; that the time for a European 'balance of power' had gone; and that he saw the future in terms of a Germany which was a function of European policy and, as such, a component of Atlantic policy.

If these words mean anything, they mean that the problems of Berlin, of the future relationship between East and West Germany, and—above all—of the nuclear deterrent, can only be resolved in the context of a general agreement between the N.A.T.O. Powers as a whole, and the countries adhering to the Warsaw

Pact, accompanied—we must all hope—by some form of military 'disengagement'. This could result, a generation hence, if not in union at least in a very much closer association between Western and Eastern Europe, which was the original objective of the European Movement. But it also means that the old Dulles policy of promising, always ambiguously, that Dr. Adenauer's Government, backed by the might of the United States, would somehow cause the Soviet Union to surrender East Germany, after 'free elections', is not only dead but buried. That policy has rightly been described by Walter Lippmann as a shabby hoax. It was never serious, and it was never sincere, because the Western Allies—including West Germany—never had the slightest intention of going to war to re-unify Germany or to liberate Eastern Europe; and proved it when the Berlin wall was erected. It is hard on the East Germans that, for the time being, they should have to pay the major part of the price for the hell which Hitler loosed on Europe and the world. But someone had to pay it.

What of the long-term future? Much depends on the United States. When Woodrow Wilson was forced to abandon 'isolation', he set out to reform the world according to American ideas and ideals. He failed, and fell, with calamitous consequence. But the tradition lingered on, through and beyond the second world war. It was the messianic element in Dulles's policy of brinkmanship that caused me most anxiety. This now seems to be waning. President Kennedy said recently: 'We cannot always prevail.' Equally, it is quite unthinkable that the Americans, now deeply committed to the Western Alliance, should ever fail it. As so often happens the answer to the lurking suspicion in some European minds, and particularly that of General de Gaulle, has been found by Walter Lippmann; 'It never could enter the conscious mind of Americans to do it. We have no Machiavellian tradition. The idea of switching alliances is something that is quite alien to our way of thinking.' If Adenauer and de Gaulle are able at this moment to pursue intransigent foreign policies, it is only because they are both under the shield of American nuclear power. This is what Lippmann has justifiably described as 'hitch-hiking' diplomacy. But fair is fair. Adenauer has held steadfastly to the West. And de

Gaulle, despite illusions of grandeur, has pressed on with the liquidation of the French Empire; and, in so doing, rendered yet another inestimable service to his country.

For my part I believe, and have said and written, that the Western Alliance, including Britain, would be well advised to confide the ultimate nuclear deterrent exclusively to the United States; and then give them all the aid—technical and financial—that we can. We need have no fear that this awful power will be used recklessly. The Americans are an emotional people, but a glance at history proves that they do not embark on major wars with precipitation. It took three years of German ruthlessness to get them into the first world war: and they had to be blown into the second at Pearl Harbour. What we should be worrying about is not whether the United States will plunge the world into nuclear devastation, still less whether, in an hour of crisis, they will let us down; but the absence of adequate consultative machinery for the Western Alliance as a whole. And this, in the final analysis, depends on the will of the peoples and Governments of the West to co-operate and to agree with one another.

So far as this country is concerned, I think that Sir Charles Snow laid his finger on our greatest danger when he wrote in his book *Science and Government* that we are becoming an existential society, living in the same world with future-directed societies. 'This existential flavour,' he added, 'is obvious in our art. In fact, we are becoming unable to accept any other kind of art. ... We seem to be flexible, but we haven't any model of the future before us. In the significant sense, we can't change. And to change is what we have to do.'

For example, we avert our gaze from the indisputable if unpalatable fact that the British Commonwealth is, at this moment, in the process of political and economic disintegration. Yet such an association of free multi-racial States, scattered around the globe, can still be of enormous potential value; and the Queen, as its symbolic Head, has proved it over and over again. The best way to pull the Commonwealth together is to go into Western Europe as quickly as possible. For two reasons. We should become, once again, a Great Power—or at least part of one. And the

Commonwealth countries themselves want some access to the richest and most rapidly expanding market in the world. Churchill's three 'concentric circles' never added up to much. The Commonwealth has gone its own way; Western Europe has gone hers; and our relationship with the United States, although mercifully close, is not as 'special' as he supposed. We have to carve out new paths for ourselves, in a changing world. As I said in my Radner Lectures, for the last ten years the West has been conducting a global struggle against the centrally directed forces of Communism without any central organs of decision to direct military strategy, political policy, or economic policy upon a global scale; and that is why, on balance, it has been losing it.

I look to the future with modified but sustained optimism. If the human race is to survive, we must reach agreement with the Communist world about nuclear weapons, and the establishment of some kind of world order, or government, before the end of the present century. I hesitate to estimate the chances of this; but it will certainly be easier if there are two nuclear Powers rather than ten. On the other hand, I believe that men, on the whole, are wicked little animals. When you think of the vile crimes and cruelties they have inflicted upon one another in the name of the one man, Jesus, who mastered the secret of living because he was utterly unafraid of 'rules', of Sin, and of Death, it makes you shudder. The great hope is that, today, they are frightened. Frightened of their own cleverness and wickedness; and of the fearful things they have again done to each other in this terrible century. They now face their own extermination, if they do not mend their ways; and they don't like that prospect.

Peaceful co-existence between the Communist world and what we call the Free world would not only be possible, but easy, if mankind was not so wicked. What struck me most forcibly when I was behind the Iron Curtain last year[1] was not the antagonism, but the latent similarity between modern Communism and modern Capitalism. We are all 'planners' now. It follows that, if competitive co-existence continues, the two systems will, as Mr. Michael Shanks has said, increasingly come to mirror each other.

1. 1961.

The problem facing every country is no longer one of choosing between the abstract alternatives of nationalization or free enterprise, but of finding the proper balance between the two.

There is yet another hope. Youth. And here I come to an article of dazzling brilliance by Arthur Koestler, entitled 'The Age of Paradox'.[1] In it he pointed out that the movement towards a uniform and stereotyped culture-pattern had become irresistible, because of what he described as the 'back-feed' of modern transmitting and receiving apparatus. They all want, roughly, the same thing. In the West and in the East. In the Communist world and the Free world. The boys and girls who travel across Europe, and as often as not across the Iron Curtain, on bicycles and scooters, have much in common; and understand one another. It may not be a very high kind of culture—'the Twist', for me, has limited attractions. But it is the same kind of thing. And it can be made much better. 'After the ideological debauches of the first half of the century,' says Koestler, 'a process of sobering up seems to have set in, leading to a somewhat dreary, rather tasteless and standardized world—but at least a world that acquiesces in its own survival.'

To use a favourite expression of modern youth, I am 'with him'. But, if you ask me what the future holds for the world, I can only answer in the words that Turgenev put into the mouth of one of his characters when he was asked, at the end of *On the Eve*, what the future held for Russia; 'Uvar Ivanovitch flourished his fingers, and fixed his enigmatical stare into the far distance.'

1. *Observer*, August 30, 1959.

1962.

BEHIND THE IRON CURTAIN

HAVING just returned, with Sir Leslie Plummer, from a visit to Poland, Czechoslovakia, Hungary and Rumania, I am sure of only one thing—that no facile generalizations are possible. The four countries adhere to no uniform pattern of Communism, save in two respects. These are the political power of the Communist Party, invisibly but relentlessly exercised through the medium of the secret police, which in the final analysis is absolute; and the concentration of ownership of the means of industrial production in the hands of the State, which is total.

Apart from this the differences between them, and within them, are great. I had much sympathy with one of our diplomatic representatives when he told us that he found considerable difficulty in writing a dispatch in which most of the sentences did not contradict the previous one.

Let me make it plain at the outset that, with the exception of the prisons (which were never on our visiting list) we saw everyone and everything we wanted to see; and, if truth is to be told, a bit more. We travelled many hundred of miles by road through towns, villages and a countryside which could not be concealed; and were under constant pressure to go farther afield, to visit more farms and more factories. In each country we had interviews with Foreign Ministers, Trade Ministers and Planning Ministers, all of whom talked to us with the utmost frankness.

The conclusion I have reached is that the régimes established in what we call the satellites may well be modified in the light of experience and events; but are no longer likely to be overthrown. The Dulles policy of 'liberation' is dead, if indeed it ever lived;

and we had better face that fact. Successive and wholly abortive rebellions in East Germany, Poland and Hungary put paid to it.

In a recent article Sénor de Madariaga wrote: 'The satellites are as restive as ever, and therefore forbode more trouble than help (for Russia) if it came to a European crisis.' With all respect, I must differ directly with him. Apart from East Germany, the poorest and the least successful, the satellites are solidly behind Mr. Khrushchev in his present attitude towards Germany.

Not to put too fine a point on it, the Poles, the Czechs and even the Hungarians fear and hate the Germans to an extent which we cannot even begin to comprehend in this country. I am referring not to members of the Communist Party, nor to Ministers, but to the people. They are horrified by the prospect of Western Germany getting atomic weapons; and have no desire to see Germany reunited. This gives to the Soviet Union a massive psychological support throughout Central and Eastern Europe, which we shall underestimate at our peril.

The reason is understandable when you see and hear of it at first hand. Warsaw and Budapest were destroyed by Hitler's orders. Prague received the personal attention of Heydrich. And in all four of the countries we visited the Germans killed and killed and killed, for five interminable years. The killing was not confined to the Jews; and it is not forgotten.

In Poland, for example, the Ministers put the problems now confronting them in the following order: The German menace; the standard of living, which is generally too low; and the relationship between State and Church. To Polish minds the first is dominant. In defence of the Oder-Neisse line they are ready to fight at any moment—preferably with cavalry. Every time Herr Willy Brandt, who is held in higher regard than any other West German political leader, talks about a 'rectification' of the Oder-Neisse line, or says that it is simply not possible for the German people to recognize a dictated division of their country, every Polish peasant reaches for his harness and his gun.

The moment of truth came when we confronted Mr. Fierlinger,

the Chairman of the National Assembly, in Prague. I am content to record what he said, with clear intent, and with the stated concurrence of the Foreign Offices of all four countries:

'Sooner or later Mr. Khrushchev will recognize the East German Government. Control over access to Berlin will then be transferred to them; but he is prepared to negotiate the terms on which appropriate access to West Berlin will be guaranteed to the Western Powers. We shall all support him. We reckon that the West will not drop nuclear bombs on us over this issue; and that, if conventional N.A.T.O. forces are used for an invasion of East German territory, they will immediately be defeated. At a later stage we should like to see an agreement for some form of military disengagement, on the lines suggested in the Rapacki Plan. If Poland and ourselves [Czechoslovakia] are prepared to give up nuclear weapons, and submit to reciprocal inspection on the part of the East and the West, why should the Germans, who were defeated in the war, not do the same?'

It was as simple as that.

My worst enemy can hardly accuse me of being an advocate of what used to be known as 'appeasement'. It was, for me, a poignant moment when I walked into the Hrâdcany Castle in Prague three weeks ago. The last time I had been there was when I lunched alone with Beneš in July 1938, two months before Munich.

I had motored over from the Sudetenland where Henlein, under Hitler's orders, was working his supporters up to frenzy; and my secretary has since reminded me that when we passed the Skoda Works, and she asked what was being manufactured there, I replied: 'Bombs for Hitler to blow you up, if we haven't the guts to stand up to him now.'

After lunch the President took me to a window to show me the view over the city, which was and remains almost unsurpassed in Europe. 'We don't want that destroyed,' he said: 'What am I to do, if Hitler uses force? What will you do? What will the French do? Will you stand by us?'

I replied, with truth, that I did not know what we or the French would do: but that if he fought, as he should, we would be obliged to come to his aid. It was at least a realistic view.

Today, it seems to me, there is very little realism about our attitude towards Germany in general, and Berlin in particular. We are ourselves largely responsible for the present situation. With the Americans—but not the Russians—we proclaimed the terms of 'unconditional surrender' which made a negotiated peace settlement of any kind impossible.

If West Berlin is now marooned in Communist territory we have ourselves to blame rather than the Russians, who not unnaturally took full advantage of our folly. That we have clamant obligations to the inhabitants of West Berlin is not to be denied. But we shall not save them by policies based on illusion; or, indeed, with nuclear bombs.

Ten years ago Walter Lippmann said to me: 'Sometimes I wonder whether we can repair the enormous mistake of having tried to rearm the Germans before we had made a political settlement with them.' It was Dean Acheson who did this. And it is Acheson who is now reported to be urging President Kennedy to mobilize for an all-out war over Berlin.

There is no road through this way. The only road is hard negotiation based on acknowledgement of the political realities of the present situation, and the necessity of changing them by a process of give and take.

The basic reality, which hit us with unexpected force on the other side of the Iron Curtain, is that they all fear German rearmament; and are prepared to risk world war to prevent the reunification of Germany, as a member of N.A.T.O., because they are convinced that, in that event, the Germans will come back to kill them again, this time with nuclear weapons.

Only twenty years ago the satellite countries were under the Nazi jackboot, and the Russians had the Germans at their throats. They are not prepared to take this, or the threat of it, again; and Khrushchev was not bluffing when he told Lippmann that he was in a hurry because he wanted the frontiers of Germany, the status of Berlin, and the demarcation line between the two German states fixed, 'before Hitler's generals in West Germany get the atom bomb.'

For sixteen years the policy of the West has been based on the fiction that somehow or other, after 'free elections', Germany can be reunited. For the last ten years no one has seriously believed it; and the bluff has now been called by the 'sealing-off' operation of August 13, which forced the Western Allies to acknowledge tacitly the partition of Germany as one of the results of the second world war.

We can, I believe, negotiate a temporary settlement which will guarantee access to Berlin on the part of the West, perhaps by means of the corridor suggested by Mr. Emery Reves, in return for the abandonment of the Dulles policy of 'liberation', the *de facto* recognition of the East German Government, and the firm acceptance of the Oder-Neisse frontier. It is a pill which will take some swallowing by both sides; but the alternative—nuclear war —is not open to either.

Such a settlement could bring a relaxation of the present world tension, and a diminution of the danger of nuclear annihilation. It would not bring the struggle for the mastery of the world to an end; but it might turn it into different, and less lethal, channels.

So far as the West Germans are concerned, the ultimate choice can be made only by themselves. If they believe, with Herr Strauss, that their future lies with the West in terms of a German policy which is a component of Atlantic policy, the division of Germany must be accepted as permanent. If they regard reunification as their primary objective, they will have to negotiate a peace treaty which imposes 'neutralization', in some form, upon them. In either case the policy of military disengagement, originally propounded by Mr. Rapacki, never rejected by Sir Anthony Eden, and now advocated by Field-Marshal Lord Montgomery, has much to commend it.

These are long-term issues, which cannot yet be decided. My immediate purpose is to call attention to the indisputable fact that, so far as the German problem is concerned, the satellite countries of Central and Eastern Europe are solidly ranged behind Mr.

Khrushchev; and that it would be a pity to make any mistake about this, since it might put an end to all of us.

I see no reason for a craven policy of 'appeasement' on the part of the West; and every reason for hard bargaining, from a position of military strength. The realities of the present situation are harsh. But, in the long run, realism is a better basis than illusion for the conduct of foreign policy; and less dangerous.

Poland remains, basically, a country of peasants and horses. Only the landlords have gone, and they are not spoken of with any bitterness. Wherever possible their castles have been restored, and are tended with care as museums; and those who have remained in the country are permitted to work quietly in offices, on incomes only a fraction of what they once enjoyed, provided they take no part in politics.

I had forgotten (if I ever knew) what the world lost when the horse was replaced by the internal combustion engine—the most disastrous invention that ever afflicted mankind until the advent of the atomic bomb.

On a Sunday morning we drove from Warsaw to the Poznan Fair, a distance of nearly three hundred miles. In every town and village through which we passed the peasants were pouring in to Mass from the countryside in the wooden carts which have served them for centuries, drawn by two beautiful animals in gleaming harness, and dressed in their best.

'Their lives haven't changed much,' remarked my Polish companion. 'They cultivate the soil, not very efficiently by modern standards, and often live to a great age. To them the doctor and the priest are the significant figures in town or village, and there are not enough of the former. They don't think much about politics unless they are invaded, or someone tries to collectivize their land or take away their horses. Then they resist as best they can.'

In Poznan I had a talk with the Minister of Foreign Trade, Professor Trampczynski, and his deputy, Mr. Kutin. They were justifiably concerned about the state of the national economy, but not unhopeful. They needed, they said, a higher general standard of living; and this depended on more mechanization and more consumer goods. Increased trade was the answer; and an increase in our bacon quota, even a small one, would help. I replied that, as an island, we were practically submerged in bacon; but that I would do my best. The Fair itself was less ambitious than that at Leipzig; but the British firms which exhibited put up not a bad show, without any Government support.

The question of the tourist trade arose, as it did in every country we visited. When you arrive in Poland you are presented with a form requiring you to report within 24 hours at a Registration Office; report in person at the District or City headquarters of the Militia within three days, with two photographs; report every change of residence. It also requires you to possess a return ticket, otherwise 'it will be necessary to stay in Poland until your family in Great Britain sends a ticket to Poland for the return journey.' For good measure the form ends: 'Failure to comply with the above requirements shall render any further journey impossible.'

It is not encouraging. Nevertheless there was an atmosphere of personal freedom in Poland which we did not find elsewhere. Everyone criticizes the Government.

The power of the Church is nowhere disputed—Poland, as a whole, remains an ardent Roman Catholic country; and the argument between Cardinal Wyszynski and the Communist Party is sustained at a high level. The struggle between the two theologies is unlikely to result in the total victory of either; but an ultimate *concordat* is not beyond the bounds of possibility.

Two remarks made to me in Warsaw stick in my memory. 'In this country we have something of everything, and not enough of anything'; and, 'You can say that we are a nation of patriots, peasants, Socialists and Catholics, and that these things are incompatible; but you cannot deny that we are a nation of romantics.' It is true. The birthplace of Chopin, with his piano and a plaster cast of his hand, is a national shrine; and the city of Cracow is of breathtaking beauty.

The peasants remain uncollectivized, and the gypsies unharried. As one Minister said, rather sadly: 'We have thousands more horses than we need, and it is frightfully uneconomic. Each one eats three hectares of fodder-crop a year. But they love their horses in a way you cannot love tractors; and there is not much we can do about it.'

By way of contrast, Czechoslovakia. The Czechs remain what they have always been, a nation of *petit-bourgeoisie*, without much zest for romance or adventure. The rich industrialists have left the country for good; but the standard of living in the towns is not far below what it was before the war. On balance the social pattern established by Thomas Masaryk holds; and there was no need for Jan Masaryk to die, unless he was assassinated.

As against Warsaw, Budapest and Bucharest, Prague has emerged from the fearful convulsions of the last twenty years almost intact. In lovely surroundings its inhabitants continue to eat fat pork and dumplings, and drink beer. They are genial and apparently contented. Their shops are the best-stocked that we saw, and they take good care not to become involved in politics.

The sheer administrative competence of the technical Ministers, notably Mr. Krajîr and Mr. Hloch, of the Ministry of Foreign Trade, was impressive. The rise in industrial output, from 1959 to 1960, was 11·7 per cent.; and they are now looking for 'know-how', with a view to the construction, under licence and guidance, of factories for the production of a wide range of capital goods. I see no reason why we should not provide some of it.

Budapest, reached in an hour from Prague in an Ilyushin 18, seemed like another world. This is where Hitler ordered his troops to fight it out after the great tank battles of the Transylvanian plain; and where, for five weeks, the Russians and the Germans shelled each other across the Danube. The five bridges over the river, and a substantial portion of Pest, have been rebuilt, but Buda is still in ruins.

On the face of it, Hungary is a conquered and occupied country. There are, however, ameliorating features. The Russian occupying troops, which we were told amounted to three divisions, are kept well out of sight. They live in partially concealed barracks in the countryside, and are not allowed to enter the towns in uniform.

The Hungarians themselves are suffering from what can only be described as a pervading neurosis caused by the tragic events of 1956. They talk freely about 'the rising'—without declaring their allegiance. All of them assure you that, in the sense that the conditions of life have greatly improved since, good came out of it. The Government which drove them to rebellion is openly condemned, but the neurosis which still grips them arises partly from a sense of their own folly, in expecting active support from the West, and wildly overplaying their hand. 'We drove Khrushchev to send his armour back to Budapest'; 'Compare the wisdom of Gomulka's policy with the stupidity of ours'; 'Believe it or not, Mindszenty said on the radio that the Church was going to take back all its land—that put an immediate end to the rising of the peasants.' These are the kind of things you hear if you keep your ears open and your mouth shut.

Kadar moves around in the style of Khrushchev—his mentor, protector and hero. I did not gather that he was personally unpopular, although the régime is severe. 'Quite a number of political prisoners,' we were told, had been 'quietly released.'

The general attitude towards the Dictator was best summed up in a remark made to me by an ex-Social Democrat: 'He has spent much of his life in prison. He has been tortured, and in the circumstances which prevailed in 1956, there was not much inducement for him to take on this burden.' The enormous statue of Stalin, torn from its granite plinth during the rebellion, has not been replaced; and Nagy is never mentioned, although we drove several times past the prison in which he was executed.

At the request of Sir Leslie we were given a private showing of an Hungarian film. It was a simple story of love and jealousy in which the hero and heroine finally reach the shores of Lake Balaton for an idyllic honeymoon.

Suddenly the telephone goes dead. Budapest is cut off. The rising has begun. They go to the road and pick up an armoured car. The choice, they are told, is simple: to escape to Vienna where the frontier is still open or return to Budapest where the fighting is on. The girl says she has had enough and goes to Vienna. The hero says, 'My duty lies in my country.' He is left standing in a bullet-swept street to the strains of the Hungarian National Anthem. And we are left to guess which side he is on.

The countryside showed every sign of the struggle which goes on in all four countries—a struggle not so much with the peasants as with the land. The answer has not yet been found, in terms of modern mechanized agricultural production, to a problem which bears hardly upon the national economy.

In the Babolna State Farm alone was the going really good. Here we were greeted with a fanfare of trumpets from four splendid fellows, in medieval uniform, mounted upon superb white Arab ponies; and driven in carts, drawn by four horses at a spanking pace, to see crops and livestock of high quality. The old Magyar spirit is by no means dead; and it would not take much to revive it.

To my surprise, I was invited to take part in an unrehearsed television discussion from Budapest. Among other questions, they asked me on which programme I appeared most frequently at home, and I replied: 'One with which you will not be familiar. It is called "Free Speech", and we say exactly what we think—and anything we like.' This was accurately translated.

Rumania was the biggest surprise. I had expected to find it the poorest of the four countries. On the contrary, in natural resources it is by far the richest. The increase in the gross annual product last year amounted to no less than 17 per cent. Production of cement and ships rose by 40 per cent., of oil tankers by 50 per cent., of power transformers by 80 per cent., and of ball bearings[1] by 100 per cent.

Here as elsewhere, the shortage of housing accommodation is acute, and agricultural production is wholly inadequate for their needs. But I have never seen a comparable industrial expansion.

At the technical level Mr. Florescu (Oil and Chemical Industry) Mr. Petri (Trade), and Mr. Posteuca (Construction, Architecture and Town Planning) seemed to me to constitute the central force behind the economic drive, which is terrific. I don't know whether they liked me, but I liked them. They didn't talk politics. They talked their jobs.

1. Needless to say, on our prohibited 'strategic' list of goods for export.

Mr. Posteuca, who is a peasant of Russian origin with close Russian connections, was at the Ministry of the Interior until he was drafted to the Committee of Construction. I was warned that he was the toughest of the lot, and might not take easily to a British Lord—or 'Lordel' as they call us in Hungary; but all was well. He looked exactly like Khrushchev. He took me to see two concert halls, one seating over 3,000, the other 1,000. Both have been built within the last 18 months; and, when you think of the hangar which is ironically called the Festival Hall, they put us to shame. In the former, Maestro Georgescu was rehearsing the Choral Symphony, with an orchestra of 100 and a choir of 300. The acoustics were superb, and the performance first-rate.

Afterwards Mr. Posteuca invited me to shoot geese and duck in the Danube delta at the end of October. 'We can guarantee you 100 a day,' he said, 'with excellent bouillabaisse cooked by the peasants, and sturgeon from which we get good caviare. You will also see many pelicans and flamingoes. You should then go to the Carpathians and shoot bears.'

I said I would be glad to go, provided the shooting was strictly confined to birds; but that I would be frightened of the bears. 'Oh!' he replied, 'our bears are very nice; and we only shoot them in the mating season.'

In the circumstances I decided to give the bears a break. But I would like to go back to Rumania; and to visit the Danube delta, if possible in the company of Peter Scott.

The first question you ask yourself when you leave the satellite countries of Europe is—Why have they all got Communist régimes? If there were to be free elections, as we understand them, it is doubtful whether the Communist, as against the Socialist, vote would exceed five per cent. in any one of them. This is an infinitely smaller proportion than the Communist vote in France or Italy after the war, or even today.

The answer is clear; but it is so unpalatable that many people on both sides of the Iron Curtain will not face it. Communism has been imposed upon the satellites by Russian military power, and whenever necessary by the physical presence of Russian troops. The deal was done, in fact, if not with intent on the part of the Western democracies, at Teheran and Yalta; and sealed at Potsdam.

It disposes of the claim that Communism is sweeping the world on an irresistible tide generated by its own success. It does not dispose of the *fait accompli*. If there is a lesson to be learned from the events that have taken place in Central and Eastern Europe during the past sixteen years it is that political decisions involving the destinies of whole nations and races should not be taken in a hurry, and in secret, by three men, however 'Big' they may be; but equally that such decisions, once taken, cannot be reversed without war, or modified by any means other than patient diplomacy.

Is any such modification possible? The chasm between the contending creeds is deep. As G. D. H. Cole himself admitted, the contrast between Eastern Communism and Western Democracy is between a basic individualism which asserts, and a basic collectivism which denies, the priority of individual values. Between these two creeds there can be practical agreement on a *modus vivendi*; but no theoretical compromise, because they are essentially contradictory.

Sir Leslie Plummer and myself were primarily concerned with the development of trade between East and West. Our business lay with the Presidents of the Chambers of Commerce, and the Ministers directly concerned with trade, rather than politicians; but we could not be unaware of the political power wielded in every country on the other side of the Iron Curtain by a handful of dedicated Communists. As I have already said, it is absolute; and it hit us at every turn.

I am not one of those who believe that wars can be prevented by cultural exchanges and personal contacts. But the effect of this political dictatorship, which varies from one country to another only in degree, is disastrous for the tourist trade, which could do so much to raise the standard of living in all of them by the provision of much-needed foreign exchange. We were accorded special treatment. The ordinary tourist simply will not take the whole paraphernalia of visa difficulties, registrations, inadequate hotel accommodation, inefficient service, and—on occasion—the circumspect attention, by means of microphones or 'shadowing', of the secret police. Nor is most of it necessary. The political power of the Communist Party is nowhere seriously in danger. The lesson of Hungary has been well learned by all. That is why I maintain that the Dulles policy of 'liberation' is dead.

After a time, the absence of individual political freedom gets a Westerner down. But when did political democracy, in the Western sense of the term, exist in any of these countries, with the exception of Czechoslovakia? I asked, in Bucharest, whether they were not irked by the domination of the Soviet Union, which, in Rumania, covers the economic as well as the political field. The reply I got was illuminating: 'We were under Turkish domination for 500 years, and they took from us far more than the Russians have ever done!'

Of greater interest is the part still played by the Christian religion. In Rumania and Bulgaria the Orthodox Church has come to terms with the State, as it always has done; and continues to function without political interference. In Poland and Hungary the Roman Catholic Church has not; but it is accepted as an indestructible element in the life of the people. Only in Czechoslovakia, the ex-social-democracy, are the churches empty; and this I believe to be due simply to lack of interest.

The fact remains that, in all my life, I have never attended so many crowded churches as I did on the other side of the Iron Curtain. In Budapest I heard a Mass sung in the Basilica—the third in one morning—of such exquisite beauty that I could hardly believe my ears. It seemed as if an entire symphony orchestra was playing in the organ loft; and this turned out to be the case. There were many young people in the vast congregation, who did not look as if they had come for the music alone. The priests do not walk the streets in clerical garb; but inside the churches you get the full works.

Another thing that struck me most forcibly was that they no longer regard Western capitalism as being in a state of decline, verging on collapse. On the contrary, they have a great admiration for the recent industrial achievements of France, Italy, and—

above all—West Germany. We do not realize the extent to which the Federal German Republic has succeeded in forging close economic links with all the satellite countries, including East Germany, and breaking into their markets. We have the goodwill. They have the trade.

The figures speak for themselves. Last year we exported £14·5 million to Poland against West Germany's £25·8 million; £7·7 million to Czechoslovakia against West Germany's £23·2 million; £4·3 million to Hungary against West Germany's £18·8 million; and £3 million to Rumania against West Germany's £12·7 million. Proximity, language, custom and more flexible credit terms provide no adequate explanation for this. It is, I am afraid, due to superior 'intelligence', salesmanship and driving power on the part of the West Germans. When I was in Poznan, Herr Beitz arrived in his private aeroplane, with plenary powers, and signed a very large contract on behalf of Krupps within twenty-four hours. There were no British industrialists of comparable stature; and, if there had been, they would have had to consult the Board of Trade, the Export Credits Guarantee Department, and their own Boards before taking effective action.

So far as economic planning, industrial productivity and capital investment are concerned, all four of the countries we visited have reason for considerable satisfaction. Where they fail is not in the production of capital goods but in the lack of consumer goods, which is general. Agriculture is their Achilles heel. And here the Communists have something. They know that an undisturbed and undisciplined peasant system is not the answer to modern agricultural production; and Herr Ulbricht has taught them that forcible collectivization does not pay. They are therefore seeking a compromise in the shape of 'voluntary co-operation'. So far it has not succeeded. One day it might.

Meanwhile the contrast between the standard of living of Western and Eastern Europe cannot be denied or eluded. Only two hundred miles up the river from Budapest, Vienna gleams, basking in the sunshine of a roaring tourist trade. The watch towers all along the frontier are heavily manned. No one can get through except the Big Shots. But as a symbol and shop-window of Western prosperity and culture Vienna presents a far more formidable challenge than West Berlin, which is regarded, with some justification, as artificial. In Budapest they talked of Karajan, with unconcealed admiration, as 'a truly modern man'.

Let me return, in conclusion, to the 64,000-dollar question—the future of Germany. In every country we were asked, with an interest tinged with anxiety, whether the United Kingdom was going to join the Common Market. We soon discovered that the anxiety was political rather than economic. They have not forgotten Dr. Adenauer's pronouncement, in a speech delivered only a year ago, that if the German people stand firm with the West, the day will come when East Prussia is united once more with Germany; or that of Dr. Hans Seebohm, one of the leaders of the Sudeten German Landsmannschaft, and a Minister in the Federal Government: 'We are the vanguard in the fight to shake off the yoke of Bolshevik colonialism from Eastern Europe.' They know well enough that the *Drang nach Osten* was not an invention of Hitler's; and fear an all-out attack on the part of a rearmed Germany, with full support from a united Western Europe and the United States, to recover the 'lost provinces'.

We may say that these fears are groundless, but they are passionate and utterly sincere, and there is only one way to allay them. That is a firm declaration on the part of the Western Powers, deferred if necessary until after the Federal German elections, that they have no intention of challenging or changing the present frontiers in Eastern Europe. If this were followed by a provisional agreement on the status and security of West Berlin, which is not impossible if Mr. Khrushchev means what he says, there would be an immediate relaxation of tension; and the way would then be open for negotiation on the only practical form of disarmament that can at present be envisaged—disengagement.

In a letter to the *Sunday Times* Mr. Ratiu has said that the West should press for, and eventually secure, the total withdrawal of foreign troops from the whole of Eastern Europe—an aspiration most certainly shared by every country in Eastern Europe. He did not add that the only method of securing this is by means of a corresponding withdrawal of foreign troops in Western Europe.

Unless and until something of this order of magnitude happens, it is pointless to talk of the reunification of Germany as a practical proposition in the foreseeable future; for, one way or the other, it would upset irretrievably the balance of power upon which the peace of the world now precariously depends.

July 1961.

PART II

People and Politics

APPEASEMENT: FIVE POLITICAL
SKETCHES

i. KEYNES

MAYNARD KEYNES was the cleverest man I have ever known. He revolutionized our economic thinking, and provided the theoretical background for the defeat of mass unemployment. The phrases he brought into existence—liquidity preference, propensity to consume, marginal efficiency of capital—are now part of the stock-in-trade of every economist. And the basic theories adumbrated by him—that the rate of interest by itself is powerless to equilibrate savings and investment, that savings are governed by total community income and its distribution, that investment is governed by the expectation of profit, that the demand for labour will not necessarily absorb the supply—are now generally accepted. The expansion of world trade and the *spread* of prosperity which has taken place during the past decade is primarily due to the tools which he put into the hands of men who had the sense to use them: socially controlled investment coupled with consumer stimulation or retardation, as required; planning à la Monnet; international clearings (copied by the Warsaw Powers); the creation of an international currency; investment in backward countries. If his ideas had prevailed at the time of Bretton Woods, against those of Mr. Vinson and Mr. White, we should all be in even better economic shape; but, ultimately, they will prevail.

As an economist Keynes was an empiricist, in the great British tradition. His objective was: 'the transition from economic anarchy to a régime which deliberately aims at controlling and directing economic forces in the interests of social justice and social stability.' His method was reason not evangelism. To him both private enterprise and social control were no more than devices by means of which he could reach his goal. Neither was a moral imperative. He wrote, and said, that the economic problem was nothing but a frightful muddle—a transitory and an *unnecessary* muddle. He sought always to harmonize conflicting interests by offering, on an expansionist basis, abundance, liberty and stability to all. He never felt that there was anything 'sacred' about either socialism or privately owned property. He was in his private life a daring and successful speculator, who lost and made two fortunes; and it is a pity that this fascinating side of his character and career has been so inadequately dealt with by Sir Roy Harrod in his otherwise excellent biography.

All this aroused the anger of political extremists on the Right and the Left. When I first entered Parliament the 'die-hard' exponents of *laissez-faire* feared and hated him. On the other hand Aneurin Bevan, whose intuitive intelligence was seldom at fault, had no use for him at all. He had laid idolatrous hands on the Ark of the Socialist Covenant. Worse still it looked as if he had salvaged the capitalist system.

It is, however, with Keynes the politician that I am chiefly concerned in this essay; and in the political field it is almost inconceivable that a man of his commanding intellectual stature should have been so fatally wrong.

It was the fashion, in the 'twenties and 'thirties, to deplore the Treaty of Versailles. Keynes set it. He wrote *The Economic Consequences of the Peace* in passion; and woke up to find himself, like Byron, famous overnight. It was a political pamphlet—and a scurrilous one at that. But the public thought that he had done for economics what his friend Lytton Strachey had done for biography. They were dull no longer. On the contrary, they were wildly exciting; and all mixed up with the most delectable scandal, polemics and 'debunking' of famous men. It was tremendous fun to find, in the middle of a table of reparation payments or coal deliveries, Mr. Lloyd George described as a siren and a *femme fatale*, and President Wilson as an old Presbyterian whom it was impossible to de-bamboozle. The controversial sweep, the imaginative power, and the brilliance of the writing, combined to make the book an irresistible best-seller. There had been no comparable piece of sustained invective since Swift. Every teacup in Bloomsbury rattled with pleasure. But, if you examine it in the cold aftermath of the second world war, you find that, although the invective was sustained, the argument was not.

The Treaty of Versailles was, in fact, a generous treaty. After inflicting on the world unfathomable misery, and upon France, Britain and Russia greater casualties than they had ever suffered, Germany was defeated and laid down her arms. Nevertheless, she was left intact. And, if you add up the figure of reparations paid, and loans from Britain and the United States subsequently repudiated, you find that she made no reparation at all.

The only trouble about the Treaty of Versailles was that the vital clauses affecting disarmament and the demilitarization of the Rhineland were never enforced; and the only valid criticism that can be made of it is that it left a vacuum of small and impotent States in Central and Eastern Europe. But, like Humpty-Dumpty, the Habsburg Empire had fallen off the wall; and the most consummate statesmanship could not have put all the pieces of that addled old egg together again.

The truth is that, where politics were concerned, in sharp contradistinction to economics, Keynes allowed himself to be governed by personal likes and dislikes, and even more by emotion. Where Germany was concerned he was an irrational evangelist.

Look at what he wrote, in cooler blood, about Lloyd George:

'How can I convey to the reader, who does not know him, any just impression of this extraordinary figure of our time, this siren, this goat-footed bard, this half-human visitor to our Age from the hag-ridden magic and enchanted woods of Celtic antiquity? One catches in his company that flavour of final purposelessness, inner irresponsibility, existence outside or away from our Saxon good and evil, mixed with cunning, remorselessness, love of power, that lend fascination, enthralment and terror to the fair-seeming magicians of North European folklore. Prince Wilson sailing out from the West in his barque *George Washington* sets foot in the enchanted castle of Paris to free from chains and oppression and an ancient curse the maid Europe, of eternal youth and beauty, his mother and his bride in one. There in the castle is the King with yellow parchment face (Clemenceau), a million years old, and with him an enchantress with a harp singing the Prince's own words to a magical tune. ... Lloyd George is rooted in nothing; he is void and without content; he lives and feeds on his immediate surroundings; he is an instrument and player at the same time which plays on the company and is played on by them too; he is a prism which collects light and distorts it and is most brilliant if the light comes from many quarters at once; a vampire and a medium in one.'[1]

This of the man who laid the foundations of the Welfare State; who was, by common consent, the principal architect of the Allied victory in 1918; and of whom Churchill said: 'When the English history of the first quarter of the twentieth century is written, it will be seen that the greater part of our fortunes in peace and war were shaped by this one man.' It is childish. It is mad. The madness of genius, if you like; but none the less dangerous for that. As you read, you can feel him being carried away from all sense and reason by the intoxication of his own vivid imagination, and his power over words.

It was Smuts who first advised Keynes to write *The Economic Consequences of the Peace*. Some years later he sadly summarized the result: 'When I encouraged him to write that book, I knew his views about the statesmen at Paris. But I did not expect a personal note in his book. I did not expect him to turn Wilson into a figure of fun. These few pages about Wilson in Keynes's book made an Aunt Sally of the noblest figure—perhaps the only noble figure—in the history of the war. ... Every paper I saw quoted the part about Wilson's bamboozlement. Wilson was already going down in America. In their hearts, the Americans wanted him to go down; they wanted to evade the duties he imposed upon them.

1. *Essays in Biography.*

The book was absolutely to their purpose. It helped to finish Wilson, and it strengthened the Americans against the League.'[1]

If this had been the only damage it would have been bad enough. Far worse was to come. The most disastrous of all the consequences of *The Economic Consequences* was the establishment of the legend of the *Diktat*, which became the basis of Nazi philosophy, reduced the Western democracies to paralyzed impotence, and enabled Hitler, only twenty years later, to trample the continent of Europe underfoot. 'That the mistake of Versailles had to be paid for by the Allies,' says the *History of the Times*, 'remained one of Barrington-Ward's[2] deepest convictions.'

On April 29, 1945, Etienne Mantoux was killed in action against the Germans in Bavaria, at the age of thirty-two. The year before, in an exceptionally able book,[3] he had written: 'Without the guilt-complex, without the loss of faith that paralyzed their will, the pathetic succession of surrenders which culminated in the catastrophe 1939–40 would never have been possible. "We do not," once said Clemenceau, "have to beg pardon for our victory." He could not have better described what was to follow. *Meaculpism*—for such is the name that this school of thought invites—loomed large in Great Britain and France during the interwar period. The Treaty, Mr. Keynes had written, was "a breach of engagements and of international morality" comparable to the invasion of Belgium. "Those who sign this Treaty will sign the death sentence of millions of German men, women and children." Such words ate deep into many consciences. Long before Hitler made his appearance on the European scene, meaculpists were agitating for the revision of the Treaty.... And if anyone was likely to forget it, Hitler would soon remind him. Abuse of the *Diktat* was a favourite gag in his grandiose nerve war. But now his invective sounded in many ears like some ghastly echo from *The Economic Consequences of the Peace*.'

In 1939 Keynes turned away, with horror, from his erstwhile political disciples. 'The *intelligentsia* of the Left,' he wrote, 'were the loudest in demanding that the Nazi aggression should be

---

1. S. G. Millin, *General Smuts*.   2. The Deputy Editor.
3. *The Carthaginian Peace*.

resisted at all costs. When it comes to a show-down, scarce four weeks have passed before they remember that they are pacifists and write defeatist letters to your columns, leaving the defence of freedom and civilization to Colonel Blimp and the Old School Tie, for whom Three Cheers.'[1]

It was too late. The Golden Age of 'debunking', of the denunciation of Versailles and the appeasement of Germany, was about to go up in the smoke and flames of Dunkirk. Maynard Keynes was the first 'appeaser'—and the worst. The world owes much to him, but it had to pay too heavy a price for his hatred of Lloyd George, and his love of Doctor Melchior.

1961.

ii. BALDWIN

The first time I saw the late Lord Baldwin was on Sports Day at my private school in the year 1911, when my father beat him in the Father's Race by inadvertently winding him with his elbow. He took this with perfect equanimity, and I knew then what a nice man he was. The school was St. Aubyns, Rottingdean; the headmaster an Ulsterman called Stanford, with a strong personality and an ungovernable temper; and politics of the deepest blue governed our small lives.

Sir Edward Carson lived at the end of the street; and every time he returned from one of his campaigns—'Ulster will fight, and Ulster will be right'—we all turned out, with Union Jacks, to cheer him as he drove down the street. With one exception. The Vicar's son, a day boy, was the only Liberal in the school; and resolutely refused to play any part. We much despised him for this act of courage.

In those days Rottingdean was a remarkable little village, although acute homesickness prevented me from appreciating its charms. Opposite the church, for which Sir Edward had designed a stained-glass window of Sir Galahad, was the Burne-Jones house; and, almost next door, the house of Baldwin's cousin Rudyard Kipling. Baldwin's two sons, and Kipling's only son, later to

1. *New Statesman and Nation*, October 14.

be killed, were all at St. Aubyns. Apart from choir 'feasts', our two big events of the year, to which we all looked forward passionately, were Trafalgar day and Empire day. We dressed in grey sweaters and shorts, and grey felt hats with our colours round them, and shot off blank cartridges in tiny rifles, and sang the school song which began:

> St. Aubyns boys are we, are we,
> And we live by the side of the sea, the sea.

The school motto was an unpronounceable Greek word which, translated, meant 'Quit you like men'. We lived in an atmosphere of health, simplicity and security which we were never to know again; and Baldwin's kindly smile and cherrywood pipe brought added strength to it. No one then suspected that he was destined to be the political master of Britain for nearly twenty years, least of all himself.

After my Orkney and Shetland fight in 1923, which he had encouraged, he sent for me (as Leader of the Opposition) and asked if I would like to join his secretariat. I jumped at it. There was, at that time, a streak of impetuousness in his nature, which gradually died with the consolidation of his political power and the passage of the years. The decision to bring down the Coalition Government in 1922 was the result of no premeditated plan. He blurted out the terms of the American debt settlement, which he negotiated as Chancellor in Washington, before they had been submitted to the Cabinet, and before his private secretary, Grigg, could stop him. And the General Election of 1923 was the result of an apparently casual remark at a meeting in the country when he said, with truth, that if we went pottering along as we were doing we should have grave unemployment with us to the end of time.

The kindliness and simplicity remained with him to the end. One day a gentleman arrived at the office in Palace Chambers for a chat. I showed him in. Baldwin talked freely, and at length, to his agreeable visitor. Next Sunday an 'interview' appeared in one of the newspapers containing frank and caustic comments on the character and abilities of practically every member of his own

Shadow Cabinet. Lord Birkenhead was reported to have said: 'The bloody fool has done it again!'; and the secretariat was in a flat spin. Baldwin was merely amused.

On another occasion I accompanied him, on duty, to Edinburgh, where he was to make an important speech. It was not until the last crumb had gone down my throat that I realized I had eaten the lunch which had been prepared for him as well as myself. He had watched the process with a twinkle in his eye; but it never occurred to him to take remedial action while there was still time. Herein, perhaps, lies a clue to his own character. Later in the journey he said, suddenly and *à propos* of nothing, that the main ambition of his life was to prevent the class war from becoming a reality; and in this, to a remarkable extent, he succeeded. He added that our only hope was protection; and if he had stuck, with conviction, to that view, we should be living in an easier world. Alas, he thought, as later on he was to do about rearmament, that it might be a vote-loser.

The only thing that caused me any misgiving was his addiction to political gossip. Whenever J. C. C. Davidson breezed in with the latest story of what 'the Goat'[1] was up to, he listened with evident enjoyment and interest. I regretted this because I thought it was a great pity that these two men had ever parted. I think it still. Lloyd George would have served under Baldwin. He, too, was an economic empiricist; and there is every reason to believe that, in 1923, he would have accepted protection and Imperial Preference as necessities. If Baldwin had put that 'dynamic force' in charge of economic policy, and set Churchill to look after our defences, they would have formed an invincible political triumvirate which must have carried us safely through the tumultuous years that lay ahead. Moreover, he would have been spared those phases of exhaustion, amounting to prostration, which so disastrously followed any major personal effort.

No adequate portrait has yet been painted of this remarkable man. G. M. Young clearly came to dislike him in the course of writing his biography; and his son, inevitably, was too involved emotionally to give us an objective picture. The contradictions in

1. Lloyd George.

his character were astonishing. To the basic simplicity was added a sensitivity not far removed from neurosis. He had all the gifts of a great diplomat, yet took no interest in foreign affairs; and told this writer, on his last night in the House of Commons, that it was the one thing he regretted. Geneva was an hour's drive from his beloved Aix-les-Bains. And there, at the League of Nations, he could have exercised an influence comparable to that of Briand. He never went.

He despised oratory, and was himself a great orator. He mistrusted brains, although he was unquestionably the ablest politician of the day. He loved political power; but it was the love of a miser, and, when he had it, he showed no great desire to do anything with it. He spoke often of the missing generation, but I do not think he missed it very much.

He well understood the psychological problems of the industrial revolution of our time, and his speeches on this subject revealed a broad and deep humanity; but he showed less concern over the long agony of the miners in 1926, and the plight of the distressed areas, than, for example, Churchill. On the morrow of the General Strike he could have done anything. He did nothing. A letter from Steel-Maitland, the Minister of Labour, urging a conference with trade union leaders of the calibre of Pugh and Bevin 'to propound the terms of a genuine industrial peace now, while the country still has confidence in the Prime Minister' remained unanswered. He went instead to Aix-le-Bains—leaving the miners still out on strike. He had had enough.

Above all, he understood middle-class England. There was no call here for experiment and adventure, for bold imaginative leadership, for greatness. He knew that the middle-classes wanted only to feel safe, and to be let alone; and saw to it that they were kept undisturbed. As Acton said of Liverpool, the secret of his policy was that he had none. Is this a fair portrait? Not quite. There were occasions, such as the famous speech on the Trades Disputes Bill, when he reached great heights. I believe that the secret of his long, tenacious and successful hold over the electorate is to be found in the simple fact that he *was*, fundamentally, a nice man; and the country knew it. Hitler, Stalin and Mussolini had still to prove, conclusively, that in this century niceness is not enough.

Hitler! Here was Baldwin's Achilles heel. After my own interview with him in Berlin, in January, 1932, I never doubted the danger. 'Somehow,' I wrote, 'he has managed to communicate his passion to masses of desperate people. And therein his power. The cry *"Heil Hitler!"* re-echoes through Germany today. We should not underestimate the strength of the movement of which he is the living embodiment.'

In the autumn of that year Baldwin, whose political instinct was seldom at fault, sensed danger. 'No power on earth,' he told the House of Commons, 'can protect the man in the street from being bombed.' He went on: 'This is a question for the young men far more than it is for the old men. When the next war comes and European civilization is wiped out, as it will be and by no force more than that force, then do not let them lay the blame upon the old men. Let them remember that they principally and they alone are responsible for the terrors that have fallen on the earth.'

There can be only one explanation of this extraordinary statement on the part of the most powerful politician in Britain at that moment. A deep subconscious desire to avoid personal responsibility. And only one lesson to be drawn from it. No man should seek to govern his country unless he has clear political objectives, supported by sincere conviction; and is prepared to use all his efforts and energies in selfless pursuit of them—and go when he succeeds, or fails.

After the 'blood bath' of 1934 there could no longer be any doubt about what was happening in Germany. I told my own constituents, on October 24, that the life and soul of democracy, and the freedom of the individual, were being challenged as they had not been challenged for two thousand years; and that the issue which would shortly confront us was whether we were prepared to fight for freedom, or submit to tyranny.

What did Baldwin tell the nation? Nothing. Where was the moral imperative which he, above all men, was fitted to proclaim? Compare his silence with Gladstone's denunciation of

Turkish atrocities which were trivial by comparison with those of
the Nazis:

'That burden of woe and shame—the greatest that exists on
God's earth—is one that we thought united Europe was about to
remove; and in the Protocol united Europe was pledged to remove; but to removing which, for the present, you seem to have
no efficacious means of offering even the smallest practical contribution. But the removal of that load of woe and shame is a
great and noble prize. It is a prize well worth competing for. It is
not too late to try to win it. I believe there are men in the Cabinet
who would try to win it, if they were free to act on their own
beliefs and aspirations.

'It is not too late, I say, to become competitors for that prize;
but be assured, whether you mean to claim for yourselves even a
single leaf in that immortal chaplet of renown, which will be the
reward of true labour in that cause, or whether you turn your
backs upon that cause and your own duty, I believe for one that
the knell of Turkish tyranny in those provinces has sounded. So
far as human eye can judge, it is about to be destroyed. The
destruction may not come in the way or by the means that we
should choose; but come this boon from what hands it may, it
will be a noble boon, and as a noble boon will gladly be accepted
by Christendom and the world.'

Apart from Duff Cooper and Swinton, who ordered the Spit-
fires off the drawing-board and was sacked for his pains, there
were no men in Baldwin's Cabinet who would try to win anything. They were all in the conspiracy of silence, up to the neck.
Churchill deluded himself when he thought that Baldwin wanted
to bring him back. He said to my father at this time, and with an
implication not intended to be missed, 'Churchill is a very bad
guide for youth.' But the real reason for Churchill's continued
exclusion was, of course, the fact that he would have roused,
alarmed and re-armed the country. Worse still, he would have
deluged Baldwin with letters, forced him to take decisions, and
made him do some work. As A. L. Rouse has truly pointed out,

Doctor Jones's Soothing Syrup, always at hand and in plentiful supply, was very much more to his taste.

At the conclusion of his biography of Baldwin, G. M. Young wrote: 'To have succeeded, so unexpectedly and so greatly; to have seen the amusement, the tolerance, the contempt even, of his early associates giving way to the admiration and affection of a whole people; and in its turn this affection, this admiration converted to the bitterest hatred: to have staked everything on that one virtue, integrity, and to know that far and wide throughout his own England men and women under the rain of death were cursing him as the politician who, to gain a few months or years of office, had lied to the people and left them defenceless against their enemies. There was not much to comfort him in those years.'

These are terrible words, which I cannot think are fully justified. Baldwin did not deliberately lie to the people. Like them, he did not want to know the truth—for too long. But in the end he faced up to it, and demanded the mobilization of all the industrial resources of the country to meet the growing menace. He was a far bigger man than those who served him. And I am convinced that, if he had remained in power, there would have been no Munich. Apart from anything else, he would never have bothered to fly to Berchtesgaden!

Nevertheless, on the crucial issue of life or death, he failed the country. He told the House of Commons, on November 28, 1934, that the Government were determined in no conditions to accept any position of inferiority with regard to what Air Force might be raised by Germany. Subsequently the Air Staff laid it down that the minimum number of fighter squadrons required for our defence was 52. In 1939, when war was declared, we had 34. The final word lies with J. L. Garvin:[1] 'It is bad enough that air equality has been promised by successive governments, but not provided. Far worse that performance has not reached one half of promise. Considering our vast manufacturing resources, our famous wealth, our access to the world's materials, our 1,800,000 people on pay without work; and considering what we have at

1. Editor of the *Observer*.

stake near and far—the present position, which leaves us still so far outstripped in overhead power, must be fairly described as the gravest wrong to a people and an Empire in the whole of British history.'

For this wrong Baldwin, as Prime Minister, must bear the primary responsibility.

I must end this chapter on a personal note. In February 1941—the darkest hour of my life—I received a letter from Astley Hall, in a familiar hand-writing:

Dear Bob,

If you feel it would be good to get away for a day or two from the crowd, and just rest, and have only an old man to talk to, come down here. Whether you will or not I shall quite understand: do just as the spirit moves you. But if you do care to come you will be welcome.

Yours sincerely,
Baldwin of Bewdley.
(once known in a previous state of
existence as S.B.)

Owing to the death of my father, I could not go. But a fortnight later came another letter, again in his own handwriting.

'I don't want your visit to fall through. You will be coming to two people who had a real affection and regard for your parents, and who can realize what such a shock as you have suffered means to you at this time.'

Again, in the turmoil of those days, the visit fell through; and to the end of my life I shall regret it. But how could one help loving such a man?

Lloyd George's methods were different. From him I received one morning a peremptory summons to lunch at Churt the same day. When I arrived I found, to my astonishment, a man white with anger—on my behalf. The fire had not yet gone out. With flashing eyes he said, what I myself shall always believe, that I had been the victim of malevolent forces bent upon my political destruction; and denounced those whom he held responsible for

123

this in terms so scathing that they can never be repeated. He then gave me some advice. It did not differ markedly from that which I had already been given by Lord Birkenhead, nearly twenty years before: 'You will always be in and out of trouble. But so long as you stick to your constituency, and they stick to you, no one will ever be able to break you.'

But Lloyd George gave me something more valuable than good advice. He contrived to impart to me some fraction of the moral courage which was his own supreme quality, and which reached white-heat in the spring of 1918. Thus I survived, when I might so easily have given up.

Churchill, as a War Minister in the class of Cromwell or Chatham, comes into a different category. Lloyd George and Baldwin had all the elements of political greatness; and their qualities were completely different, and entirely complementary. Mutual admiration and fascination as well as mutual suspicion entered into their tortuous relationship. It remains a tragedy, for Britain and for the world, that men and events combined to prevent them from joining forces.

1961.

iii. NEVILLE CHAMBERLAIN

I cannot understand why Mr. Iain Macleod, with laurels still fresh upon his brow and a career of dazzling promise ahead of him, has chosen this moment to dredge the evil-smelling political pond of the 'thirties. Some of us had to swim in it. He did not. If his object was to rehabilitate Mr. Chamberlain, he has failed; because he has nothing of substance to add to the melancholy story which has already been recorded, at tedious length but with meticulous accuracy, by Sir Keith Feiling.

In private life Neville Chamberlain was affectionate and sensitive, with a great love and knowledge of country pursuits and of the music of Beethoven. These are endearing qualities which were rewarded by the complete devotion of a small and intimate family circle. In public life he was aloof, arrogant, obstinate and limited. He was also a failure. 'Everything I have worked for,' he told the

House of Commons, with absolute truth, in September 1939, 'has crashed in ruins.'

Mr. Macleod tries to paint a picture of Chamberlain as a great radical social reformer. It is unconvincing. He was a first-class municipal administrator, who well understood and radically changed the structure of British local government; and he was the first prominent politician to grasp the power of the political machines in the modern age, which he reanimated and subsequently used for his own purposes.

There it ended. It so happened that this writer was parliamentary private secretary to the Chancellor of the Exchequer in 1929, and saw something of what went on behind the scenes. The mechanics of the Local Government Act were the work of Chamberlain, devised with faultless efficiency; but the vision and drive which underlay the whole conception of de-rating came from Churchill; and in this field the efforts of the Minister of Health were confined to attempts to whittle it down. Chamberlain was a miniaturist who had no use for large brushes.

It was the same when he went to the Treasury. An inherited belief in protection, and the fact that we had fortunately been driven off the gold standard, enabled him to pull us out of the depths of the worst depression in our history and set the stage for an economic recovery. There it stopped. The Lloyd George 'New Deal', of which Keynes was the principal architect, was—in Mr. Macleod's own words—'sniffed at as the poorest stuff imaginable'; and on pages 172 and 173 of his book we find a contemptuous and total rejection of the Keynesian economics which have enabled capitalism in a free society to survive in the modern world.

As Chancellor he tinkered with the cancer of massive unemployment. A couple of million pounds for tramp steamers, a couple of million pounds for pigs, a bit for milk, a trifle for beef. It was all small, haphazard, essentially palliative, and unrelated to any long-term constructive economic policy. There was no serious attack on the problems of the slums, the distressed areas or the roads—he actually 'raided' the Road Fund at a time when nearly two million men stood idle. But the invincible conceit persisted. Those inside the Government who wanted more strenuous and

effective action, such as Elliot and Ormsby-Gore, were sardonic-
ally christened 'the Boys' Brigade'; and those outside, including
the present Prime Minister, were dismissed as: 'fellows who think
they ought to have had office and want to show the Government
what a mistake was made in leaving them out.' Meanwhile he was
writing to his sister Hilda that it amused him to find a new policy
for each of his colleagues in turn, and that he was more and more
carrying the Government on his back.

When Chamberlain became Prime Minister he found himself
at the head of a country with inadequate armaments and vast
responsibilities, in a turbulent world of naked power politics. In
order to avoid attack, and possible defeat, he had to achieve a balance of power; and this could only be done by means of instant
rearmament on the greatest scale, and an alliance with Russia. He
rejected both and turned instead to the ill-starred policy of appeasing the Fascist dictators. Hence the failure to build the Grand
Alliance in time. Hence Munich. Hence the second world war.
The logical conclusion of his policy was a total British withdrawal
from Europe; and, to do him justice, this was what Lord Beaverbrook assumed and desired. To commit us, as he finally did, to the
defence of Poland—much farther away than Czechoslovakia—
without any assurance of Russian support and with Hitler by then
in strategic control of the Continent, was a gesture of such reck-
lessness that it very nearly encompassed our destruction.

Oliver Stanley once said that to Baldwin Europe was a bore,
and to Chamberlain a bigger Birmingham. It was too true. Confronted by a frantic and ferocious madman with a destructive
genius of unparalleled malignity, he dealt with him as if he were
a recalcitrant town councillor who could nevertheless be relied
upon to keep his word—to him. As a result Hitler pulled off, at
Munich, one of the biggest bluffs known to history.

Unlike most Prime Ministers Chamberlain always saw people
who wanted to see him, however unimportant they were. He invited me to call upon him at Downing Street on August 24, 1938,
after I had returned from a Continental tour, and listened with
courteous attention to all I had to say. When I had finished he remarked, in his brisk way, that the Germans were attempting to

impose a reign of terror upon the whole Continent, and added: 'I gather that you are of the opinion that the gangster element among the Nazis is now in complete control, and that they will stick at nothing.' I felt encouraged by this, but it made no difference. He held to his course. 'I like,' he said, 'to stick to things even after there seems no chance of success.' That, and a quite unreasoning optimism, was his undoing. Even after war was declared he thought that Hitler had missed the bus, and had a 'hunch' that it would be over before the spring. The final phase of his life when he passed, within the space of a few months, from the dizziest heights of apparent success to the depths of public and personal disaster, had something of the nobility of Greek tragedy.

Winston Churchill once wrote that life is a whole, and luck is a whole, and no part of them can be separated from the rest. As Alan Taylor has truly pointed out, Neville Chamberlain had no luck at all. Not even Mr. Macleod can bring him that.

1961.

iv. HALIFAX

If you fall under the spell of Lord Halifax, as so many have done, including the present writer, criticism becomes a kind of sacrilege. Even when you are shocked, and there are passages in his autobiography by which I was deeply shocked, he compels you to accept him for what in fact he is—a grand *seigneur* and a great gentleman: one of the last products of what is rather naïvely called on the jacket 'a remarkable civilization that has already passed away'.

As an intimate picture of family life in one of the great Victorian country houses the opening chapter, drawn with great delicacy of touch, can hardly be surpassed. So it continues. Whenever the author describes the Yorkshire or the Indian scene, his friends, Oxford and All Souls, above all his father and the faith which inspired him, the book glows. Only when it touches politics does it go dead. It is difficult to believe that he held high office, almost continuously, for over twenty years. On the contrary, as you read on you begin to feel that it was jolly good of him to leave, even for a while, the life he loved and lived so well at Garrowby; and that he himself would probably concur in this view.

A cursory reference to the fall of the Coalition Government in 1922 gives a significant indication of things to come. After quoting with approval Baldwin's warning that Lloyd George was a dynamic force, and that this could be a 'terrible thing', Lord Halifax continues: 'It was the last straw when the general public came to think that the three ablest members of the Cabinet, Lloyd George, Churchill and Birkenhead, were pursuing a personal policy, involving a fair risk of getting the country into war with Turkey.' The group of young Tories who came to dominate the Party were frightened by what had happened, although it was successful; and still more by the methods which had been used to make it happen. Here, in a nutshell, is the issue and the argument which culminated in Munich and the second world war.

As Viceroy Lord Halifax nearly succeeded. The cast of his mind enabled him to comprehend the spiritual forces and complex intellectual processes which animated Gandhi as no other British statesman could have hoped to do; and he was bewildered by the reaction in Parliament to the agreed announcement regarding Dominion status. 'I cannot doubt,' he writes, 'that the choice by public men in England of an attitude and language so lacking in imagination and sympathy was not without its influence at a formative moment, and strengthened the demand for independence.' Nevertheless there was another chance. The blueprint of Indian Federation emerged from the Round Table Conference of 1930 and, as a result of the vehement efforts of Hoare, reached the statute book. It never came to life.

For India as a whole, says the author, the failure of Federation was a disaster; and again lays the blame upon the diehard opposition in Parliament. It is an inadequate explanation. On this issue the Labour Party was supporting an overwhelming Conservative majority. If in the early 'thirties Baldwin, with Halifax restored to the Cabinet, had exhibited only a tithe of that dynamic force which he found so 'terrible' in Lloyd George, there might have been a different story to tell.

One approaches, with justified trepidation, the stony road of appeasement; and reads with wide-eyed amazement the following: 'The criticism excited by Munich never caused me the least surprise. I should very possibly indeed have been among the critics myself, if I had not happened (*sic*) to be in a position of responsibility. .... They ought to have criticized the failure of successive Governments, and of all parties, to foresee the necessity of rearming in the light of what was going on in Germany; and the right date on which criticism ought to have fastened was 1936, which had seen the German re-occupation of the Rhineland in defiance of treaty provisions. I have little doubt that if we had then told Hitler bluntly to go back, his power for future and larger mischief would have been broken.'

This fairly leaves one gasping. Lord Halifax was a member of the British Cabinet from 1932 onwards. In 1935 he became Secretary of State for War, and as such the recipient of a whole series of cogent warnings from our Ambassador and Military Attaché in Berlin, not to mention a formidable memorandum from Sir Robert Vansittart in which all the evidence of the conquering aims, plans and rearmament of Germany was marshalled and brilliantly deployed. In 1936 Flandin, the French Foreign Minister, came to London to ask for moral support from the British Government in resisting the German occupation of the Rhineland; and even this was denied him.

There are occasional disconcerting indications of the author's attitude of mind. Of Goering, for instance, he writes: 'I was immensely entertained at meeting the man. One remembered all the time that he had been concerned with the "clean-up" in Berlin on June 30, 1934, and I wondered how many people he had been responsible for getting killed. Like a great schoolboy, full of life and pride in all he was doing, showing it all off, and talking high politics out of the setting of green jerkin and red dagger': and of Goebbels, 'I had expected to dislike him intensely, but am ashamed to say I did not.' Despite this, you would never glean from these pages that he became the willing accomplice and principal instrument of Chamberlain in his policy of rabid appeasement; that in 1938 he wrote private letters to Sir Nevile Henderson (who had succeeded Sir Eric Phipps as British Ambassador in

Berlin, and whose name does not appear in the index) which to this day make one hot with shame; or that, as Foreign Secretary, he acquiesced in the displacement of Vansittart by Sir Horace Wilson.

Whom does he blame this time? Believe it or not, Churchill—for laying down, when he was Chancellor of the Exchequer in 1924–29, and before Hitler had even been heard of, that no major war was to be expected for ten years; and the poor old British public for 'a wholly irrational pacifist sentiment'. I believe this to be profoundly untrue. I was myself active in politics throughout this period, as representative of a Scottish constituency with a strong radical tradition extending over a century. They never cavilled when I supported Churchill's demands for massive rearmament, nor even when I advocated compulsory national service in January 1938. All the country needed in these fateful years was resolute and courageous leadership; and that it never got. The alleged pacifist sentiment was eagerly deduced from a freak by-election at Fulham, and used as an excuse for palsied inaction by the Government.

Towards the end of his book Lord Halifax gives us, as an illustration of Baldwin's 'firm faith and simple goodness,' a letter written by him in July 1940, in which he says that God's plan must be incomprehensible; and goes on to describe what amounts to a 'Vision' in which he was told that he could not see the plan, but that there was a purpose in stripping him of all the human props on which he depended, and leaving him alone in the world. 'You have now,' said the Voice, 'one upon whom to lean, and I have chosen you as my instrument to work with my will. Why are you then afraid?'

So now it is not only the Conservative diehards, and Churchill, and the British electorate, but God Himself who has to take the blame. If the Almighty bears any resemblance to the God of the Old Testament, I doubt if He will accept it. It was not by means of appeasement that Moses led the children of Israel to the promised land; or, indeed, that they got back there. The verdict of the Deity and of posterity will, I fear, be hard on the pre-war Establishment; on Baldwin, Halifax, Simon, Chamberlain and Hoare,

who constituted its political core; on Geoffrey Dawson, its Secretary-General; on Montagu Norman, its Treasurer; and on Cliveden (Philip Lothian and Tom Jones), which constituted, with All
Souls, its G.H.Q. Between them they conducted us to disaster.
Why? I thought then that they were a pack of unmitigated humbugs—and cowardly humbugs at that. The more charitable, and
probably the correct, view is that they were all too nice and too
high-minded for the very rough world in which we have to live.
They found themselves confronted by a gang of bloodthirsty
ruffians, and behaved like gentlemen. The result was catastrophic.
Much can be said about Hitler and Mussolini, but by no stretch
of the imagination can they be described as gentlemen; and
it required something more than a gentleman to deal with
them.

This in conclusion. In Washington Lord Halifax achieved what
he had so narrowly missed in Delhi—spectacular success. And,
although it might be a shade duller, the world would certainly be
an easier place to live in if it consisted of people like Baldwin and
himself.

1957.

v. DAWSON

It is a humbling experience for anyone who was a Member of
Parliament between the two world wars to read the biography of
the man who, throughout that fateful period, occupied the central position in the small group which wielded effective political
power in this country. Geoffrey Dawson was not only editor of
The Times. He was also Secretary-General of the Establishment.
This had its origins in Milner's South African 'Kindergarten'; and
one of its earliest and most remarkable achievements was to make
Milner, who had no experience of British politics and was at the
time comparatively unknown, a member of the War Cabinet in
1916. The appointment was abundantly justified by events, and he
played a decisive part in establishing unity of command on the
Western Front; but he owed his success to the fact that he had a
leader. Milner was a superlative bureaucrat. Without the dynamic

leadership, inspiration and political support of Lloyd George he would never have reached the position or exercised the power that he did within the political hierarchy.

His disciples were in similar case. They needed personal leadership. Dawson spent much of his life looking for it—from Milner himself, from Northcliffe, from Lloyd George, and finally from Halifax. For one reason or another, it never satisfied him. And when, in the absence of leadership, the Establishment finally achieved almost unchallenged power, they found themselves in the position of eminent Civil Servants without political direction or control. As such they became increasingly complacent and, when it came to the supreme test, they failed the country.

It is interesting to reflect that, before 1914, no group of the kind existed in England. There was no need for it. The country was then governed by Asquith's Cabinet, in the teeth of fierce opposition in Parliament. A Prime Minister who could turn for advice at any moment to men of the calibre of Lloyd George, Grey, Crewe, Morley, Churchill, Haldane, McKenna and Samuel, required no guidance from outside. Nor were Balfour, Lansdowne, Bonar Law, Austen Chamberlain, Carson, Robert Cecil or F. E. Smith in urgent need of external assistance. This may be one of the reasons why, in the years between the wars, the group of which Dawson became the centre strove always—as part of its subconscious drive for power—to eliminate party politics, and bring into being 'National' Governments without strong political personalities, policies or point. This was one of the main objects of the so-called 'National' Government of 1931. Dawson played a leading part in its formation.

Thereafter the Establishment assumed, to an extent hardly realized at the time, control of our affairs. Within a decade they had brought us to the most fearful abyss we have ever seen. Why they did it God alone knows. In themselves they were the antithesis of decadence; high-minded, self-effacing, hard-working, acutely conscious of their own moral rectitude and intellectual superiority. Dawson's own character was fairly summarized by Bishop Headlam at his Commemoration Service in All Souls:

'He had a deeper sense of duty than anyone else I have known. ... It did not matter, he said, what your reputation was—it did not matter whether what you did was known or unknown, it did not matter whether you obtained any recognition for what you had done; *what mattered was that you should be conscious yourself of having tried to do what was right.*'

That they all were. What, then, went wrong? Probably the basic reason for their failure to measure up to events was that they never had to fight their way in politics; and few of them could claim even a nodding acquaintance with the hustings or the rough-and-tumble of parliamentary debate. Their horizon was therefore restricted. Round they hopped, like birds in an enormous cage, from shoot to shoot, from Cliveden to All Souls, to the Athenaeum, to the Travellers, to Grillions dining club, to Round Table 'moots', and back again; with the result that they were out of touch with ordinary people, with all that was happening in Europe, and finally with reality. There never was a Cliveden 'set' in the generally accepted sense of the term. Lady Astor cast her net too wide for that. But, as Dawson himself acknowledges, there was a Cliveden 'front', animated by Philip Lothian and Tom Jones; and Sir Evelyn Wrench quotes a description of All Souls as: 'an unofficial club for running, or helping to run, the destinies of the British Empire.' I saw them both at their fell work in the 'thirties.

A large part of this lengthy book reflects nothing but credit on Dawson's character and judgment. His first decisive intervention in public affairs of supreme consequence was in the autumn of 1916, when Asquith was overthrown and Lloyd George became Prime Minister. It was the 'uninspired' leading article which he wrote alone at Cliveden on December 2 that precipitated the crisis; and when it was all over, he recorded with justified satisfaction that the new appointments, and the creation of a small War Cabinet, were 'a real triumph for the paper'.

Then, after the breach with Northcliffe and his recall to the editorship of *The Times* on his own terms, he is to be found throwing the full weight of his increasing influence against any attempt to keep the Labour Party out of office in 1924, and subsequently to introduce repressive legislation against the trade unions. The only puzzling thing about these years is the apparent indifference of himself, and those who were now working closely with him, to the plight of the unemployed. As they shot and rode over the Yorkshire moors they never seem to have felt the impact of the suffering and smokeless industrial towns beneath them. And this is the more surprising in that their intellectual mentor, Milner, was himself tormented by it. 'Did I not say,' he wrote, 'when there was all that rotten talk about ruin and bankruptcy, the burden of debt, etc., that "the only thing which terrified me in looking ahead was the possibility of a restriction of credit"? I always knew this mad nonsense would come. ... I am up against theories strongly entrenched in the Treasury, the Bank of England, and certainly the greater part of the whole banking world; and supported by tons of literature from the abstract school of political economists who have held this country in their baneful grip for nearly a century.'

Alas, the Establishment was content to leave the direction of economic policy to the Governor of the Bank of England. The consequences remain with us to this day.

With the advent of the 'thirties deeper shadows begin to fall. Dawson was an uncompromising advocate of the policy of appeasing Germany, and to this he came to subordinate all else. 'I do my utmost, night after night, to keep out of the paper anything that might hurt their [German] susceptibilities.' It involved slashing the dispatches of Norman Ebbutt from Berlin to a point which drove that great foreign correspondent to despair. Even so, he was expelled by the Nazis. It drew from Dawson a mild editorial protest, followed by an 'interesting talk' with Sir Nevile Henderson about a project for getting Goering over for the Grand National!

The long-drawn story comes to a tragic conclusion, with everything for which Dawson stood reduced to ashes, and he himself working quietly on through the 'blitz'. A final incident deserves to be recorded. On the day after Hitler launched his attack on the West, and the night that Churchill received from the King the truncheon as High Constable of Britain with which he was to save what was left of Western civilization, Lady Oxford and Asquith called on the Chamberlains at 10 Downing Street. Afterwards she wrote to Dawson, the man who, with full conviction, had engineered the political downfall of her husband: 'I looked at his [Neville Chamberlain's] spare figure and keen eye, and could not help comparing it with Winston's self-indulgent rotundity.'

Here endeth yet another lesson of the Establishment—with a question mark. Why did Geoffrey Dawson, one of the few men with the courage to stand up to Northcliffe, refuse to stand up to Hitler? The answer is wrapped in impenetrable mystery. With all his virtues, and they were many and great, he goes down to history as an architect of the Decline and Fall of the British Empire, to the service of which he dedicated his life.

1955.

SCOTS AT WESTMINSTER

THROUGHOUT the half-century preceding the outbreak of the first world war Scotland was solidly Liberal. Gladstone, alive or dead, dominated all; and memories of the Midlothian campaign never faded. The hiatus between Gladstone's death and the advent of Campbell-Bannerman, with Rosebery a fading political figure, was easily surmounted. Joseph Chamberlain was regarded as a shocking renegade; and the torch passed, with hardly a flicker, into the firm grasp of Asquith.

In some aspects Asquith suited the Scots better than any other politician of modern times; and, prior to 1914, his grip on the Scottish electorate was unshakable. They admired his massive intellectual power. They knew precisely where he stood on the great political issues of the day; four-square, come fair weather or foul, like one of the rocks off the coast of East Fife which he represented for over thirty years. And they did not mind in the least that he was a Yorkshireman. On the contrary, they cared not where their politicians came from provided they were men of proved ability; and they liked to send to the House of Commons those whose names were household words. Asquith and Churchill, Haldane and Bryce—all were equally welcome; and, so long as they stuck to the pure milk of the true Faith, equally secure. For Balfour they had a certain admiration, as a philosopher and man of letters rather than as a statesman. For Ramsay MacDonald they never had much use. And about Lloyd George they were apt to use one of their favourite expressions—'I hae ma' doots.' The doots were amply confirmed when he deliberately shattered the Liberal Party in 1918; and for this they never forgave him.

Nevertheless, they accepted the inevitable. The Scots are a logical people; and saw, before the English or the Welsh, that under our two-party system there was no room for a third. The General Election of 1922 settled the issue. A few tattered Liberal banners survived in the more remote areas—just as Roman Catholicism survived the Reformation in the Outer Hebrides. But, in the main, the Scottish electorate plumped for Socialism or Conservatism; and the political pattern then established has not since changed. This accounts for the remarkable absence of pronounced swings, to Right or Left, in subsequent elections. Scotland is almost equally divided between the Labour and Conservative Parties. There are not more than ten 'marginal' seats.

From the General Election of 1922 a new political phenomenon emerged—the Clyde group. They exercised a political influence far in excess of their number, comparable to that of the Irish, and much greater than that of the Fourth Party. They became, for a time, the conscience of the nation—at a moment when it was badly needed; and brought to the resentful attention of the House of Commons, as it has never been brought before or since, the desperation of the slum-dwellers and of the unemployed. John Wheatley was their leader. I still believe him to be the ablest politician the Labour Movement has yet produced, with the exception of Aneurin Bevan. Handicapped by short-sightedness, which prevented him from being a good mixer, he had a brain like a nut-cracker which reached out eagerly and unerringly for the heart of the matter.

Wheatley's premature death was a heavy blow to the Labour Party and, in particular, to the Clyde group. Maxton was no successor. Like Lloyd George he was an artist expressing himself through the medium of politics. But he was indolent, and totally devoid of political ambition. He was a great natural orator. The lean emaciated figure, the raven locks, the deep resonant voice, the stabbing forefinger, the vehement but always controlled passion, the flashes of humour that lit his bitterest speeches made him, at his best, incomparable as a debater in the House of Commons and in emotional appeal from the platform. But he never aspired to be more than an agitator; and the mellowing influence of Parliament blunted the edge of his attack. He was too loving and lovable a man to play, with any hope of success, the revolutionary part for which he cast himself.

Gradually the Clyde group disintegrated. Tom Johnston, the scribe, among them but never quite of them, went off to plough a lonely albeit highly successful furrow, greatly to the benefit of Scotland; Kirkwood, the firebrand, to become fairy godfather to the *Queen Mary* and finally a Peer; Shinwell to Seaham and office. The fire went out of Neil Maclean and Campbell Stephen. And Buchanan had to wait for a quarter of a century before he was given the chance to exercise in administration the qualities of mind and heart which made him a great Chairman of the National Assistance Board. It is an ironical reflection that the only traceable practical effect on British political history produced, as a group, by some of the most vivid parliamentary personalities of our time was the election of Ramsay MacDonald as Leader of the Labour Party.

Meanwhile, it devolved upon the Scottish Tories, hitherto a small band without many personalities or traditions, or indeed much hope, to provide the main opposition to the Socialists; and to imbibe a sufficient quantity of the spirit of Liberalism to make themselves acceptable in that rôle. On the whole they succeeded remarkably well; and this was largely due to the enthusiasm and unquestioned brilliance of a great political teacher, the late Noël Skelton. Neither Sir Robert Horne, the effective spokesman of big business, nor Walter Elliot with his diversified interests, ministerial pre-occupations and doubtful political antecedents—had he not been a Socialist at Glasgow University?—could have been a comparable mentor for the new Unionist Party, or done as much.

Like Elliot, Skelton was a superlative talker, with a tremendous gaiety and zest for life; but in the more concentrated Edinburgh tradition. He stimulated every gathering he joined; and in a flash generated the sparks of animated and provocative talk by means of audacious sallies and improvisations, flung out with reckless prodigality. Among others, the phrase 'property-owning democracy', which has now passed into general political currency, was originally coined by him. Fortified by the pawky humour of Fred

Macquisten—a 'card' if ever there was one—the Scottish Unionists put up a good show in the 'twenties; and held their own, better than their English colleagues, in the General Election of 1929.

From then on a steady decline took place in the political life of Scotland which has not ceased, and for which no rational explanation has ever been forthcoming. With the exception of Hector McNeil, who was happier in the field of foreign affairs, and of Sir William Darling, who was content to follow in the footsteps of Macquisten, no new figures of consequence emerged on either side. Lord Attlee was in continuous difficulty over his Scottish appointments; and Mr. Macmillan has solved his problem only by excluding from the Cabinet, and even from office of Cabinet rank, every single Scottish Unionist M.P. Who can blame him? Even *The Scotsman* was driven to remark, in an acid leader, that whereas in the old days Members of Parliament made speeches of interest and importance during the recesses, now they seldom spoke at all—and, if they did, what they said was unreadable. In recent days (and nights) it has seemed that the Labour Party has found a formidable debater in the shape of Mr. William Ross; but for some unaccountable reasons the Scottish Members, as a whole, have fallen below the level of the nation they represent.

Yet Scotland herself does well. We continue to produce the best ships, the best beef, the best oats and the best whisky known to man. Our engineers, craftsmen, miners, farmers and fishermen still hold their own against all comers. And, when all is said and done, no nation of her size has ever exercised a comparable impact and influence upon the outside world. As Barrie said to the students of St. Andrews: 'You come of a race of men the very wind of whose name has swept to the ultimate seas.' Wherever you go, from the Far West to the Far East, you find Scotsmen running the show. Only at home do they seem to be unsure of their destiny; and to have lost some of the buoyant self-confidence which is their most admirable and endearing characteristic abroad.

A political revival is urgently required. I believe it can be achieved with the material at present available. We need a greater conceit of ourselves; and a less parochial outlook. If I had ever been offered the Scottish Office—and at one moment, long ago, it was conceivable—I should have asked for an official residence in Edinburgh; and with the assistance of my old friend Sir Compton Mackenzie, striven to revive the pristine glories of a society which once commanded the attention of Europe. I should have driven round Scotland in an enormous black car, with the rampant lion flying proudly in the wind, and—if possible—outriders on motorcycles. I should have steamed round her coast every year in the fishery cruiser, rechristened a yacht for the purpose, with more flags. And all this not for the purpose of self-aggrandisement; but just to show that the Secretary of State for Scotland is, in his own right, a tremendous political figure whose presence at the British Cabinet table must be counted an honour to them. The offer would, of course, have been precipitately withdrawn when I made my terms. But something very real, and very necessary, lies behind them. Without Scotland the English would be sunk.

1957.

PART III

The Art of Economics

INTRODUCTORY NOTE

I AM not a professional economist; and my only claim to include the following speeches on economic policy, in one or other Houses of Parliament, is that in the past I have so often been proved right, and the so-called 'experts' wrong. If you doubt this, or consider it an unduly arrogant assertion, read them!

I was opposed to our return to the gold standard in 1925, at the pre-war parity of exchange. I was opposed to the monetary deflation which inevitably followed, and which caused first the General Strike of 1926, and then massive unemployment for fifteen bitter years. I was opposed to Snowden's Mad Budget and Economy Bill of 1931, rightly described by Keynes as 'replete with folly and injustice'. I was opposed to the American Loan on the terms we got, and to the Bretton Woods Agreement, for reasons hereafter set out. I was the only member on either side of the House of Commons who vehemently denounced the lunatic attempt to make sterling convertible in the summer of 1947—an extract from my speech on this occasion appears in the chapter on *International Liquidity in the Free World*.

Finally, I have been opposed to what have been called the 'Stop-and-Go' tactics of recent years, due to an excessive reliance on Bank Rate as the main regulator of the National Economy. Our export performance over the past decade, by comparison with that of the Common Market countries, has been disgraceful—an average increase of 10 per cent., as against 70 per cent. Here is proof positive that exports will never rise except in the context of general economic expansion, industrial growth, and increased efficiency. The truth is, as Mr. Rees-Mogg has pointed out, that British export costs were actually forced up by the disin-flationary measures which were introduced in order to keep them steady. The crucial economic problem confronting this country is that of the balance of payments; and no one can persuade me that it will ever be solved by stagnation.

On some of these issues almost my sole supporter was Lord Beaverbrook—that invincible champion of lost causes. We lost a number of battles: but have not yet lost the continuing fight for economic expansion. If he now wants to do it one way, and I another (through the Common Market), that is of little conse-quence so long as it becomes accepted economic doctrine. And there are signs of this. For nearly half a century the Treasury has been the nigger in the woodpile; and is now on pretty shaky ground. In the 'thirties Keynes felt able to write: 'Scarcely anyone in England believes in the pre-war Gold Standard, or in the Policy of Deflation. These battles have been won—mainly by the irresist-ible pressure of events and only secondarily by the slow under-mining of old prejudices.'

A similar process now seems to be taking place. It will be accelerated by the staggering revelations in the third volume of Lord Dalton's autobiography. What terrible advice he got! Hugh Dalton was an economist, but made no pretensions to be a market man. They should have told him that the right policy was to keep money as cheap as possible, but that there were limits. They told him no such thing. He himself had some misgivings, when he called 3 per cent. Local Loans stock for redemption, in January 1947, about issuing an undated stock at $2\frac{1}{2}$ per cent. The Governor of the Bank of England, Lord Catto, had 'slight hesitations'. The Treasury had none. He gives the names. Sir Richard Hopkins said: 'Chancellor, you must be resolute. We must all speak outside as though we were quite sure we could carry this thing through.' The result was 'Daltons', now cursed, together with $3\frac{1}{2}$ per cent. War Loan, by everyone who bought them. Again, on converti-bility, the Chancellor was 'gravely informed', as late as July 1947, that it had been discounted; and that when it came it would make very little difference. Small wonder that he writes: 'I am still surprised, looking back, by this profound error of practical judgment.'

In this light the criticisms of the Treasury which follow may not be deemed altogether ill-founded. There is a certain amount of repetition. I have deliberately kept it in. Forty years of public life have persuaded me that, if there is to be the slightest chance of your ideas being ultimately accepted, you must repeat them over and over again.

THE AMERICAN LOAN AND
BRETTON WOODS

I FEEL rather strongly about this question, and I would like to say to my friends that, as no amendments are being called in this debate, I propose myself to seek to divide the House on the main question tomorrow, and to ask as many of them as I can get to do so, to vote with me against the proposals of His Majesty's Government. The main ground on which I do that, among many others, is because I conscientiously believe that this country is not, and will not be, in a position to discharge the obligations she is being invited to undertake by the Government; and if one believes that, I do not think one has any alternative but to carry one's beliefs into the Division Lobby. I have never believed that you can get out of debt by getting into more debt; and I do not think this is going to make our position any stronger.

We spent £10,700 millions over and above what we could provide ourselves on the war; and of this sum £9,200 millions was spent during the war, leaving us on 'V-J Day' with another £1,500 millions of inevitable war expenditure to be paid, unless we had suddenly demobilized every soldier, sailor and airman in the field at that moment. I submit to the House, and I think the Chancellor of the Exchequer will agree with me, that this extra £1,500 millions should have been included in Lend-Lease. It was essential war expenditure, for it was Lend-Lease that produced our war effort, and turned our national economy completely upside down, and is therefore largely responsible for the position in which we find ourselves. Lend-Lease was passed in the United States as an: 'Act for the defence of the United States.' That is ex-

actly what it was, comparable precisely to the subsidies we ourselves paid to various European countries during the Napoleonic
Wars, with great success, when we wanted them to fight our
battles for us.

Unlike the last war which was officially terminated by Presidential proclamation on July 2, 1921, this one came to an end
within three weeks of the termination of hostilities. I can see no
justification for this. It was like giving a man a lift in an aeroplane,
as Mr. Roosevelt gave us under Lend-Lease, taking him nine-
tenths of the way across the Atlantic Ocean, and then, when
100 miles from the shore, throwing him out of the aeroplane and
telling him to swim for it. That is, roughly, what has happened.

I submit that the conditions put forward for our approval are
far too onerous. It is not untrue to say that comparable terms have
never hitherto been imposed on a nation that has not been defeated in war. To get through, and pay our debt, on the admission
of the Government, we shall have to increase our exports by
75 per cent. over pre-war. If there ever was any chance of our
achieving this aim, it has been removed by the conditions attached
to the loan which is now being given us. Lord Baldwin has been
much criticized for the 1923 debt settlement; but the terms he obtained were princely in comparison with these terms. And our
position was incomparably better then. But we were compelled to
repudiate, as we shall be compelled to repudiate this time. Look
at the inevitable effect of our undertaking to convert sterling into
dollars on our trade. No doubt hon. Members on both sides of the
House have read the letter of Sir Hubert Henderson in *The Times*
this morning. He wrote:

'... all incentive to other countries to buy from us because we
buy from them will be removed in about a year from now. Moreover, any part of the huge accumulated sterling balances which
countries in the sterling area are allowed to spend at all must be
made equally available for dollars as for sterling purchases.'

As to the conditions that attach to this loan, I will make a con-
cession to the Chancellor of the Exchequer. I will not say we have
to go back to the gold standard, I will say simply that we have to

go back to gold. I hope to say a few words on this subject on the Second Reading of the Bretton Woods Bill, the rejection of which I am moving, so I will content myself on this occasion by quoting from Article IV, Section (1), paragraph (a) of the Final Act:

'The par value of the currency of each member shall be expressed in terms of gold as a common denominator, or in terms of the United States dollar of the weight and fineness in effect on 1st July, 1944.'

If that is not going back to gold, I do not know what going back to gold is. Under the Bretton Woods Agreement, gold will purchase any currency. A member may, in defined circumstances, be called upon by the Fund to redeem his currency either in gold or in gold currency. In addition, exchange rates between member currencies shall not vary from official parities by more than 1 per cent. There are many other articles I could quote. I will content myself with one quotation from the *Economist* on this question of gold, on which I have been challenged so often. The *Economist* said last week:

'The differences between the Bretton Woods system and the gold standard have often been pointed out, but the similarities are perhaps even stronger. The aim of both is free convertibility, and though the Bretton Woods system is more elastic than the gold standard of 1925–31, it is being introduced at a much earlier stage and in a much more tumultuous world.'

Then there is this cutting down of the transitional period from five years to one, to which reference has been made in previous speeches this afternoon. I ask hon. Members to look at the world today, and say whether final and long-term decisions of any kind can be taken. What are the governing factors which should be taken into consideration in the fixing of an exchange?—national income, wage rates, trade, imports and exports. Do we know them? Can we prophesy them? He would be a very clever man who would dare to prophesy what conditions will be one, two, three or four years hence. Even the Treasury, great though their intellectual capacity is, are taking on a little more than they can chew if they assure the Chancellor that they are satisfied that a rate of 4·03 is 'O.K.' They were satisfied after the last war with a rate of 4·86 and it did not turn out very well. I confess I think that to anchor ourselves to gold at this parity of exchange, at this juncture in world affairs, is an act of absolute insanity.

I am opposed to gold only because I believe that if you make it the monetary basis, and the basis of credit, with a fixed price, as Bretton Woods does, sooner or later it will exercise a contracting influence on the world. I believe it is the greatest obstacle to the one thing which will get the world to its economic goal, which is a continuous policy of economic expansion. Many hon. Members will remember vividly the Debates of 1925, and the old days of the gold standard of the 1920's; this debate is like living the whole thing over again. We finished the last war a prosperous country, with a prosperous agriculture. It took ten years of deflation to turn it into a really poor country, with a derelict agriculture, the workers migrating to the United States, factories, dockyards and workshops closed down, and with nearly 3,000,000 unemployed. That is what the gold standard did to us last time.

Another condition that we are now asked to swallow is the acceptance of the principle of non-discrimination in trade, involving the elimination of imperial preference and of quotas on imports. I do not think there is any need for me to dilate on this. I think that if it is persisted in—and I hope it will not be—it will involve the break-up of the British Empire.[1] I say to my hon. Friends above the Gangway, before they abstain from voting, to reflect on the words of Polonius:

'To thine own self be true.'

If the Tory Party ceases to believe in the Empire, and in the economic expansion and development of the Empire, it ceases to have any meaning in this country. Nearly half our exports before the war went to the British Empire. Look at the effect which this proposal will have on the Colonies. What will be the effect, for instance, on Jamaica, which enjoyed a preferential price on sugar amounting to £11. 5s. a ton prior to the war, in 1938? I agree that

1. It has. B.

149

the countries within the closed economic system of the United States, including the sugar countries—Puerto Rico, for example—enjoyed an even greater preference. But the Customs Union of the United States is absolutely preserved under this agreement. The doctrine of non-discrimination of trade is based, in my submission, upon the altogether fallacious assumption that, as trade is, or should be, conducted by individuals, the size of national markets is of no consequences. According to this doctrine, from the economic point of view, there is no difference between the United States of America and Monaco. What nonsense! This doctrine will not stand investigation in the modern world of mass production.

I am going to speak bluntly, and say that there are two main objectives underlying the agreement which we are being asked to approve. The first is to get back as quickly as possible to the economic system of the nineteenth century—the system of *laissez-faire* Capitalism. The second is to break up, and prize open, the markets of the world for the benefit of the United States of America, who have an intense desire to get rid of their surplus products, which will be enormous, at almost any cost. If this is not so—and the Chancellor was continually asking us to put forward alternatives—why did they not give us a commercial loan to enable us to get through the next year or two, without conditions attached, as they did to France? Were they asked to do so? Did they refuse to do so? The rate offered to France, without any conditions attached, was only five-eighths per cent. more than the rate which we are being charged under this Loan Agreement. Even an Aberdonian would hesitate to sacrifice as much as this for the sake of an additional five-eighths per cent. I suggest that it would have been far better for the Chancellor of the Exchequer to have said, when the negotiations took the shape they did, 'All right. Let us scrap the long-term agreement for the time being, and let us have a straight loan on reasonable terms.' I believe that would have been his right course. Furthermore, if we had then appealed to the Dominions and the countries in the sterling area to help us through these difficult years, I believe that they would have rallied to our side. I ask the Chancellor of the Exchequer, did he ever put that suggestion directly to the Dominions, the Colonies, or to other countries in the sterling area? If he had, I do not believe we should have been short of anything except tobacco, cotton and films.

I want now to put two propositions to the Chancellor of the Exchequer. The first is that multilateral trade, fixed exchanges and free convertibility, to which this Agreement admittedly commits us, are impractical in the modern world. The philosophy underlying the old Liberal doctrine of enlightened self-interest and the free-market economy depended for its success on the existence of empty spaces and continually expanding markets. The spaces are filling up. The era of uncontrolled capitalist expansion is drawing to a close. I never thought I should live to teach these things to hon. Members who sit on the Government side of the House. The *laissez-faire* economy of the nineteenth century, I would remind the Chancellor of the Exchequer, who used to think this himself, has now to give way to the planned international economy of the twentieth century.

My second proposition is that we cannot have a planned national economy with international economic anarchy. It has been left to a Socialist Government to lead us back to international economic anarchy and to the economic system of the nineteenth century, the system of *laissez-faire* Capitalism, which crashed to destruction in 1929.

How does their policy square with:

'There must be no return to the gold standard. It cannot be in our interests or in anyone else's, to join in a policy of collective suicide.'

That is from the Labour Party pamphlet of 1944, endorsed by the Blackpool Conference. What about the Foreign Secretary[1] who, only a month or two back in this House, during the 'caretaker' Government, and in those flashing few weeks when he was relieved for a spell from the cares and responsibilities of office, said:

'I take the line, and my party takes the line, that, neither directly nor indirectly, will we again be anchored to gold in any circumstances.'

1. Mr. Ernest Bevin.

I would remind the Chancellor of the Exchequer that these agreements mean positively opening the sluice-gates of exchange restriction. It is no use the right hon. Gentleman drawing this tremendous distinction between letting capital out and letting money out for current transactions. That distinction is extremely difficult to draw; and many people will be able to evade it. There will be plenty of people in the City of London who will find a method of opening the gates, and will be able to get their money out.[1] I would also remind the right hon. Gentleman that it was the export of money from this country which brought down the Labour Government in 1931, and later brought down the Blum Government in France. I am not at all sure that it will not also bring down this Government. Although that might be some compensation, it would not be sufficient to offset these proposals.

These terms are hard. They are very hard. As the *Economist* truly says:

'Our present needs are the direct consequences of the fact that we fought earliest, that we fought longest, and that we fought hardest.'

The Americans have had full value from Lend-Lease. In addition, they have made a substantial capital profit on the securities which we were forced to sell in order to save them in 1941. We made nothing out of that transaction, because we shot off what we got in defence of the United States of America.

For the hardness of the terms I blame very much the method of approach. I think the hon. Member for Ipswich (Mr. Stokes) will agree with me when I ask, 'Why is it that we should always talk about money, and not about goods?' I always said we should approach these matters from the angle of goods, not gold. I should like to quote from old Clemenceau—and how wise he was—because his words show clearly the point to which we have arrived:

'We have come to such a pitch that, for want of a Government, we blindly entrust our most vital interests to so-called independent

1. As, in 1947, they did. B.

152

"experts", that is to say experts free from governmental responsibilities; with the result that we take haphazard resolutions that will be a heavy burden on us to the end of our days.'

Every word applies to the present situation. I should like to put my alternative, but I am not proposing to occupy the time of the House any longer. (Hon. Members: 'Go on.') It is the alternative of the sterling *bloc*, based upon the British Empire, and fortified by the countries of Western Europe.

There was a chance for a middle unit, standing between what my hon. friend the Member for Chippenham (Mr. Eccles) and I call the 'knock-about' capitalism of the United States of America on the one hand, and the rigid, socialist, closed economy of Russia on the other; free to expand, by multilateral agreement within that economy, with like-minded nations. That arrangement might have provided a balancing *bloc* which would have been of very great value in the world. I do not want to see the world divided into two, and only two, opposing systems. I think there is danger in it.

This is the great argument of goods *versus* gold. It is an argument between those who think of human welfare in terms of the essentials of human welfare—light, heat, food, clothing and shelter—and those who think of it in terms of money. I have said before in this House that I am a goods man. I do not believe that money is, or should be, anything more than a convenient medium for exchanging goods and measuring their value. One day the myth of gold as a separate entity, and as the pivot around which the whole economy of the world revolves, will be exploded. The ultimate solution of our economic problems lies in increasing effective demand, by clothing the desperate needs of masses of people with sufficient purchasing power to enable them to buy the abundance which modern science has placed at their disposal.

Are we to throttle production of goods by making gold the basis of international credit? Are we to accept the doctrine of non-discrimination, based on the fallacious assumption that all sovereign States are of equal economic importance? Are we to hand over absolute economic power to the great creditor nations, by accepting the bargaining power of export surpluses, and rejecting that of markets, which is our only asset? Are we to try to solve the economic problems of the twentieth century by applying the ideas of the nineteenth? I never thought I should feel again as I felt at the time of the Munich Agreement, but I feel just the same as I did then. This is our economic Munich. I believe that we are at the parting of the ways. 1940 and 1945: they are two critical dates in the long and almost incredible story of the British Empire. We took the right road in 1940; are we going to take the wrong road in 1945? Lord Keynes once described Mr. Lloyd George as a witch flying on a broomstick through the twilit air of Paris from the hag-ridden woods of Celtic antiquity. My description of Lord Keynes is a siren, beckoning us to our doom from the murkier depths of Bretton Woods. That is the danger. He is a siren, with his persuasive tongue. In defiance of all his teachings and the precepts that he has told to us for years, he has now driven us into this position. We have heard a lot about mandates recently, especially from the Chancellor of the Exchequer. It may be that the Government have a mandate to nationalize the gas works. I do not deny it. And on the question of whether this will be good for the gas works, or the public, I would not venture to dogmatize. But there is one mandate which His Majesty's Government never got from the people of this country, and that was to sell the British Empire for a packet of cigarettes.

December 1945.

THE ECONOMIC CRISIS: 1956

I INTEND to devote the first five minutes of my speech to a visit which I have paid just recently to the U.S.A. I think that it might be of some interest to the House. I discovered, rather to my surprise, that over there a planned economy was being pretty well run. I was not altogether expecting that. I want to tell the House, first of all, about the team. The team consists of an Economic General Staff, for which the Chancellor of the Exchequer and I pleaded in vain for about twenty years in this House between the wars, headed by a very remarkable man, Mr. Arthur Burns; a special department of the Treasury under the Under-Secretary, Mr. Randolph Burgess; and the Federal Reserve Board, of which the Chairman is Mr. William McChesney Martin, a very young and brilliant man whose reappointment was recently confirmed by the Congress.

The methods are, first, the management of money and control of credit, through the discount rate and open market operations, far superior to those which exist in this country. I admit that they are greatly assisted by the fact that the reserves of the commercial banks in the U.S.A., expressed as a ratio of their deposit liabilities, are fixed by law. I was interested to see that Professor Erhard, the Economic Minister in the Government of Federal Germany, is now introducing legislation to do that very same thing.

I am not at all sure that it might not be worth very careful consideration on the part of the Chancellor whether the minimum reserve requirements of our own joint-stock banks should not also be fixed. It would have one very desirable result. The discount rate would operate over a much wider field; and it would no longer be necessary to use the bank managers of this country as fiscal agents of the Treasury, which they dislike very much and which, if I may say so to my friends of the Tory Party, constitutes the most intimate and unpleasant form of Government interference with private life that it is possible to imagine.

They are also assisted by the practice of the United States Treasury of distributing its cash balances and short-term borrowings very widely through the commercial banking community. We do not do that. We have our Treasury bills, to which reference has already been made; and I will not go into that.

The second method is what they call 'built-in stabilizers'. That is a good American expression. It means frequent variations in taxation, and expenditure on social security, public works and farm support prices. The third—and this rather surprised me—is a control over the use of credit in security speculation, and for housing loans insured or guaranteed by the Federal Government which now amount to over two-fifths of the total home mortgage debt. The fourth is a control over imports which, though far less necessary there than here, is extremely effective.

Finally—and this brings me to the end of the first part of my speech—they have something which we have not got on any comparable scale, and that is a most wonderful statistical service. I suppose that Mr. Burns himself is one of the greatest living statisticians. After years of research, although he is not so very old, he has reduced about 600 indicators of economic trends in the national economy to twenty-one 'key factors'. The fact remains that they have statistical information in the Treasury and the Federal Reserve Board about the national economy of the United States incomparably superior to anything we have even thought of in this country. That is why we are so behind the times, and they are so up to date.

Mr. Martin, the Chairman of the Federal Reserve Board, gave evidence before Senator Fulbright's Banking and Finance Committee while I was in Washington. He thinks that things will be fairly good for at least another twelve months, although slightly less surging than last year. But they will be pretty good, and still on the up. To the question, 'What is your policy going to be for the next six months?' he replied, 'Lean against the wind; timing is of the essence.' He can do it. Who can do it in this country?

I have always had a theory that we have never won the Walker Cup because we have never sent our team over to study the methods of the United States, with the result that our golfers are amateurs and theirs are professionals. I think that much the same applies to the Treasury and the Bank of England. The Chancellor should send a deputation from the Treasury and the Bank of England to study the methods of the Treasury and the Federal Reserve Board of the United States. I am firmly convinced—and I have worked quite hard at this—that we are amateurs and they are professionals in these matters.

Certainly, their results have been impressive. They stopped the impending recession of 1953–54 to the consternation and surprise of every economist in this country who had predicted it with varying degrees of certainty from Right to Left—from Clark to Balogh.

They checked successfully the impending inflationary boom of 1955–56. They have kept the national economy upon a level keel, and prices amazingly steady; and have produced an economic climate of opinion which has resulted in a productivity without parallel elsewhere.

I now come to the second part of my remarks. Having seen how it should be done, I am more than ever convinced that the economic policy of successive Governments since the war has been, well, let me content myself by saying, 'Jolly bad', all the way through, and by the lot. We got off to a bad start with the American Loan, which was used as a drug. I never wanted to have it on the terms we got. Then we had Daltonian buoyancy, accompanied by ridiculously cheap money, after which the right hon. Gentleman ran us into convertibility and there was an almighty crash, and that was that. This was followed by Crippsian austerity and controls; and the result of that was devaluation, which was not so hot. Finally, we have had the Lord Privy Seal's 'dash to freedom', which has landed us in our present position.

All I can say about it is that four major crises within a decade are nothing to make either party very proud. There is not much to go on slamming each other about. The record of both parties in this matter is pretty lousy. I do not believe that the problem that confronts us today will be solved by the dogmas either of socialism or of *laissez-faire*, but only by radical revisions of thought and policy, and by courage.

Now let us have one look at causes. What are the four main causes of our present trouble? The greatest of them all has been excessive public expenditure, ever since the war. I am going to say something with which hon. Members opposite will not disagree. I am oppressed by the thought of the wasted expenditure on defence. I am not blaming anybody for the moment. In this sphere, science has been working too fast for humanity. We have been scrambling along desperately and trying to catch up, but we have never caught up.

Obviously, the Royal Air Force is the most important of the three services, but think of the amount of money that has been spent, for example, on Fighter Command since the war. What have we got to show for it now? This has been an expenditure, not of £10 million or £20 million like the bread or milk subsidies, but of hundreds of millions of pounds, absolutely wasted. I sometimes lie awake at night and think of the money that has been wasted, and is still being wasted, on defence, with the best intentions. Sooner or later the Prime Minister and the Chancellor of the Exchequer will have to make up their minds what sort of defence forces we want in three years' time, and say to the Minister of Defence, 'That is what we need. Scrap everything else.'

On my second point I may not carry all hon. Members with me. A system of progressive taxation on earned incomes which, in the words of Professor Lionel Robbins, 'amounts to a discrimination against enterprise and ability such as has never before existed for any long time in any large-scale civilized community,' is the greatest hamper to our economic advance. No man in this country can save out of earnings, even if he is right at the top of his profession. He can only save out of successful speculation or real property deals. That is all wrong.

Thirdly, there is the point to which Lord Beveridge drew attention in *The Times*, the day before yesterday. He referred to the actions of associations of employers and workers which are equally responsible for determining competitively the money rates of wages and the prices which inevitably follow, by bidding up for ever higher wages and scarce labour, in conditions of full employment. Employers have tried to bribe labour away from one industry to another, and the trade unions have been tempted—I do not altogether blame them—to take advantage of full employment to force up wages to heights which the national economy cannot stand.

I now come to excessive imports. The most significant are coal, steel and feeding stuffs, all of which we should be producing ourselves in far greater quantities. To the Chancellor I say, 'I do not think you can go on dishing out dollars indefinitely to the commodity markets.' Sooner or later we shall have to cut our dollar imports to the level of our dollar earnings.

We live in an expanding world and are losing, at the moment, our share of an expanding trade. In the circumstances a policy of national economic expansion is essential, and a long-term policy of restriction would be suicidal. There was a thing—I think the Chancellor may remember it—called the Strasbourg Plan. So far as trade policy is concerned it was designed to harness the industrial resources of Western Europe to the raw material resources of our associated overseas territories, and by providing assured markets for both to expand the production and the trade of the whole.

That plan was dismissed—I am bound to say contemptuously dismissed—by the Lord Privy Seal.[1] I minded a bit because I had had a hand in the drafting of it and I think that my right hon. Friend might at least have given it a more civil farewell before kicking it down the chute. But I know well why it was dismissed. It was dismissed because it involved planned international investment, preferential arrangements, and therefore discrimination in trade. I say to the Chancellor of the Exchequer that, in one form or another, he will have to come back to it.

Finally I want to say that if, in the name of *laissez-faire* and non-discrimination, the Chancellor refuses to give the national economy the positive strategic direction which the Americans are giving to theirs, we cannot hope to survive in the modern world.

1. Mr Butler, when Chancellor of the Exchequer.

February 1956.

THE CRISIS DEEPENS: 1957

THE House will have listened with great interest and considerable amusement to the stimulating speech of the hon. Member for Cheetham (Mr. H. Lever). I hope to come back to it in a moment or two. At the outset, I would only say that the hon. Gentleman complained about the economic lectures that so many people give to the House, and I must warn him that I am about to deliver an economic sermon.

Mr. H. Lever: I was complaining of the Minister's lectures, not those of the hon. Gentleman.

Sir R. Boothby: What I propose to say will be worse than a lecture; it will be a sermon. A sermon demands a text, and my text is taken from Walter Lippmann:

'A society cannot stand still. If it loses the momentum of its own progress, it will deteriorate and decline, lacking purpose and losing confidence in itself.'

At present, we are losing out to the Communists in almost every field, and nowhere is this more dangerous than in the economic field. Together with the United States, who bear by far the greater load of responsibility, we are at this moment taking certain steps which are calculated to intensify any pending economic recession, which I think was on the way anyhow.

Industrial production has been sagging, both here and in the United States. Commodity prices have been falling steadily, while the cost of manufactured goods has been rising. The underdeveloped countries have, in consequence, been feeling the pinch. These three factors, in combination, provide, in the words of *The Times*, a classic setting for an international trade recession.

Yet we continue to pursue restrictive monetary and credit policies. It obliges me to say, 'This is where I came in.' I have been
through it three times—in 1925–26, when we went back to the
gold standard, and went on to the General Strike; in the crisis of
1929–31, when Snowden introduced the maddest Budget ever
presented to this House; and again in 1937, when we were only
saved from a serious recession by the advent of the second
world war.

I am now going to do a shocking thing. I intend to quote, at
some length, from a speech I made almost exactly twenty years
ago to the night, on November 2, 1937. It will not bore many
people, because very few can have been in the House at the time,
or will have heard it before; although I see one or two hon.
Gentlemen opposite who might have been around. Anyway, it
will give the Official Reporters a bit of fun, getting it out of
Hansard. They will probably have to send to the cellars for it.
I said:

'Under a Capitalist system, prosperity can be maintained only
through the steady flow of capital into industry under the stimulus
of confidence and anticipated profits. There is no other way in
which you can get the wheels of Capitalism to go round satis-
factorily. Today, the rate of investment in capital goods is falling
off in the United States and, to a lesser degree, in this country....
There is another disquieting factor. My right hon. Friend the
President of the Board of Trade said, rightly, that we had no right
to interfere in the internal affairs of the United States. Nevertheless, it cannot be said that they are no concern of ours. The fact
remains that whether it is President Roosevelt in America, or the
Chancellor of the Exchequer in this country, any man with power
and authority who makes a speech, or gives a Press interview
which brings about a diminution of confidence does, by that very
fact, deal a blow not only at the economic system of the United
States and this country, but also at the democracies of the world.

'Another lesson which we can learn is that whether we have
a Socialist or a Capitalist Government in this country, managed
finance is here to stay; and the power of the managers is almost

unlimited—far greater than any of us ever imagined it would be. Bad management and lack of co-operation between the United States and this country were, in my opinion, largely responsible for the slump of 1929; and they are almost entirely responsible for the recent recession.

'Just think of the ultimate forms that co-operation might take—a *de facto* stabilization of the pound and the dollar, to which the currencies of all those countries of the world which are not behind a closed system would ultimately link themselves; the maintenance on both sides of cash reserves and credits at the banks, sufficient to maintain commodity prices and the volume of international trade; and last, but not least, as an ultimate aim, is there any reason why, in co-operation with the United States, we should not use some of the vast stocks of gold that we possess in a joint lending policy to try to re-establish a measure of prosperity in those countries which are still impoverished as a result of the war, and of the slump of 1929–32? There are countries which are crying out for purchasing power, to whom gold loans would be invaluable. We could quickly increase international trade, and purchasing power, by acting thus together with the United States.

'I have not touched, and have not time to touch, on the political advantages of economic co-operation between the English speaking peoples, as others already have done. I would only say that I believe it is by far the best hope, and perhaps the only hope, of saving our civilization from war and destruction.'

(OFFICIAL REPORT, November 2, 1937.)

Every sentence of that speech, made in 1937, applies exactly to the present situation. I find this a little disheartening. One bats away and does one's stuff, and, everybody says, 'Jolly good speech,' and stands one a drink; but nothing happens. That is the depressing thing about politics. Here I am again, saying exactly the same thing. However, I never give in, and I am not giving in now.

I turn, for a moment, to the Chancellor. He said, in April:

'There are some who say we should depress demand to a point at which employers cannot afford to pay, and workers are in no position to ask for, higher wages. If this be the only way in which to contain the wage-price spiral, it is indeed a sorry reflection on our modern society. To slash production, to drive down investment, to push up unemployment is a high price to pay for price stability.'

(OFFICIAL REPORT, April 9, 1957.)

That is a clear statement.

In September, the Chancellor introduced a new economic policy. My remarks will not be as critical as some hon. Members opposite may imagine. I think I understand how it all happened. The essence of the Chancellor's new economic policy was, in his own words, to put the present fixed exchange rate of the pound ahead of economic growth as an economic objective. In short, the level of our industrial activity is now to be varied, rather than the level of the pound sterling in the exchange markets of the world.

It is no use my right hon. Friend or anybody else pretending that this does not constitute a pretty sharp change in policy, over a comparatively short period. What caused it? It was the run on sterling. In this respect a great deal of nonsense is talked—I am not referring to the hon. Member for Cheetham—about speculation. Sterling is one of the great trading currencies of the world, and every day thousands of perfectly legitimate traders have to take a view about it, in order to conduct their ordinary business transactions. A great deal depends on the view they take. Latterly, they have taken the view that sterling would depreciate in value, and they have acted accordingly. Those who are responsible for this are not a lot of mad gamblers sitting round a table drinking whisky in Zürich. They are, to a large extent, traders of the world who have to take a view about sterling. We talk in a rather loose way about speculation. The fact remains that these traders have taken this view about sterling, just as they have taken views about the D-mark and the dollar.

What, we must ask ourselves, caused them to take that view about sterling? The answer is twofold. One reason is our wage-cost inflation; and the other—I believe this to be the primary and basic cause—is our terrifying lack of reserves, as bankers of the sterling area. The rise in the Bank Rate to 7 per cent. was regrettable. I do not say that, at that moment of time, it was avoidable. I know that the pressure brought upon the Chancellor by the Bank of England was not wholly dissimilar from the pressure brought on the Labour Government in 1931. I know what a Chancellor must feel when he is told by the Governor of the Bank of England that, unless he does something drastic, there will be no reserves left in another five days.

There is no doubt at all that inflation is like Munich and Suez. It is an inflammable and emotional topic. It arouses passionate emotions in the breasts of everybody, and most people find it difficult to take a steady view of it. However, Professor James Meade had a good sentence in a letter in *The Times* this morning. He quietly said:

'It remains very desirable to find some way of preventing a continuous inflation of prices without stopping economic growth.'

That is not, on the face of it, a very startling sentence; but it is a profoundly true one. It represents the dilemma confronting the Chancellor, for it is what he has to try to do.

I dislike dear money, for various reasons. First, it costs a lot in the form of higher rents and increased interest payments on the sterling balances and the service of the National Debt. Amounts of £50 million or £100 million here and there may not seem much, but they add to the total burden. Secondly, dear money as such has never yet succeeded in bringing about any substantial or lasting improvement in our balance of payments, which is one of the things that matter most. On the contrary, it brings a reduction in export orders. Thirdly, and worst of all, it must involve cuts, of varying severity, in public and private investment; and thus retard economic growth.

In the long run, production is the real, and only criterion of wealth. If I had been Chancellor, I should have adopted from the start a policy designed to maximise productive investment in this country; and in order to do it I should not have hesitated to limit our dollar imports to the level of our dollar earnings, and to retain the system of building licences. I am sorry to have to make that last remark, but I am on the record as having said it for years. However, I believe that this horse has now bolted the stable, and the buildings have already been erected—offices, hotels, and petrol stations, and, I might add, some schools which might well have been designed as 'de luxe' hotels for the Nassau beaches. I regret, bitterly, that building licences were ever dispensed with. I shall never change my view. It has done a lot of damage to the economy of this country.

Mr. Ian Mikardo (Reading): That is why the hon. Gentleman was never Chancellor of the Exchequer.

Sir R. Boothby: Despite the loss of two stones, I remain a convinced and unrepentant expansionist. I shall never change. In my heart, I agree with an American friend who wrote to me the other day:

'The attempt to cure a wage-cost inflation by drastic deflation is like trying to cure a sore thumb by cutting off your arm.'

Let me add that confidence is easier to undermine than to revive.

I would say this to my right hon. Friend. An essential corollary to an expansionist policy must be the relief of taxation for those who have to live on small fixed incomes. As my hon. Friend the Member for Tynemouth (Dame Irene Ward) has consistently said, we in the Tory Party have failed in not relieving these people from taxation five or six years ago, to a far greater extent than we have done. As the hon. Gentleman the Member for Cheetham said, people living on small fixed incomes are bound to suffer from an expansionist or, if the word be preferred, an inflationary policy. We have not looked after them; and I ask my right hon. Friend whether he will, at any rate, bear these words of wisdom in mind for the next Budget.

That being said, it is essential that the Chancellor's policy at the moment should succeed. If it is not accompanied by a reduction in wage increases, it could easily result in prices rising faster; for it is at least possible that some industrial firms will find it easier to provide the money to pay increased wages by cutting their investment programmes. If they do that, consumption will be increased at the expense of capital development, which is the last thing the Chancellor wants. That is a real danger.

We listened this afternoon to what I thought was a characteristically sensible and level-headed speech from the Minister of Labour.[1] The Government are large, if not the largest, employers of industrial labour; and on the most vulnerable front. I believe that the Government, in these circumstances, have a direct and inescapable responsibility, and must give a lead on this matter of wages. I do not want to get into trouble here with the Opposition. Though I have had a number of cheers up to now, I do not think that this part will go over quite so well. I believe that, in general, wage increases must now be found from increased productivity; that is to say, from increased efficiency.

The dollar gap has, for the time being, reappeared; and, with it, the problem of the United States balance of payments with the rest of the world. The thing is hardly ever in balance. On top of this, outside the dollar area and Germany, the free world is suffering from a terrible shortage of liquid resources. This problem of international illiquidity derives, of course, from Bretton Woods and the ill-starred American Loan, which we should never have taken. The hon. Member for Cheetham was quite right. The theoretical price paid at Bretton Woods for fixed exchanges was adequate and well distributed gold and dollar reserves for the free world as a whole; and they were not provided. That is really the root of the trouble.

To raise international reserves to an adequate level in relation to trade, we need an international conference of the kind suggested yesterday by the right hon. Member for Huyton (Mr. H. Wilson). I support his plea that such a conference should be held at the earliest possible moment. We face just as serious a Communist challenge in the economic field as we do in the nuclear or in the diplomatic sphere. The Capitalist economy of the twentieth century is on test now against the Communist economy; and Russia does not have to restrict production in order to maintain the exchange value of the rouble under a Bretton Woods agreement. Russian production is going straight ahead.

1. Mr Macleod.

It does not matter how many changes there may be in the Kremlin; there is no check to Russian production. It marches on; and Russia can also offer stable prices to the uncommitted primary producing countries of Asia and of Africa. If they think that we are now going back to the old 'boom and bust' system of the 'twenties, these countries will leave us and come to terms with the Communist world, as some of them are doing now; because the Communists can say, 'We will give you X amount for your rubber, your cotton, your tin, your copper or whatever it may be, and that stands. We do not mind what happens in the commodity markets. It will not make any difference to us.'

We have ourselves to devise a new and more flexible monetary system under which some of the economic pressures can be taken by variations in exchange rates, and in which international reserves and credit facilities will be sufficient to enable it to function in the context of sustained economic expansion. We have also to co-ordinate monetary policies and plans for investment in the underdeveloped countries, which we have not done at all since the war.

Finally, we have to work out various schemes for securing greater stability in the prices of primary products, because it is the instability of the Capitalist world that gives the greatest ground for criticism of it. All these things ought to have been tackled at Bretton Woods in 1945. We let them go. We have been able to carry on largely through American generosity, but that cannot last for ever. We have also to accept the necessity for some discrimination against dollar imports if our deficit with the United States exceeds a certain limit; and the dollar countries themselves have to recognize that fact.

That was precisely what the Strasbourg Plan sought to achieve. We wanted to bring the Commonwealth into Europe altogether, united; and to link the raw material economy of the sterling area with the industrial economy of Western Europe by preferential and other arrangements. It was a much better plan than the proposed European Free Trade Area. We would have come in altogether as a Commonwealth, or at least with a large number of Commonwealth countries, with our raw materials, and reached good arrangements with Europe, because the basic problem there is no longer one of trade, but of payments and of investment. The trade would flow all right if the means of payment were available.

The right hon. Member for Huyton yesterday asked, towards the conclusion of his speech, who was the *eminence grise* behind the economic policy of the Government. He thought that some strange figure, shrouded in the recesses of the Treasury, or perhaps not in the Treasury at all, might be directing the economic policy of the Government. Let me assure the right hon. Gentleman that it is just the dear old Treasury, and nobody else.

I hope that my right hon. Friend the Chancellor of the Exchequer will not take umbrage if I say that sometimes, when I lie awake at night, I think what a good Chancellor I would have been myself; and when I do this I feel quite sorry for the country. Then I remember something that was told to me by a high Treasury official thirty years ago, just after I first got into the House. He said to me, 'There is something which you, as a young promising politician'—that is what I was then—'ought to know. There is only one man who has ever made the Treasury do what it did not want to do, and that was Lloyd George. And let me tell you something else; there will never be another.'

It is all very well for the right hon. Member for Huyton to laugh, but I understand that he has designs on that office. He may well find himself in the same position, and, if so, I shall be very interested to see what happens. I am inclined to think that it will be the same old story.

However, I must end on a cheerful and optimistic note. I also remember that, despite all the hammer blows that the Treasury have delivered to this country in the last thirty years, we have survived. It is a tremendous tribute to the resilience and strength of our people. And, after all, there is always the off-chance that the Treasury may do better in the future.

October 1957.

THE ECONOMIC CRISIS: 1960

My Lords, I should like to begin by saying that I feel that the crux of the problem has been succinctly put by the noble Lord, Lord Brand. It is, in fact, the insufficiency of our liquid reserves. By and large, as the noble Lord pointed out, they have remained at under £1,000 million over the past decade, as against liabilities, in the form of overseas sterling holdings, of over £4,000 million—that is to say, our reserves are only 25 per cent. of our short-term liabilities. And the fate of all bankers who accept deposits with inadequate cash reserves is the constant nightmare of every Chancellor of the Exchequer and of every Government. We met it in 1947, and we met it again in 1949 and 1951.

The remedy is clear enough. It is, as the noble Lord, Lord Brand, said, to build up an excess of exports, both visible and invisible, not only over imports but also over what we find it desirable or necessary to lend abroad. And it is easier said than done. The Prime Minister has been exhorting industrialists to do just this: to export more. But I want to examine for a moment what the Government have been doing. So far as imports are concerned, they have dismantled all our defences. I protested vehemently against this in another place. I have no dogmatic views, one way or the other, on the subject of physical controls. Where they are unnecessary, as the noble Lord, Lord Fraser of Lonsdale, said, they are obviously undesirable; but I have always thought that they should be kept in reserve, to be used in case of necessity. And they are not now in reserve.

The Government have also failed to reduce expenditure above the line. I know that this is an old theme; but the fact remains that a certain part of our expenditure on the Welfare State is wasteful. I do not think that there has been nearly enough pruning in sheer administration; but, of course—and this is not going to be very popular—the real enemy here is defence. We are no longer a great world Power in the nineteenth century sense of the term; and ever since the war successive Governments, both Labour and Conservative, have tried to behave as if we were—for example by having what has been called hitherto an 'independent deterrent'. I want to ask the noble Viscount, Lord Hailsham, who I believe is going to reply, what we have spent on defence since the war, and what we now have to show for it. But I would beg of him not to look up the figures now, because I am anxious that he should reply to this debate; and I believe that, if he did look at the figures of what we have spent on defence since the war, and what we have now got to show for it, he should be rendered unconscious and would therefore be unable to make any reply at all.

But that is not all. Despite repeated appeals, Her Majesty's Government insist on maintaining the 2 per cent. stamp duty on Stock Exchange transactions. It does not bring in all that amount of revenue, but it does discourage investment in productive enterprise by those with moderate incomes; and, worse still, it discourages investment in this country from abroad, and therefore has an adverse effect upon our invisible exports and on our balance of trade. It is not without significance that a great deal more foreign money is at the present moment being invested on the continent of Europe than in this country. While I do not say that this stamp duty is the only reason for that, it certainly plays a part.

Finally, there is the bank rate. I hope that the noble Lord, Lord Fraser of Lonsdale, will not take it amiss if I say that dear money is expensive. It is a platitude. It is expensive for the Government; it is expensive for local authorities; and it presses very hard on those who have entrusted their savings to the Government.

I will not comment on the present condition of the gilt-edged market, with which the noble Lord, Lord Pethick-Lawrence, has already dealt very well. I will content myself by saying that the two biggest swindles that have ever been perpetrated on the British public were the $3\frac{1}{2}$ per cent. War Loan, and what have since become known as 'Daltons'. As one of those swindles was perpetrated by a Conservative Government and the other by a Labour Government, your Lordships will observe that I am preserving the impartiality which becomes a member of the Cross Benches.

Dear money also directly hits the export trade, for the conduct of which industries—both large and small—require capital for the provision of credit to their purchasers overseas, and also for the purchase of stocks to ensure prompt delivery. I should like to suggest that the policy of attempting to increase exports by repressing industrial investment and development at home is, in the long run, a suicidal policy. Bank rate is the clumsiest of all methods of controlling monetary and credit policy; and that was brought out clearly in the Radcliffe Report. It hits the small man rather than the big; it acts as a restraint on productive investment which is desirable and necessary; and at the same time it does not necessarily curb loan expenditure on those products which are neither desirable nor essential. It is, in effect, wholly non-discriminatory. It is a clumsy, blunt-edged weapon, as the noble Earl must know. I was therefore horrified to hear him say yesterday—and I am referring to the noble Earl, Lord Dundee—that the Government intend to use the weapon of bank rate more frequently (I think that is a fair expression), as one of the main weapons of their economic policy. It reminds me of nothing so much as Alice and the mushroom. First a nibble one side, then a nibble the other side; and never the right size. How do they expect the business community to plan ahead against this kind of background of constant change?

The noble and learned Lord, Lord Radcliffe, is one of my oldest friends and no one has ever questioned his great abilities. But he has also great failings; he is modest, he is reticent and he is discreet. For my part, I have never been able to see that these alleged virtues are anything but grave defects. I wish that he were standing here in my place today, and really setting about the Government and the Treasury.

A Noble Lord: He is sitting here.

Lord Boothby: He may have been sitting here, but I do not think he is now. Oh, I see that he is. Dear, oh dear! If I had realized that the noble and learned Lord was here I do not think I should have said what I have said. Anyway, having started off, I may as well plunge on and say that he must be aghast at the man-handling of the Report of his Committee by the Treasury, who have clearly never read it.

In the last analysis it is the physical use of our available resources that matters—and I am now nearing an end. Look at what confronts us. In the Common Market they have set themselves a rate of expansion—that is to say, an increase of productivity—of between 4 and 5 per cent. per annum, and are now achieving it. In the United States, the Eisenhower policies have been jettisoned by both the Presidential candidates; and they now aim at an annual rate of economic growth of not less than 5 per cent., to be achieved by increasing both public and private investment. This is the measure of what we are up against, we who are doddering along at a $2\frac{1}{2}$ per cent. rate of increase at the present time. Do we aim to tag along like this for ever?

What is the aim of Her Majesty's Government? It does not clearly emerge from any Government statements—still less from the Opposition. I listened the day before yesterday in another place to the speech of Mr. Harold Wilson. He accused the Government of being inept, of giving no leadership, and of having no policy. Then what did he do? He chased his own tail for nearly three-quarters of an hour. The whole of the second part of his speech flatly contradicted the first part. He put out for half an hour all the advantages of going into the Common Market, and then all the disadvantages. At the end, he came as near as a toucher to saying—if your Lordships will forgive this expression—that he did not really know what the hell we ought to do. This is the final impression that was given to me by Mr. Harold Wilson's speech. The Government were a shade more comprehensible, but Mr. Wilson sat down in a state of complete mental chaos, to which he had also reduced the whole of the House of Commons.

As I see it, three broad choices confront us. We can make another attempt to go back to the *laissez-faire* multilateral system of the nineteenth century; or we can relapse into the rigid national economic autarchy so dear to the heart of Socialist purists who want nothing better than to go back to the utmost misery and austerity in order to be able to get the chance to impose upon us their true-blue Socialism. That was implicit in Mr. Crossman's pamphlet: we do not want prosperity; we want misery, and only then shall we have a chance of getting real Socialism.

Viscount Alexander of Hillsborough: My Lords, this speech, and many others made in the House during the last few years, forget that if a Tory Government had been returned in 1945 there would have been no recovery at all. We are living today upon the foundations that were laid then.

Lord Boothby: We are living today, if the noble Viscount will forgive me, on the foundations which were laid by Marshall Aid. That is what brought about our recovery; and nothing else.

There is a third choice, which I know is distasteful to the noble Viscount, and that is to build up regional, economic units capable of standing on their own feet in the modern world, through effective economic co-operation within and between various groups of nations. That is what everybody is jibbing at at the present time—on both sides, let me admit. I reject the first choice, because it is quite impracticable. We cannot go back to nineteenth century *laissez-faire*. I reject the second, because it would involve a drastic cut in our standard of living. But let us be under no illusion as to what is required by the third. It will demand greater surrenders of national sovereignty, both in the political and economic fields, than either side in this country has yet been willing to contemplate. There is no doubt about that. There are the three choices, and which one we will take I do not know. I am quite sure in my own mind about which one we ought to take.

Let me conclude with a quotation—a most remarkable quotation—from Barbara Ward's book, *The West at Bay*, which was published some years ago, but which is still as up to date as ever. It is as follows:

'The British, the French, and the Low Countries, all assumed that the inter-war world'—that is, the world between 1918 and 1939—'could be a recognizable version of the nineteenth century with a gold standard, with free trade, with national sovereignty (only slightly limited by the League of Nations), with liberal ideas and capitalist economics. The possibility that the first war had torn a gaping hole in the old fabric was not considered. Even the portent of the Russian revolution was tidied away behind explanations of the backwardness and barbarism of Russian society. Over these days the last light of the Victorian sun still streamed, the light of a safe world of order and progress, the light of great certainties and greater wealth. But the illusion cannot be re-created after this struggle. For this time, it seems, all the pillars have fallen. The last ray of the old sun has been extinguished, and if we of the Western world do nothing but look backwards, then "we are for the dark".'

July 1960.

INTERNATIONAL LIQUIDITY IN THE
FREE WORLD

LORD BOOTHBY rose to call attention to the lack of liquid reserves in the Free World, and the consequent effect upon currencies, economic growth, the development of emergent countries, and the volume of international trade; and to move for Papers. The noble Lord said: My Lords, I beg to move the Motion standing in my name on the Order Paper. I must tell your Lordships that I am at the moment full of penicillin and passion: penicillin on account of a germ that I picked up last week in New York; passion on account of the shortage of liquid reserves in the Free World.

It may seem odd to your Lordships that anyone should feel emotional on the subject of liquid reserves of the kind I have in mind,[1] or indeed on the subject of monetary policy; but I have done so throughout my adult life. The reason is that I have always believed that our failure after the 1914–18 war to devise an international monetary system which would meet the requirements of the modern world is the primary cause of most of the evils which have since befallen us, including the second world war.

The tragedy is that we very nearly did it. The Genoa Conference of 1922, in a series of currency resolutions, recommended a conference of central banks of issue, and the subsequent practice of 'continuous co-operation' between them. It also recommended a monetary convention based on a gold exchange standard; restriction of the circulation of gold; and a redistribution of gold reserves. Finally, it recommended the regulation of credit, with a

1. As opposed to whisky. B.

175

view not only to maintaining currencies at par with one another, but also to preventing undue fluctuations in the purchasing power of gold.

For these resolutions the late Sir Basil Blackett and Sir Ralph Hawtrey were primarily responsible; and they were subsequently described by the late Sir Laming Worthington-Evans as a financial code worthy to rank with the legal code of Justinian. The Genoa Conference, alas, crashed to political ruin. This led to the fall of Lloyd George, the assassination of Rathenau, the French occupation of the Ruhr, and the abandonment of the Genoa currency resolutions. All were serious; but perhaps the last was the most serious of all.

In 1925 this country returned to an uncontrolled international gold standard at the pre-war parity of exchange. As a boy of twenty-five I had the temerity to oppose this step in another place. Only four other voices were raised against it; three Conservative, one Liberal—none Labour. In fact, Mr. Snowden was one of its most passionate advocates.

Lord Pethick-Lawrence: My Lords, has the noble Lord verified that fact? Because I took a very strong view against it.

Lord Boothby: My Lords, I am delighted to hear that. I do not think my noble friend made a speech, because I looked it up; but it may well be so. However, he will not deny that the leading financial pundit of that time in the Labour Party, Mr. Philip Snowden, was strongly in favour of our return to the gold standard. In any case, whoever supported or opposed it, the consequences were catastrophic. There was inflation in the United States, and deflation in Europe, culminating in the greatest economic collapse known to history. By 1931 the number of unemployed in this country, never less than a million during the 'twenties, had risen to 2 million; and the German unemployed amounted to 6 million. It was upon the backs of these 6 million unemployed that Hitler climbed to power.

In 1945 we had another chance. We did not take it. The theoretical price paid at Bretton Woods for fixed exchanges, and a fixed price for gold, was adequate monetary reserves and adequate liquid reserves for the Free World; and these were not in fact provided. Keynes wanted to provide them in the form of 'Bancor'. He was brutally defeated by Mr. Harry Dexter White and Mr. Vinson, and died in near despair; but his ideas live on, mercifully for us all.

I moved the rejection of the Bretton Woods Agreement in another place, on the grounds that it failed to provide sufficient liquid reserves, and put the whole onus of restoring a balance of payments not upon the creditor nations but upon the debtor nations. I very much regret to say that I was gagged, and that the House of Commons was gagged, in that debate by Mr. Dalton, now the noble Lord, Lord Dalton. We had a debate on the American loan. We were denied a debate on the Bretton Woods Agreement. Nevertheless, I managed to get nearly 100 Members of Parliament, including some of the Labour Party, into the Lobby against it; and also into the Lobby against the terms on which we had to take the American loan.

I also managed—and I think it is rather important to go back over the history of the past, because it enables us to see what is wrong with the present—to get in a few words when the Motion for the convertibility of sterling, to which we were committed by the Bretton Woods and American loan Agreements, was debated in another place on July 31, 1947. I then said:

'The agreements we are discussing tonight shackle us more firmly and more relentlessly than ever to the gold standard. In practice, what they do is to make sterling convertible into dollars and therefore into gold. And in so doing, they enormously increase the danger of sudden withdrawals of foreign balances from London ...'

That is what we have been suffering from, of course, during the last few years. I went on:

'We are now financing the world dollar deficit. This convertibility of sterling is imposing upon us an unbearable burden which we are simply not capable of carrying. We cannot afford to lose dollars at this rate. As long as the holders of sterling were entitled to withdraw their balances only by the purchase of British goods, we had a chance of getting through; now I think we have no chance of getting through. All these arrangements will be very short-lived. They will all fall to the ground, and have to be abandoned.... It is sheer, stark insanity, in our present position, to embark upon this ludicrous course.'

My Lords, again I regret to say the Labour Government vehemently opposed these views, and Mr. Glenvil Hall, then Financial Secretary to the Treasury, said that he could see not the slightest justification for them. Sir George Benson also said that I was guilty of the grossest exaggeration; that there was no reason why we should not go back to free convertibility at that time. But in fact I was right and they were wrong; for after five frightening weeks, in the course of which the balance of the American loan was washed away, we were compelled to abandon convertibility. This, in turn, was followed by the enforced devaluation of sterling in 1949, and by an economic collapse in Western Europe, due largely to the rigid arrangements which were made at Bretton Woods, from the consequences of which we were all rescued in the nick of time by Marshall Aid.

So much for the 'forties. During the past decade we have been subjected, and above all this country has been subjected, to what have been widely described as 'Stop-and-Go' tactics; and to my mind, the reason for them is obvious. Every time we have encouraged economic growth within this country we have run into balance-of-payments difficulties; and nobody should be more aware of that fact than my noble friend Lord Amory, who I am very glad to see is to participate in this debate. I am sure he will agree that the results of this 'Stop-and-Go' policy have been most unsatisfactory.

In recent years the rate of our industrial investment, and in consequence the increase in our productivity, has been much slower than that of other countries in Western Europe, particularly the Netherlands, West Germany, France and Italy. At present, there is little dynamism in the British economy comparable to that of France, West Germany or Italy. The rate of economic growth in the United States is also considerably below that of France,

Italy and West Germany; and until quite recently the steel industry of the United States has been running at about 50 per cent.
capacity, at a time when the demand for capital goods in every
under-developed country in the world has been steadily increasing.
The reason for this is surely perfectly simple. The gold reserves
available to the Free World are inadequate to support the volume
of production and trade which the two major international currencies, the dollar and the pound sterling, have to carry. It is
manifestly absurd that a country with the vast natural resources of
the United States should be compelled to throttle down economic
growth and overseas investment because of a temporary balance-
of-payments difficulty.

I have said over and over again that any attempt to increase exports by repressing industrial investment at home is a policy of
desperation and madness. Many such attempts have been made in
this country by means of what has been called the 'credit squeeze'.
Some of them have been resisted. I cannot quote information
which I have been given in confidence, but I can tell your Lordships that some of the 'Big Five' joint stock banks have succeeded
in resisting pressure by the Treasury and the Bank of England not
to grant loans to great engineering firms to enable them to carry
on with modernization, which is essential if we are to be able to
hold our own in the modern world. The pressure has been very
great. The 'Big Five' have often been able to resist it—I could
quote at least two cases from my personal knowledge. But the
'little 500', of course, are not in a position to resist such pressure.
The result of these 'credit squeezes' and high bank rates, to which
we have been intermittently subjected during the last ten years, is
that the modernization of British industry has been held up; and
that has done a great deal to diminish the efficiency of our economy
in relation to that of France and Germany, and indeed of Italy and
the Netherlands, all of whose industries have been brought right
up to date.

The fact remains that, according to the Report of the United
Nations Economic Commission for Europe, which meets in
Geneva, we are the only industrial country in the West at the
beginning of this year, 1961, where a high increase of the gross

national product seems unlikely in the course of the year; and where exports are expected to be 'sluggish'—and I quote the word actually used in the Report. Great Britain and the United States have not at present the liquid reserves necessary to maintain the industrial potential of the West at full capacity; to expand world trade; and to develop the emergent and impoverished countries of Asia, Africa and South America, which I believe to be absolutely essential. The very fact that, in order to prevent more severe restrictive action, the United States have lost some 4 billion dollars in two years proves this. As for us, so long as our own reserves are only 25 per cent. of our overseas liabilities, we must always be living on a knife-edge.

Meanwhile, during the last two or three years, the tenuous liquid resources of the Free World have been drained off to Germany, which is becoming virtually a 'Fort Knox' of the 'sixties—with this difference: that the D-mark is not, like the dollar and the pound, an international currency, so that these reserves are being put to no good use but are, in effect, sterilized. There are not enough aggregate reserves in the Free World anyway.

What is to be done? Various proposals are now being canvassed. The basic and the primary one is an increase in the price of gold. This, of course, would bring immediate, if temporary, alleviation; for, as Sir Frederick Leith-Ross has pointed out, the dollar of 1960 is not the dollar of 1934 and by maintaining an artificial price for gold, you reduce the volume of international liquidity. Gold is the only commodity in the world which was pegged at an artificial price at Bretton Woods: every other commodity has since risen. This argument is very compelling. Nevertheless, I must confess, having been twice to the United States recently, I believe that the project of raising the price of gold now is politically impossible. I think that they simply will not do it. There are good reasons. An increase in the price of gold would be of greatest benefit to the Union of South Africa and the Soviet Union, and we are not particularly anxious to bring especial benefits to either of those countries. There are also other objections which I think are understandable and which, so far as the United

States is concerned, are at present invincible. Therefore, I think that we must turn elsewhere for a solution.

For my part, I believe that an enlargement of the conceptions of Bretton Woods, and the transformation of the International Monetary Fund into an International Central Bank offer by far the best solution. I am not going into details. They would bore your Lordships, I think; although sometimes when one gets into the middle of them, into their mesh, as it were, they have a fascination of their own. However, they are all there for study, if your Lordships wish to do so. There is Professor Triffin's scheme, a modernized version of Lord Keynes's original proposal at Bretton Woods for a Clearing Union. There is the suggestion of Mr. Maxwell Stamp for the issue of Fund certificates. There are the proposals of Mr. Bernstein. There is the forgotten scheme, evolved by the Oxford Institute of Statistics during the war, for the automatic use of persistent surpluses of 'mature' creditor countries for the economic development of 'undeveloped' countries. For your Lordships' sake, I will not go into these schemes today. I am concerned more with the growing volume of support for my own views; and this I find extremely encouraging.

The Radcliffe Report, while doubting whether the 'scarce currency Clause' (Article VII) of the International Monetary Fund Agreement is workable in practice, saw great merit in the proposal for the transformation of the International Monetary Fund, along the lines originally proposed by the United Kingdom, into an International Central Bank, with its own unit of account, free to accept deposit liabilities or to extend overdraft facilities to the central banks of member countries.

It was my noble friend Lord Monckton of Brenchley, Chairman of the Midland Bank, who said, in his Annual Report to the Bank, that what was required was:

'a thorough re-examination of the functions and mechanism of the International Monetary Fund.'

He went on:

'There remains the deeper question whether the Fund should not itself be remodelled into what might be called a true Central

Bank for central banks, equipped like them with powers of credit creation and contraction.'

Sir Oliver Franks, Chairman of Lloyds Bank, has also advocated the transformation of the I.M.F. into a Central Bank for the Free World. And last, but by no means least, there is President Kennedy, who in his Message to Congress on February 6, 1961, said this:

'Increasing international monetary reserves will be required to support the ever-growing volume of trade, services and capital movements among the countries of the Free World. Until now the free nations have relied upon increased gold production and continued growth in holdings of dollars and pounds sterling. In the future, it may not always be desirable or appropriate to rely on these sources. We must now, in co-operation with other lending countries, begin to consider ways in which international monetary institutions—especially the International Monetary Fund—can be strengthened and more effectively utilized, both in furnishing needed increases in reserves, and in providing the flexibility required to support a healthy and growing world economy. I am therefore directing that studies to this end be initiated promptly by the Secretary of the Treasury.'

So, my Lords, all the things that I was saying as a rebel, fifteen years ago, are now being said by the Establishment in this country and in the United States. I beg of your Lordships to believe that this is no new experience for me. All I am asking now is: for how long must the Free World suffer from the rigid monetary rules imposed at Bretton Woods? It is becoming increasingly clear that our international exchange system has broken down; and that unco-ordinated monetary policies, non-discriminatory multilateral trade, and fixed exchange rates cannot be made to mix. We are shackled—the whole Free World is shackled—by Bretton Woods. That is why our productive capacity is running at much less than it should be, right through the Western world, but above all in this country and the United States; and that is why we are not able to afford to the emergent and under-developed countries of Asia and Africa the assistance that we should be affording to them if we are to save them from Communism. We need a monetary system which is at once more comprehensive and more flexible.

There are two concrete suggestions that I should like to make. The first is that the International Monetary Fund should be instructed at its next meeting to consider ways and means by which more international liquidity can be created, and holdings of national reserve currencies can be converted into holdings of reserves with international backing. The second is that, thereafter, an international economic conference should be summoned to consider a radical reorganization of the international monetary and payments system; and, indeed, of the whole Bretton Woods set-up.

The objectives have been well defined by Dr. Balogh: first, the automatic use of an increasing portion of persistent creditor balances for long-term investment in under-developed areas; and secondly, the gradual transformation of the two Bretton Woods institutions—the Fund and the Bank—into an effective force to stabilize economic growth in the non-Soviet orbit.

Meanwhile, I think that we in this country should consider seriously the possibility of flexible managed exchange rates, which worked reasonably well after we had been driven off the gold standard in 1931, with the aid of an Exchange Equalization Fund; and, still more, the necessity of keeping our overseas investments within bounds until a more satisfactory international monetary system has been brought into being.

My Lords, I have done; I have kept you too long, and I am sorry. But I feel strongly on this subject. I believe that it is the most important question that now confronts us. I am sure that the main Communist challenge to our world will be an economic challenge and not a military one, at any rate over the next decade. I am well aware that the Communists are not shackled by Bretton Woods or anything else; and that they have a considerable production of gold which enables them to grant credits on easy terms, without conditions, wherever it seems politically desirable to do so. I think that if the problem I have attempted to adumbrate this afternoon is not solved in the pretty near future the Communists may win this struggle, simply owing to our own stupidity; because it stares us in the face, and it is by no means incapable of solution. Some stabilization of raw material prices at remunerative levels is essential. A fall will only increase the fearful discrepancy between the comparative prosperity of the industrial countries of the West and the abject poverty of the non-industrial countries in Africa, South America, and the East. International commodity schemes, and also the relationship between the price of gold and commodity prices, cannot—in the long run—be ignored or escaped; but the root cause of our present troubles lies in the lack of adequate liquid reserves to buttress the two great trading currencies of the Free World—the dollar and the pound. It is with the object of directing your Lordships' attention to this very great problem that I have tabled my Motion.

March 1961.

THE CRISIS DEEPENS: 1961

My Lords, I must confess at the outset of my remarks that, unlike the Lord President, I do not feel any sense of personal inadequacy; I just feel a sense of personal despondency, because this has happened all too often before. This is the sixth balance of payments crisis since the war; and I remember that four times I have gone down to the House of Commons after a tremendous Press campaign warning us against the dreadful things that awaited us, and all the sufferings and sacrifices we should have to take and make; and then nothing much happened. We just got the same old rise in bank rate and left the House of Commons feeling a little sad at having been braced to do so much and called upon to do so little. It does not hit the individual in the same way as it hits industry. Then everything gets better; the 'hot' money comes back; and then it happens all over again.

These proposals have, of course, little relevance to the basic long-term economic problems confronting this country. They are designed simply to get us through yet another balance of payments crisis—as I said, the sixth that has happened since the war. The method is the old one and, I think, the bad one, of attracting 'hot' money to this country to see us round the corner. Many years ago Keynes wrote:

'Unless the aggregate of the new investments which individuals are free to make overseas is kept within the amount which our favourable trade balance is capable of looking after, we lose control over the domestic rate of interest.'

This is precisely what has happened; hence the rise in the bank rate. I think we probably had to do it. But we had to do it only because once again we have in fact lost control—because the balance of payments has gone wrong. I think it would have been better if the Government had taken far more strenuous steps to keep the balance of payments right, which they have never done. I believe this policy will succeed in the short run; but at a very high cost.

Let us take a brief glance at three of the main proposals of the Chancellor. First of all, the 7 per cent. bank rate, which is generally regarded as a crisis rate, in conjunction with the 3 per cent. special deposits. This is the clumsiest economic weapon of all, because it hits the lot. It will cause a diminution of productive investment in industry—it must do—and, therefore, deter economic growth at a moment when we desperately need it. It will also increase costs and rents, and decrease productivity.

What does it all really amount to? By raising the bank rate and the special deposits to the fantastic height they now are, you knock the whole national economy about, in the desperate hope that a reduction of imports will somehow or other come about as a by-product. I just do not believe that this is the way to do it. This is using a sledge-hammer instead of a scalpel knife. In so doing you impose heavier burdens, not only upon the Exchequer, and on the taxpayer who has to pay higher rates of interest, but also upon local authorities and industry throughout the country. There is not much hope for the export trade here.

The second major proposal is a surcharge of 10 per cent. on Customs and Excise duties. While it varies, of course, on different items, the effect is to put up the cost-of-living index by $1\frac{1}{2}$ per cent. Nobody is going to tell me that this is going to make it easier to hold wages during the 'pause' which is so strongly advocated by Her Majesty's Government.

I am absolutely certain that the Lord President's appeal—fervent, eloquent, and made with great sincerity—for what he called a 'certain degree of personal restraint' is very necessary; but I am going to ask him quite frankly, and somewhat brutally, what the Government have done to encourage this. They removed practically all discipline from the economic field from the moment when they started indulging in what used to be known—perhaps

the Lord President has forgotten it—as 'the dash for freedom'—
Mr. Butler's 'dash for freedom'. I never supported it. I always
thought it was a mistake. In fact what they did was to take all
discipline away from the economic field; and in so doing deride
the memory of Sir Stafford Cripps, who, when all is said and
done, exercised a greater moral authority in time of peace over
the people of this country than any Chancellor of the Exchequer
since Gladstone. I think we ought not to forget it; it is true, and
he was right.

Enough of this; let us just have a look at the record during the
last ten years. First the Government removed all building licences.
I am on the record here. I opposed it from the start. They then
abandoned all effective control over the export of capital from
this country. They have made no attempt whatsoever to plan our
industrial development in co-operation with leaders of industry
and the trade unions. They have set up no planning machinery of
any sort or kind. Nor have they made any attempt to stop the
speculative boom in land which has now got completely out of
control. Finally, they have completely failed to curb increases of
national expenditure which we can no longer afford and which
can only lead, in themselves, to further inflation.

The result, my Lords, has been, and we had better face it, an
orgy of reckless personal speculation—for example, in property
shares and television shares—which has no parallel in the history
of this country since the South Sea Bubble. In these cases one field
for speculation was allowed to continue by the Government, and
the other was actively created by the Government; and the Lord
President comes down to this House and appeals for a' certain
degree of personal restraint'! It will not do. I know the stand he
took himself about television. I am only taking it as an example;
but all this has been going on now for too long, and not the
slightest attempt has been made to deal with it or curb it in
any way.

There are one or two questions I should like to ask the noble
Earl who is going to reply. How much capital does he think has
gone out of this country during the last five or six years by way of
the escape hatches of Kuwait, Bermuda and Nassau? How much

of the Overseas Trading Corporation surpluses abroad have not returned to this country in any shape or form? How much money has been wasted—and I emphasize the word 'wasted' because I am not a supporter of unilateral disarmament—on armaments over the past ten years, which we really cannot possibly afford? How much capital and labour has been employed, and is still being employed, on the construction of quite unnecessary buildings in this country—anyone can see it going on right the way from John o'Groats to Land's End—while slums continue? Lastly, do Her Majesty's Government really think that we can afford, at this juncture, to rebuild New York and Chicago; because that is what I gather Mr. Clore and Mr. Cotton are setting out to do? I am sure it is very desirable; but I should have thought that the United States themselves could have looked after that one themselves.

My Lords, of course I blame the Treasury more than the Chancellor of the Exchequer. I blame the Treasury because for over forty years it has been the most disastrous institution this country has ever had. In fact I often wonder how we have survived it. It is a miracle. Except in the two world wars, when Keynes was there, they have never had a new idea, still less a good one. I am old enough to remember the 'twenties, when Sir Winston Churchill said, without any great conviction:

'It is the orthodox Treasury dogma, steadfastly held, that whatever might be the political or social advantages, very little additional employment can, in fact, and as a general rule, be created by State borrowing and State expenditure.'

We have long since learnt the answer to that; but if the Treasury could seriously hold it as 'dogma', what cannot they believe? They can believe anything. It is my chief regret, in a life full of regrets, that I was never given the opportunity of being Chancellor of the Exchequer. It would not have lasted long, but it would certainly have been fun while it did.

The noble Viscount, the Leader of the House, said that one of the advantages of this place is that there are some things one can say here that one cannot in another place, where there are, after all, votes to be considered. For example, one thing I should like to say is that this country is still riddled with restrictive practices, and they are not confined to one side of industry; both sides are equally to blame. The shipbuilding industry, my Lords, is dying at the present time; and this is due to the people inside the shipbuilding industry, and well they know it. They will not take any steps to put the situation right; and that is not the only industry to which this applies.

I often smile when I read some of the very pompous leading articles in our newspapers saying what a terrible thing restrictive practices are. They say how important it is that we should free the economy of them, and shoulder our responsibilities. I often feel inclined—except that one has to keep in with the Press, so long as one is in public life—to write a letter saying: 'Have a look at your own office and see what the employment situation is, and see how many redundant people you are employing.' Here is the real reason for the recent closing down of newspapers; it is because the printing industry in this country is an absolute scandal, and none of the newspaper proprietors have had the guts to stand up and say, 'Enough of this nonsense!'; just as the shipbuilders should have said, 'Enough of this!' long, long ago.

On this aspect I want to say one other thing. I wonder how many jobs in this country today are being done by three men when one man would do. I should think the number is absolutely staggering. For that I do not blame the trade unions entirely; I think the employers are also very much to blame, because it has all been too easy for them. This is something that ought to be said by somebody, somewhere—and I do not see why it should not just as well be said by Lord Boothby in the House of Lords as by anybody else—because we all know it is true. We have to face up to this problem, because it is not a comparable problem with our chief competitors.

If you ask me what I would do, I would say first that wages have to be related to productivity. One of our chief troubles is that we have never related wages to productivity. They have risen by 6 per cent. against a rise in productivity of less than 2 per cent. over the last two or three years. That is no good. But how can you get an agreed wages policy unless you have a plan, and bring into that plan the trade unions themselves—in fact both sides of industry? We want, as my friend Lionel Fraser said in an admirable letter to *The Times* the other day, a Five-year Plan for Progress; because, as he truly said, there is no alternative to a coherent, long-term economic policy.

Going back to the recent trip I took in Eastern Europe, although they have failed in agriculture because neither the peasant system nor forcible collectivization will do, they are making tremendous strides on the industrial front. Their productivity, and their gross annual national product, exceed ours in all of these countries. And why? Mainly because it is extremely well planned. But it is important not only for Communist and Socialist countries. As the noble Lord, Lord Brand, said, they are doing it in France and doing it extremely well. M. Monnet started it; M. Massé is carrying it on. The results are achieved by influence rather than by coercion; and they are startling.

France has a planned economy not far short of, and in some respects better planned than, that of the countries east of the Iron Curtain. The whole staff of the planning organization in France does not amount to more than 40 people, but they do very well. They have got 3,000 of the really important and influential industrialists together, and persuaded them to follow an agreed course. This is what we have to do. And I beg my noble friend to ask the Chancellor of the Exchequer to consider sending a small mission of inquiry over to Paris to see how they do it. And they may as well go on to Bonn, because Erhard is doing it, too. Both the economies of West Germany and France are infinitely better planned than ours, which is hardly surprising because ours is not planned at all.

We shall then have to come to grips with the problem of international reserves. With our present reserves and liabilities we cannot carry on with sterling as the second major international currency of the world. I have, on this at least, an unblemished record, because I did oppose the Bretton Woods Agreement. I opposed it on three grounds. First of all, because it put the onus of restoring equilibrium in international balances of payment on the debtor countries and not on the creditor countries; secondly, because it failed to provide adequate liquid reserves for the dollar and sterling; and thirdly, because it fixed exchanges at rates which were arbitrarily chosen, in a world of flux. I am one of those who doubt whether any democracy with a completely free economy can ever maintain, indefinitely, a fixed rate of exchange. I am not sure it can be done, because it means that economic pressures which might otherwise be corrected by variations in the rate have to be met by infinitely more difficult methods, and sometimes impossible methods, such as a substantial all-round reduction in wages.

I think we should say to the International Monetary Fund before they meet this September, 'Look here, there are the Bernstein proposals; they would help a great deal, but unless we can get more adequate liquid reserves, and unless we can avoid this agonizing biennial balance-of-payments crisis, for which a 7 per cent. bank rate seems to be the only remedy, we shall have to let the pound not be devalued, but just go.' I am not at all in favour of devaluing ever again to a fixed level, because that guess might be no better than the last one. A floating pound worked pretty well between 1931 and 1937, supported as it was by a powerful Exchange Equalization Fund. I think that if we told them that we would let it find its own level again, if adequate liquid reserves are not forthcoming, they might do something. I doubt whether we can maintain the pound, with our present wholly inadequate reserves, at this narrow fixed rate.

Thirdly, I would restore building licences. I would not do it on a big scale, but I would do it on a sufficient scale to stop the wasteful and extravagant building which is going on. We have had enough of that. Fourthly, I would reimpose some effective control over foreign investments, using a better method than that used in the past, which would not be difficult. Fifthly, and finally, I say that, since the quantitative control of investment is the core of any planning scheme, I would set up an organization comparable to that which exists in France to direct investment into channels which, from the national point of view, are the most productive and most important, and away from wasteful channels. It can easily be done by some discrimination in the granting of investment allowances; and does not require any elaborate machinery.

I would do it in consultation and collaboration with the industrialists and the trade unions. I know that I shall be accused of advocating physical controls, planning and Socialism. I do not care what I am told, and I do not care what you call it. It may be physical controls, planning and Socialism. But there is one thing that is more important than any of these things, and that is sense.

Before I sit down, perhaps I may be allowed to detain your Lordships for a moment or two with a quotation from a very trenchant paragraph by a friend of mine, the outspoken, fearless and independent financial correspondent of the *Spectator*, Nicholas Davenport, because he succeeded last week in putting into one paragraph what I have been trying to say, and saying much less well, in the last twenty minutes. He wrote:

'If anyone should repent, it is the Government itself. It should confess that it has been pursuing idiotic economic policies, refusing to plan and direct the two sides of industry, refusing to apply a building control and so allowing the building and contracting industry to over-reach itself and force up wages, relying on higher rates of interest and credit restrictions to do the impossible act of balancing the economy, encouraging the wrong domestic investment by indiscriminate investment allowances, refusing to control our overseas investment and allowing foreign exchange we have earned to stay abroad instead of coming home, trying to protect sterling with "hot money", that is, short-term foreign loans, expecting to boost exports by knocking the home trade in consumer durables, raising the price level at home by higher indirect taxes and dearer money and then complaining of the uncompetitive prices of British exports! This catalogue of ghastly mistakes is enough to make the nation rise up in anger and tell the Prime Minister that they never had it so bad—in Government administration.'

That is powerful stuff; but I think that if you read it in *Hansard* tomorrow you will agree there is more than an element of truth in it. All that we have got from the Government over the past eighteen months is economic stagnation.

July 1961.

INDUSTRIAL RELATIONS

Closing Address to the Summer School in Management Studies at the University of St. Andrews: 1959

WE stand at the moment on the threshold of a new and exciting era which can bring undreamed-of prosperity. Automation is already with us, and the development of atomic energy is well under way. We have learned how to control major fluctuations in the trade cycle by the strategic direction of the national economy. We have proved that in advanced industrial countries the problems of unemployment and poverty can be solved by policies of planned economic expansion, if managements and workers at every level co-operate in a sustained effort to increase productivity. But beneath the glittering apparatus of modern science and industry there remains a human problem, as yet unsolved. Too many workers still feel that, although they are comparatively well off, they are no more than cogs in a gigantic machine.

Here is a problem which industry alone can resolve. The demand for personal fulfilment no longer appears as a political demand for the liberation of one class, but as a social aspiration towards raising our industrial society to the level of personal responsibility. And this can only be achieved within that society. In order to do it we must face the fact that property rights no longer constitute the basis of economic and industrial power. What matters is control, which has passed into the hands of the bureaucracy, the managers, and the trade union leaders. I do not say that their vast power is exercised without regard to the public interest; but in so far as it is derived neither from property rights nor from an established democratic system, it is irresponsible. The control of Parliament over the administration of the great public corporations is, to say the least, limited; as is the control of the great private corporations by vast, shifting bodies of anonymous shareholders. And it is difficult to see how either can be made more effective without a serious impairment of efficiency. In these circumstances, I believe that it has become urgently necessary to provide the governing authorities in industry with a legitimate basis of power.

The central fact in the social crisis of our time is that the industrial plant has become a basic social unit but is not yet an integrated social institution; and the task which confronts us is to build a democratic industrial society, based on the factory, in which the workers are given status and function, a sense of personal responsibility, and therefore a direct interest in the prosperity of the industries in which they are employed. Not only the trade associations and trade unions, but the individual worker, must be woven into the fabric of our industrial life.

It was Rathenau, the original exponent of industrial 'rationalization', who pointed out that the modern State consists of a multiplicity of separate semi-autonomous States, enjoying a considerable measure of independence, but individually and collectively stunted because they lack a foundation in the soil of the people. Of these the great industrial corporations are among the most important. Owing to their origin they still bear the marks of undertakings run purely for profit; but in fact, and to an increasing degree, they serve the public interest. What Rathenau described as 'the depersonalization of ownership and the objectivication of enterprise' leads to a point where the undertaking becomes transformed into an institution which resembles the State in character; and it is significant that the methods of recruiting staff used by our public corporations, or companies of the magnitude of Shell, Imperial Chemical Industries and Unilever, are very similar to those of the Civil Service.

Sir Winston Churchill once posed the suggestion of an Economic Parliament. I think this has to be rejected, because in a true democracy there can only be one sovereign Parliament to which all other estates must be subordinated in certain cardinal respects. But there should certainly be a National Economic Council, consisting of representatives of the Government, managers and trade unions, and staffed by the best economists we can get hold of, to give a purposive strategic direction to our economic policy, and plan the growth of the national economy for periods extending over several years, on the basis of adequate statistical information. If such a Council is to function properly it will have to work in close co-operation with the Treasury and the Bank of England where the control of monetary and credit policy is concerned; and—in Keynes's own words—exercise a series of co-ordinated acts of intelligent judgment as to the scale on which it is desirable that the community as a whole should save, the scale on which these savings should go abroad in the form of foreign investments, and whether the existing organization of the investment market distributes savings along the most productive channels. The quantitative direction of investment is indeed an essential component of any planned economy; but it need not involve a multiplicity of controls. For example, if we join the Common Market, a European Clearing House for exchange and trade regulation, a European Central Bank for long-term investment in backward areas, and international schemes for stabilizing the prices of certain basic commodities will—in the first place—be all that is required.

Underneath the National Economic Council the semi-independent corporations, public and private, will continue to grow, many of them with statutory rights of their own. But in order to give them democratic roots a new code of industrial relations is required; and, in particular, a re-definition of the relationship of both craft and industrial trade unions with the shop stewards, with each other, with the managers, and with the State.

The trade unions have been rightly described by Sir Winston Churchill and the late Walter Elliot as an estate of the Realm; but, by definition, an estate of the Realm is not the whole Realm. Organized labour must now come to terms not only with itself but with the other estates. It will demand goodwill and effective co-operation from all. The abuses within the trade unions which, on their own admission, have been losing them public sympathy, are well known. Wasteful and unnecessary demarcation disputes, unofficial strikes engineered by shop stewards in breach of negotiated agreements, rigged elections, and—on occasion—the tyrannical use of the closed shop. These abuses can, and should, be dealt with by the T.U.C.

The duty of the State in the functional and decentralized industrial system that I have in mind will be to give statutory sanction to those agreements reached between Government and industry, and within industry itself, which are considered by Parliament to be in the public interest; to protect certain basic individual rights; to curb the power of bureaucracies and monopolies; to facilitate the mobility of labour; and to encourage industrial development in areas where patches of local unemployment exist or impend. We need more flexibility because, if the maintenance of the existing structure of industry and of jobs people are already doing becomes the main objective of our economic policy, we shall lose the race against the centrally directed industrial system of the Soviet Union.

What part has management got to play in building the democratic industrial society which is so much to be desired? First of all, it seems to me that the workers could and should be given longer contracts of service, in addition to the right of consultation and appeal, and an assurance of promotion on merit. We have recently been reading a lot about compensation for loss of office. This principle should now be applied to employment generally. Next, the workers should be taken into managerial confidence to a greater extent. Encourage and facilitate share ownership by the employees, as I.C.I. have done. In individual cases where their counsel would be of value, do not be afraid to seat them on the Board. It is not always necessary to wait until they have worked their way up to high managerial level, and come within striking distance of retirement age. In any event tell them what you are trying to do, and let them see what the difficulties are. As in an army, so in industry, the ultimate responsibility devolves upon the Commander; but he must explain his purposes, and the methods by which he proposes to achieve them, to his troops. It was the secret of Montgomery's success.

Above all, let us bring humanity and friendliness as well as efficiency into our industrial life. I have no desire to impinge upon the felicities of domestic life, but I would like the social organization and activities of the factory to amount to something more than canteen lunches. And I go farther than this. I think that provision should be made for union meetings in workshops when they are desired, and for workshop arbitration as the final stage of grievance procedure.

Finally, I would urge you to encourage your workers to take part in local government, and in all forms of organized recreation. Thus, and thus alone, can they be given a real share, and not merely a paper one, in determining the infinitely involved circumstances of their lives; and a sense of active participation in social decisions in factory and workshop, town and village.

In all these matters the Americans are far ahead of us. They have never suffered from the same rigid class distinctions. Whatever their positions in the social or industrial hierarchy may be, they are apt to call each other by their Christian names outside the office or the works. And since the emergence of the modern managerial society, of which the trade unions form an essential part, they have abandoned the nineteenth century conception of a class struggle in which the interests of capital and labour are necessarily opposed, and rewards for skill and hard work should therefore be resisted.

In conclusion I would wish to leave the single word responsibility in your minds, because I believe that irresponsibility is in the long run the greatest enemy of freedom, and one of the gravest dangers this nation now faces.

PART IV

Personal Recollections

EDINBURGH REVISITED

I was born at my grandmother's house, number 5 Ainslie
Place, Edinburgh, on February 12, 1900, in a snowstorm, and
in the reign of Queen Victoria. There the early years of my
childhood were spent until, in 1906, my parents moved to Beech-
wood, an Adam house on the southern slope of Corstorphine hill,
with a walled garden and a splendid view of the Pentlands.

My earliest memory is of a German band which came to play
outside the house once a week. Every effort was made to get me
to sleep before it arrived. In vain. On each occasion I had to be
carried, screaming and terror-stricken, to a back room. In retrospect, it shows remarkable prescience. I also remember sitting on my
grandmother's knee in the large drawing-room before a flickering
fire. She looked at me long and earnestly, and finally said: 'You're
a queer little fish.' I was.

Before the first world war Edinburgh society still glittered.
Lady Dunedin, the wife of the Lord Justice General, was its
doyenne; and her parties, for old and young, achieved an international reputation. I remember being taken, frightened, to some
of them, in a cab through which the street lights flashed; and how
quickly she put an end to a shyness that has never returned, for she
was one of the kindest of women in a world from which kindness
had not fled.

The dominant influences in what I suppose would now be
called the 'formative' years of my life were my maternal grandfather, Henry Lancaster, and Robert Louis Stevenson. I never saw
either of them, for the very good reason that they were both dead
when I was born. But my grandmother, in the true Victorian

tradition, mourned my grandfather and talked about him for thirty years, so that he became a part of my life. I wish I had known him. From all accounts he was brilliant, boisterous and joyous. The friend of Thackeray, of Principal Sir Alexander Grant, of Professor Sellar; and a favourite pupil of Jowett at Balliol, who wrote of him, 'Dr. Johnson has said that every man may be judged by his laughter, and those who knew our friend will have no difficulty in applying these words to him.'

Mr. Gladstone designated him for the office of Lord Advocate, but his premature death put an end to that, and to all my grandmother's ambition. A few essays on Scottish schools and universities, on Burton, Macaulay, Ruskin, Thackeray, George Eliot, Carlyle and Tennyson are all that survive. But they survive well.

Stevenson had lived just round the corner, at number 17 Heriot Row. His *Child's Garden of Verses* was the first book I ever read—the others followed pretty quickly. I put my paper boats in the Water of Leith—'Dark brown is the river'; and every evening pressed my face to the windowpane:

'For we are very lucky, with a lamp before the door,
And Leerie stops to light it as he lights so many more;
And O! before you hurry by with ladder and with light,
O Leerie, see a little child and nod to him tonight!'

Those were spacious days before Europe began, and continued, to blow itself to pieces. Edinburgh was surrounded by ducal palaces, and large mansions designed and adorned by the Adam brothers, inhabited for the most part by baronets. My parents were far from affluent; but I remember no period before the second world war when we had less than six indoor servants, two gardeners and a chauffeur. And there were only three of us!

We even had a laundrymaid. She was called Maggie Magee, and she had beautiful tawny hair, and I helped her to hang out the clothes, and loved her dearly. So it was a shock to me when I came in one evening and found my father playing and singing a song—he was always composing songs—which began:

'A terrible thing has just happened to me,
And a lass in my laundry ca'd Maggie Magee.

And noo' I'm like bitin' my tongue wi' my teeth,
  For she's wedded a chap in the police at Leith.'

Then came the chorus, to a lovely lilting air, which instantly
reduced me to tears:

'Maggie Magee, Maggie Magee,
  The sun's in your hair, and its licht's in your 'ee;
But what's to become of my washin' and me,
  Now you've married your policeman, Maggie Magee?'

For some reasons best known to themselves my parents decided
to send me to a private school in the extreme south of England.
This was hard, because I was an only child, and very spoilt. I have
never liked doing what I didn't want to do, and one look at
Rottingdean convinced me that it was no place for me. I therefore
decided to walk back to Edinburgh, a distance which I calculated
was 468 miles; and duly set off, at the age of ten, in knicker-
bockers and a bowler hat, with a walking stick, and ten shillings
in my pocket. But when I got to Roedean I thought better of it,
and took a bus back. I had a cold reception.

One other aspect of those pre-war Edinburgh days demands
respectful, indeed awe-struck attention. The preachers. They were
tremendous; and I do not think they will ever be repeated. There
was Wallace Williamson at St. Giles. There were the two Doctors
of Divinity irreverently known as Black and White. Above all
there was John Kelman, of the United Free St. George's. I can
truthfully say that, in all my life, with the single exception of
David Lloyd George on one of his good days, I have never heard
a greater natural orator than Kelman. He held his vast congregations, and for some years the bulk of the student body in Scotland,
in the palm of his hand.

The summer of 1914 was golden, but lead was in the air. By
this time I had reached Eton, and I remember my father introducing me to a small man at Lord's and saying: 'Take a good look
at him, because you will hear of him again.' It was Jellicoe; and
three weeks later he was Commander-in-Chief of the Grand
Fleet. During the first world war Edinburgh was indissolubly
associated with the Royal Navy. The battle-cruisers were based

there almost from the beginning; and in 1917 Beatty brought the entire Battle Fleet from Scapa to Rosyth. Never in history has there been a comparable armada. I remember, as a boy, counting nearly fifty dreadnoughts at anchor above and below the Forth Bridge.

When it was all over, and the High Seas Fleet had surrendered, and the Grand Fleet was dispersed for ever, there was a sense of anti-climax from which, I think, my native city has never quite recovered. In 1923 there was a General Election, precipitated by Baldwin, on the issue of protection. Noël Skelton, one of the most brilliant and original thinkers the Tory Party has produced in this century, asked me what I proposed to do; and I told him that I would like to come and help him in Perth. His reply was surprising, and characteristic. 'I could write at length,' he said, 'on the defects of your character, but I had not hitherto supposed that you were a coward.' The upshot of this was that, after an interview with Colonel (now Sir) Patrick Blair, the political secretary of the Scottish Unionist Party, I was dispatched, with a couple of sweaters, to the Orkney and Shetland Islands to fight my first election at the age of twenty-three. I scarcely knew where they were. I certainly knew none of their inhabitants; and had to be introduced to my own agent in Kirkwall by my Liberal opponent, Sir Robert Hamilton. I lost because I failed to convince the incredulous crofters of Shetland that a beneficent Tory Government was really going to give them a pound an acre every year, whether they grew anything or not. But not by much. And it was tremendous fun. Some Aberdeenshire farmers were buying cattle in Orkney, and came to one of my meetings. Their verdict: 'He knows nothing about agriculture, but when he talks he goes off like an alarm clock—and we can teach him.'

As a result, I became Member of Parliament for East Aberdeenshire the following year; and thereafter Buchan became my political base, my spiritual home, and the indispensable background to my whole life. My visits to Edinburgh were fleeting, and I lost touch with it. But I sustained the impression that, despite the presence of some formidable personalities—the names of Dr. Charles Warr, the Dean of the Thistle, who has so nobly main-

tained the traditions of St. Giles; of Lord Clyde; of Craigie
Aitchison, a great Lord Justice-Clerk and an even greater advocate; of Sir William Darling; of 'Bunty' Cadell, the artist; of
Mrs. Rosalind Maitland, the musician; and of Noël Skelton himself, immediately spring to mind—a good deal of the bloom of
my earliest years had departed.

Revival came with the advent of the Festival after the second
world war. It marked the reconciliation of Bruno Walter with
the Vienna Philharmonic Orchestra, and the emergence of Kath-
leen Ferrier from total obscurity to world-wide fame. I remember
Dr. Walter pointing to her at a small dinner party and saying to
my mother, 'She is my greatest discovery.'

The Festival has not lived up to its initial promise. Somehow or
other—perhaps because it lasts for so short a time, perhaps simply
because it *is* a Festival—it has never become an indigenous part of
the life of Edinburgh. If you go back there, as I had occasion to do
the other day, you find that—despite its undeniable beauty, and
the prodigious efforts of Compton Mackenzie and Moray Mc-
Laren—it is a bleak city. You get out of the train in the cavernous
gloom of Waverley Station, and that alone is enough to daunt the
stoutest heart. You gaze at one of the finest sky-lines in the world;
but, when you go to the new town, you see houses that are now
too large to be lived in, and too substantial to be pulled down. If
you stand on the Dean Bridge in a biting wind on a Sunday afternoon, as I did, you are overcome by a sense of desolation.

It is high time that the City Fathers came to the rescue. They
have been far too slow since the war. The Waverley Station, together with the Waverley market, should be blown up. So should
Toll Cross, and with it that terrible King's Theatre. Last, but not
least, the Calton site, including the top of Leith Walk, should be
given the full treatment of a comprehensive modern development
scheme. What Edinburgh now needs is a drastic detergent. More
brightness and lightness. Better and gayer hotels. Princes Street
alone, like patriotism, is not enough.

I don't despair. I think that, having seen what can be done in
Coventry, Plymouth and Bristol, the Town Council will at last
get a move on. I further think that our entry into the Common

Market may well mark the re-emergence of an Edinburgh society which, once again, will command the attention of Europe—less snobbish than that of the nineteenth century, and more cosmopolitan than that of London. A society, in short, of the kind once dominated and adorned by the finest mind Edinburgh has ever produced—that of David Hume, who proudly and justifiably proclaimed himself a citizen of the world.

If this happens, I might die there.

1962.

AN AFTERNOON WITH CHURCHILL

MANY volumes have been written about Winston
Churchill by himself; and many more will be written
by others. He has been the dominant influence in my
life, for good and ill; but there is little point in recalling a personal
relationship with one so great which began nearly forty years ago
in unclouded sunshine and ended in repeated thunderstorms. I can
only record my thankfulness that I stood behind him in the
desperate years before the last war when he was fighting for the
survival of this country—there were not many others; and my
gratitude to him for giving me the chance to do some work in
the cause of European unity.

This Essay makes no claim to be more than a snapshot taken on
a sunny afternoon in the South of France. I cannot even vouch
for its accuracy. I was very tired when I wrote it. But at least it was
written the same evening, when the memory was still fresh.

★　★　★

I arrived at the Hotel Roy-Reine,[1] with Malcolm Bullock, at
12 o'clock. Mary Soames met us in the hall, very pretty and
charming—as always; and up we went, in the lift, to a nice room
where we found Clemmie and Christopher Soames, and five dry
martinis. A very warm welcome from Clemmie, who seemed
somewhat relieved to see us.

Suddenly the door opened, and in walked Winston, in a blue
siren suit. Bowing low to Malcolm, he came across to me. 'Ah,'
he said, 'red trousers. Very nice. They match your tie. I've just

1. In Aix-en-Provence.

been dealing with the German armour at Dunkirk, in which you are so interested. At first I was inclined to accept Halder's version, which you first told me. But that has now to be modified. These German Generals say anything that suits their book. Pownall has unearthed the official German War Diary.

'Look. This is what happened. Kluge reported to Rundstedt that the armour was tired, and extended. He asked for two days in which to rest it. Rundstedt agreed. Then, by a piece of good luck, Hitler motored over to Rundstedt's Headquarters, and also agreed that this was necessary. In the afternoon a message came from O.K.W., Hitler's supreme Headquarters, ordering the armour to advance on Dunkirk. This order came from Keitel.' 'And, presumably, Halder, as Chief of Staff?' I interjected. 'Yes,' he said: 'It was disregarded by Rundstedt, despite Guderian's protests, who was fortified by Hitler's verbal agreement that the armour should be rested. That, and Calais, saved the B.E.F.

'I did Calais myself. I personally gave the order to stand, and fight it out to the end. I agreed to the evacuation of Boulogne with reluctance; and I think now that I ought to have ordered them to fight it out there too. But the order to Calais meant certain death for almost the entire garrison.

'It was the only time during the war that I couldn't eat. I was very nearly sick at dinner.' Tears came into his eyes. 'But, together with the Gravelines line, which was steadily flooding, it gave us two vital days; and a few of our cruiser tanks actually broke out of Calais, through the German armour, and got to the Gravelines line.

'Now look at this'—producing his proofs. 'Here is a yelp from the German Commander at Dunkirk. He says the British troops are disembarking in large ships, without equipment, but unscathed. "We do not want to have to meet them again, when they have been re-equipped." Only then was the order given for the armour to move in on Dunkirk. And by then it was too late.' He put away the proofs. 'The failure to press on with their armour, and Calais, saved us. And I did Calais. Now come in to lunch.'

This was all right: langouste mayonnaise, soufflé, a couple of bottles of champagne on ice, and a bottle of Volnay, topped up with brandy.

' I find alcohol a great support in life,' he said: 'Sir Alexander Walker, who keeps me supplied with your native brew, told me that a friend of his, who died the other day, drank a bottle of whisky a day for the last ten years of his life. He was eighty-five.' 'If you ever gave it up,' I replied, 'you'd die.' Silence.

Then: 'If I become Prime Minister again, I shall give up cigars. For there will be no smoking. We cannot afford it.' 'What,' I said, 'none at all?' 'Well, only a small ration for everyone. And then a black market in coupons, organized by the Government, so that anyone who couldn't give it up would have to pay through the nose!' 'You'd better not say that before the election,' I said. 'I shan't,' he answered.

'They said,' he went on, 'that I was wrong to go to Greece in 1940. But I didn't do it simply to save the Greeks. Of course, honour and all that came in. But I wanted to form a Balkan front. I wanted Yugoslavia, and I hoped for Turkey. That, with Greece, would have given us fifty divisions. A nut for the Germans to crack. Our intervention in Greece caused the revolution in Yugo-slavia which drove out Prince "Palsy"; and delayed the German invasion of Russia by six weeks. Vital weeks. So it was worth it. If you back a winner it doesn't really matter much what your reasons were at the time. They now say that I went to Greece for the wrong reasons. How do they know? The point is that it was worth it.' This I knew to be nonsense. It was not worth it. It did not lead to the formation of a Balkan front. It is by no means certain that it delayed the German invasion of Russia, the date of which had already been fixed. It gave Rommel his chance, and very nearly lost us Egypt. Finally, it was a classic example of what he himself had described, in the last volume of *The World Crisis*, as the commonest of all the great military errors: 'It is the error most easy to perceive in theory and most difficult to avoid in action. There are two enemies and two theatres; the task of the Commander is to choose in which he will prevail. To choose either, is to suffer grievously in the neglected theatre. To choose both, is to lose in both. ... A score of good reasons can be given

P   209

not only for either course, but also for the compromises which ruin them. But the path to safety nearly always lies in rejecting the compromises.' However, I had not been asked to lunch to argue, much as I would have enjoyed it. And anyway he was by now in full spate.

'My hardest time was the end of 1940, and the first six months of 1941'—with an odd look at me (it was the time of my troubles). 'I had to do eight things at once, with enough material and time for three or four. It was very exciting.'

'A bit too exciting,' I said.

'Not for me. I enjoyed it. The hornets were buzzing round my head. I like that.' I very nearly said, but didn't, that it was perhaps because everyone knew he liked it that he was no longer Prime Minister.

By this time the champagne was beginning to work. 'I see that poor Attlee has caught a cold in Ireland,' he remarked. 'I hope it's nothing worse than that.' This brought the whole party to attention, and a query from Clemmie. But he only burst into a song about colleens.

'Oliver Stanley,' he went on, 'said a very clever thing the other day. He said that, to Baldwin, Europe was a bore; and to Chamberlain a bigger Birmingham. Oh, those men! I got the facts from a frantic Civil Service, whose reports were continuously disregarded. But I think there was someone in the Air Ministry who deliberately withheld information from the Cabinet.'

I said that Vansittart had told me that, when he took the Secret Service reports to Baldwin, the latter said: 'Oh, take that stuff away. It gives me nightmares. I don't want to read it.' He had not heard this; and was appalled. 'You were on the right side then. How is your constituency? How are the herrings? You seem to have persuaded a reluctant public to eat them.'

I told him that my constituency had been turned into a safe seat under the new redistribution scheme. 'You deserve it,' he said. 'You have a great record there. They must love you very much. How long have you been there? Nearly a quarter of a century!'

I said that one of my troubles in life was that I was always right about public affairs, and always wrong about my private affairs.

He thought for a moment, and then said: 'No. Sometimes wrong about public affairs, and sometimes right about private affairs. That would be a fairer statement of the case.'

He got up and left the room, returning a moment later with some more papers. 'These will please you,' he said, 'It is a correspondence with Attlee about Western Union. I have put him on the spot. Max (Beaverbrook) tells me they are much upset by it. I have insisted that it be published tomorrow. You should say, at the Interlaken Conference, that you are very disappointed with the performance of the British Government about Europe, but hope for better things now—and see that it is telegraphed to London.'

The conversation then turned to the Jews. I said that they were going to win hands down in Palestine, and get more than they ever expected. 'Of course,' he said. 'The Arabs are no match for them. The Irgun people are the vilest gangsters. But, in backing the Zionists, these Labour people backed the winners; and then ran out on them. You were quite right to write to *The Times* protesting against the shelling of Jerusalem.' This brought Christopher Soames in. He said that public opinion at home was pro-Arab and anti-Jew.

'Nonsense,' said Winston. 'I could put the case for the Jews in ten minutes. We have treated them shamefully. I will never forgive the Irgun terrorists. But we should never have stopped immigration before the war.'

He went on to say that he never saw Weizmann because he found him so fascinating that, if he did, he would spend too much of his time talking to him. 'Weizmann gives a very different reason,' I replied. 'What is that?' 'Last time I saw him he said that the reason you would not see him was because, for you, he was "Conscience".' Silence.

Then back to the war.

'The Americans were not always easy to deal with. They like to concentrate on one thing. They scrap everything else—at colossal expense—to build up a single Plan. But in war nothing stands still. Everything goes on all the time. So you often lose a lot by this policy. I had the greatest difficulty in persuading them to let us capture Rome. After that, they removed nearly all Alexander's divisions for that foolish attack on the Riviera, which made no difference at all to the situation in Brittany. If they had let me have my way, we might have got to Vienna.'

This opened the way for a question I had long wanted to ask him.

'Surely,' I said, 'we missed a great opportunity in Italy when Mussolini fell? If we had at once come to terms with Badoglio, we might have got the whole country without fighting. Not only Rome, but Genoa.'

He looked sombre.

'Ah,' he said, 'there is a lot in what you say. There was a plan for the capture of Rome from the air. It miscarried.'

Finally, I asked him if he knew what was going on in Berlin. 'No,' he said. 'It might be another Munich. With this difference. We shall be far stronger this time next year. The American Air Force will be three times the size, and their bombs a third bigger. And this advantage. We shall be able to have our holiday in peace!'

'Nevertheless,' he continued, 'I would have it out with them now. If we do not, war might come. I would say to them, quite politely: "The day we quit Berlin, you will have to quit Moscow." I would not think it necessary to explain why. I am told that they are absolutely certain that we shall behave decently, and honourably, and do the right thing—according to their ideas of our own standards—in all circumstances. With me around, they would not be quite so sure.'

And—in conclusion—'They say I interfered during the war. I did. I interfered all the time.'

The moment then arrived for departure to Les Baux, which he remembered from fifteen years ago, and where he thought he wanted to paint a picture. I said I could not, and would not, take my car, unless they filled it up with petrol. This was accordingly done; and all the painting apparatus collected.

Winston than appeared in snake-skin shoes, and a Mexican sombrero hat; and off we set, before a wide-eyed crowd, in three cars. Winston and Clemmie and one detective in the first. The

Soames' and another detective in the second. Malcolm and I in the third—mine—without a detective.

We told them they ought to see the ruins (Roman) of St. Remy on the way. But they took the wrong road, so we got there first. Somewhat dazed by the combination of tremendous heat and alcohol, I found a very nice niche in a beautiful Roman arch, where I curled myself up, and went fast asleep, dreaming of centurions. I thus missed the best scene of all.

On arrival, Winston clambered out of his car, gazed for a few seconds at the ruins, and said: 'How bloody. How absolutely bloody.' 'Look at Bob asleep,' said Malcolm, hoping to divert his attention. But all he said was: 'Bloody.' Clemmie and Mary thought it was quite lovely, and decided to stay for a while. Whereupon the old boy climbed back into his car, and drove off to Les Baux; alone, except for the chauffeur and detectives.

Clemmie and Mary then looked at the ruins from every angle. Christopher confided to me, when I woke up, that he hated sight-seeing; and thanked God that he and Mary were leaving the next day for a drive along the Riviera. He called it a 'pub-crawl' but, if I know Mary, it won't be that. We all then set off for Les Baux—Clemmie, Malcolm and self in my car; Soames' following.

On arrival, the detective came up to me and said: 'There's a storm on. You'd better keep clear. It'll be over in ten minutes.' It then transpired that the painting tackle was all in the Soames's car, so he couldn't begin. He had gone off to the top of Les Baux, in a rage. The chauffeur and detectives seized the easel and paint-box and ran up the hill after him; while I looked for, and found, a *bistro*.

By this time all the sight-seers at Les Baux had turned out to see what the hell was going on.

Presently there was an uproar. I went out and found Winston striding down the street, with the chauffeur and detectives disconsolately following him, plus all the painting apparatus. 'There's nothing to paint here,' he shouted. 'There's beer to drink here,' I shouted back. So he came into the *bistro*, which was almost pitch dark, and sat down.

'Were you really asleep in that arch?' he asked. And then:

'Don't you think the Calais story is very dramatic?' By that time the beer had arrived. 'It is cool, but not cold,' he said, with truth. Two pails of ice immediately appeared. Clemmie ordered a lemonade. And peace was gradually restored. 'I hate the taste of beer,' Clemmie said. 'So do most people, to begin with,' he answered: 'It is, however, a prejudice that many have been able to overcome.' The bill was then demanded. Unthinkable, said the proprietress. It was the greatest honour they had ever had. Perhaps Monsieur Churchill would sign his name in the book? Monsieur Churchill would; and did. I went out with Malcolm, wondering whether I would ever be famous enough to pay bills with my signature. 'I think,' I said, 'that we can now b...r off.' 'It's more than we can do,' said a detective, who was standing immediately behind me. I had not seen him.

The sombrero and the snake-shoes reappeared. 'Let us rendezvous at the hotel later.' But I was too tired to rendezvous any more. I killed a dog on the way back. And collapsed on to my bed, with a sty in my eye. Thus ended an astonishing afternoon.

August 1948.

BEECHAM

Address to the Edinburgh Festival Guild, 1961

IT is a pleasure for me to address the members of the Edinburgh Festival Guild. Whether it will be an equal pleasure for you is more doubtful. My credentials are slim. I learnt my music the easy way, by listening to my father and mother play the piano, and by leading the choir with an extremely good treble voice. This is something you have got, or not got. No damned merit about it. But I was a precocious little boy; and it gave me pleasure to reduce the old girls in the front pews to tears in the solo part of 'Oh! for the Wings of a Dove', and then go back to suck a bulls-eye. So I learnt how to read my parts, and memorize a tune, if not to play an instrument. I won a prize at Eton for singing 'Rose in the Bud' and Roger Quilter's setting of 'Now Sleeps the Crimson Petal'. As I finished the latter—'slip into my bosom and be lost in me'—I heard one of the masters whisper, 'What a very inadequate bosom to slip into.' I didn't like this at all. Nevertheless, I found my love of music by singing it; and am today part of an essential ingredient of our musical life—the audience. All my life, music has been my secret vice. I say secret, because, so far as music is concerned, I have been a cat that has walked alone, I have preferred to listen to it in solitude, apart from sleeping aunts and coughing cousins—much as I have loved them all.

However, you haven't asked me to talk about myself. I must therefore tell you now that the most fortunate thing that has ever happened to me is to have enjoyed the friendship, through many years, of some of the most vivid personalities this century has produced—which means that all of them belonged to an older generation. One of them, still happily at the top of his form, lives not far from this hall.[1] Another was Thomas Beecham.

I first met him, over thirty years ago, at a dinner party of Lady Cunard's; and I remember how pleased he was when, with all the brashness of youth, I described a very modern composition as 'a cacophany of raucous dissonance which faithfully reflects the desperate Age in which we live.' Afterwards he strolled over, stroked his beard, and said in that wonderful drawling voice: 'You are the sort of chap a politician ought to be—you and Lloyd George.' From that moment I was a devotee.

Beecham was deeply rooted in provincial England. In this respect, and in others, he resembled Arnold Bennett. One from Lancashire, the other from the Potteries. Both enjoyed being thought of as 'cards', which indeed they were. I think he would have gone to the top in any profession, and certainly in business. If he had made millions, instead of spending them, his friends would have had a marvellous time; but the public loss would have been irreparable. Fortunately, he chose to become the greatest maker of music, and of orchestras, this country has ever known.

Nearly all the Beecham 'stories' are true, or almost true. I am glad that so many of them have already been recorded by Mr. Neville Cardus and Mr. Charles Reid. But you cannot get the full flavour of them in cold print. They demand the man, the voice and the occasion; now, alas, taken from us. So I forbear to repeat any of them.

When the definitive biography comes to be written, I hope that some authoritative explanation will be given of the reason why he was supreme in Handel, Mozart, Haydn, Schubert, Mendelssohn, Tchaikovsky, Puccini, Strauss, Sibelius and—above all—Delius; uneven in Beethoven and Wagner; not wholly in sympathy with Brahms; and altogether out of sympathy with Bach, Britten and Vaughan-Williams. I see the thread, but cannot trace it through. One of the reasons is, undoubtedly, his lack of interest in religion. He once recounted to me, with delight, the story of a visit paid by Elgar to Delius at Grez-sur-Loing. He told me that Delius began the conversation by saying, 'Well, my dear Elgar, have you now

1. Sir Compton Mackenzie.

set the *entire* Bible to music?' Eric Fenby gives an account in *Delius as I Knew him* which differs only marginally. According to him, Delius said he thought that it was a great pity that Elgar had wasted so much of his time and energy in writing long-winded oratorios. 'That,' said Elgar, 'is the penalty of my English environment.' 'Well, anyhow,' replied Delius, 'you're not as bad as Parry. *He* would have set the whole Bible to music had he lived long enough!' Either way, the visit turned out to be a great success. But afterwards Delius made a remark to Fenby which revealed great prophetic insight. Elgar had brought with him some records of Sibelius. 'Very good in their way,' said Delius, 'but he always uses the same procedure to get the music going, and that irritates me. A lot of his work is too complicated and thought out.... The English like that sort of thing, just as they like vogues for this and that. Now it's Sibelius; and when they're tired of him, they'll boost up Mahler and Bruckner.' Which is exactly what has happened.

Beecham himself was uncompromising. Dreadful musical crimes, he always maintained, had been committed in the name of religion. He told Neville Cardus that there was too much counterpoint in Bach—and Protestant counterpoint at that; that he would give the whole of the Brandenburg concertos for Massenet's *Manon*, and think he had vastly profited by the exchange; that nearly all the questionable works of the great musical geniuses had been prompted by religion; that Elgar's *Gerontius* had been rightly described by George Moore as holy water in a German beer barrel; and that the 'Missa Solemnis' was third-rate Beethoven.

But it is quite untrue to suggest, as some have done, that Beethoven, as a composer, was beyond his compass. When I was in New York, in 1945, Virgil Thomson, an acid critic if ever there was one, reported in the *New York Times* that he had brought 'some kind of a brass band from Rochester' to the Carnegie Hall, and given a performance of the *Eroica* which was the greatest he had ever heard.

Similarly, in Wagner, he was unsatisfying in the Ring, because he deliberately reduced its stature; but consummate in *Die Meistersinger*—for me the opera beloved above all—when in the right mood. His complaint was that everything Wagner wrote was too long. I remember going to see him after a performance of *Die Meistersinger* to which he had given all that was in him. He was lying on a sofa in a bath-towel, completely exhausted. 'Wagner,' he said, in cold and deliberate tones, 'was the most selfish man who has ever lived.'

His *Tristan*, if less intense than that of the great German conductors, was more lyrical. The first time I heard it was here, in this city, at that awful King's Theatre. It remains an unforgettable experience. Frank Mullings, a name now forgotten, dominated the performance—dominated Beecham himself. It was therefore with much satisfaction that I read, in Neville Cardus's book, Beecham's own assessment: 'The value of Mullings's interpretation of Tristan,' he said, 'was that while the music was sung with greater vitality and tenderness than by any other artist I have heard, the whole part was endowed with a high nobility, an almost priestly exaltation of mood, and a complete absence of any wallowing in the sty of merely fleshly obsession. The general effect was one of rapt absorption in an other-wordly fantasy, hopeless of realization on this earth; and this I believe to have been Wagner's own conception.' He told me, often, that, with the single exception of Chaliapin, Mullings was the greatest actor who had ever appeared on the operatic stage; and that he had tried his hardest to persuade him not to retire.

He disliked 'Festivals' as such—here the provincial side came out; but came to have an increasing regard for Edinburgh. Some of you may remember the first time he came here, and conducted an all-Sibelius concert. A well-known American critic complained that he had wasted his gifts and his time on second-rate stuff. Needless to say, there was a frightful row. He summoned a Press Conference and described the critic, to his face, as 'a musical gunman from Chicago.'

I once asked him why Sibelius was appreciated here and in the United States so much more than on the Continent of Europe, apart from Scandinavia and his native Finland. 'The feeling in France and the Latin countries,' he replied, 'is anti-northern. They want excitement, they want merriment, they want warmth, they want sunshine, they want quick response to quick emotions. You don't get that in Sibelius. What you get in Sibelius, for the greater part of the time, is an extreme reticence and a slow delivery; and that of course is very popular in England, it is our tradition. We get it, possibly, from the Government.'

'Great music,' he went on, 'is that which penetrates the ear with facility, and quits the memory with difficulty. Magical music never leaves the memory.' At once I asked him for a definition of magical music. What I got was interesting. Certain things of Handel and Mozart; the Schubert 'Unfinished', and his great quintet; the end of the *Walküre*—a 'great stroke'; and the middle of the last act of *Tristan*, when he sees the ship approaching—'not the second act which contains a lot of ordinary nineteenth-century romantic music, some of which is pure Liszt.'

He was interesting, too, on the subject of composers he had known, and known well.

About Grieg and his wife, whom he visited at their house near Bergen: 'They were perfectly delightful. Grieg sat down and played me a little piece he had just written, and his wife sang two of his songs. I can say that no one has ever sung his songs half so well. She had a small but beautiful voice and a complete under-standing of mood and nuance—quite unlike certain two-ton sopranos who bawl, scream and shout this enchantingly delicate music.'

About Sibelius: 'I was not surprised that he wrote no more symphonies. I was a little disappointed that he did not continue in his other vein; the symphonic poem, of which he gave us such splendid examples as *En Saga*, and the last one of all, *Tapiola*.

Massenet was 'the most charming of them all,' without envy, spite or malice. Debussy, 'almost dumb'. Ravel, 'lively, with curious musical predilections.' Richard Strauss, 'a very curious man.' Like Delius he had nothing to say about his own music. Delius used to say, 'You play any way you like.' Strauss didn't even say that; he said, 'You play it.' Puccini, on the other hand, talked about the interpretation of his operas at great length, and was 'consumed with profound dissatisfaction at the way his works were given in Italy—notably by the younger conductors, whom he didn't like at all.' In Beecham's opinion Puccini was the most *effective* of all opera composers. His music was quite different from that of anyone else. 'If you were to ask nine operagoers out of ten in any country in the world whose operas they like best, as I have done, the answer would be Puccini—not Wagner or Mozart or Verdi but Puccini. I think it is because he speaks to us personally in a way we understand. This is the opinion of waiters, hotel managers, taxi drivers, bus conductors, anybody you like.'

The vitality and *joie de vivre* never ebbed; but, towards the end, I detected a note of despondency about the future of orchestral playing, and of music in general.

'I like,' he would say, 'a good tune. We don't get them any more.' In his interpretation of Delius he came nearest to purely creative art because, to a degree that no other composer and conductor have ever been, they were inter-dependent; and when he told Cardus that he didn't think our Western civilization would ever again—at least not for a century of time—be refined and civilized in Delius's way, I think he was speaking from the heart. He deplored the reaction against romanticism, launched after the first world war by Constant Lambert, which he regarded as an attack on all works of art which aim at a personal expression of feeling and sensibility in terms of melody, harmony and musical diction that can be understood by the average educated listener; but came to believe that he was fighting a losing battle. I am not at all sure that he was right in this belief. There is, today, a pretty strong reaction against the reaction.

Be that as it may, I was very proud when Lady Beecham told me that he had expressed a wish, more than once, that I should become Chairman of the Royal Philharmonic Orchestra. The last time I saw him he spoke of Delius—a romantic if ever there was one—with all the old passion. 'There is in him so much melody,' he said, 'that you have to keep a tight hold on the melodic line in order to control it. But, if you do that, he is *unique* (this with a crash of clenched fist upon the table); his music, once he found himself, was underivative. He described himself as a conservative anarchist. He owed very little to predecessors. His musical ancestry was lost somewhere in the mists of the past. His vein of inspiration lasted for about ten to twelve years, say, from 1901 to 1914; just as it did in the case of Debussy.'

What more?

About Liszt: 'I know a great many stories. The most interesting of all is, I think, illustrative of his enormous capacity to read music at first sight. It was told to me by Hans Richter who, as a young man, acted as secretary to Richard Wagner, who was living outside Lucerne. For some time there had been a breach between Wagner and the gentleman who was his father-in-law, Franz Liszt, the father of Cosima, whom Wagner ran off with—Liszt did not like that at all; he was angry, and would not speak to him. Richter, who was diplomatic, prevailed upon him to call on Wagner, arousing his interest by saying that he had completed a new opera which he (Richter) had just finished copying out. So Liszt went along, and for a while the atmosphere was very frigid. Then Richter produced an enormous score, saying, "This is the new opera." Liszt looked at it. "Ah, comic opera. You have been studying counterpoint, Richard! I'll see how much you know about it." He then went to the piano, played the overture, looked around, and then continued to play the whole opera *Die Meistersinger* right through, at sight. Extraordinary! Grieg told me that he had done the same thing with his piano concerto. Probably nobody has ever played the piano like Liszt. Somebody once asked him how he was able to play so wonderfully. He said it took him ten years to do it. "But *how* did you do it?" "I did it," he said, "by listening, night after night, to the greatest singers of the day." Now the singers have to listen to instrumentalists to learn *legato*. Times have changed.'

About singers: 'There is not a voice to approach Caruso's. Gigli was a beautiful singer, and just as good an artist; but not the volume of voice, or the same quality of voice. Caruso is preeminent; and when he was young had all the top notes you want in the world, *and* the middle-range lovely register of a light baritone. It was unique. The singers of today have a certain standard of accomplishment. For instance, in the United States there are quite a number of accomplished sopranos. They all sing well, but you can't tell one from t'other. The feature about the great singers of my youth was the remarkably individual character of them all; each one was like nobody else. No one else had a baritone voice like Maurel, nobody had a bass voice like Plancôn, nor was there a mezzo-soprano like Calvé. Caruso was the same, and so was Chaliapin: the standard bass of today is as different from Chaliapin as Westminster Abbey is from Euston Station.'

About television: 'The only thing I can say is that all the music I have ever seen on television looks grotesque. You have pictures, you know, of a gentleman playing the horn and then emptying the liquid out of it on to the floor, which of course may be instructive to some people, but which I think is positively revolting. And then you have somebody sawing away on a bass fiddle. Can you think of anything less picturesque than a huge stringed instrument, called a "bull" fiddle in this country for some strange reason or other, being sawed away on like this? He can only play about ten notes on the damn thing all the time. Or a singer, coming right forward, opening a very large mouth? You see right down the larynx, almost into the tummy, the eyes go this way, the nose goes that way, and the mouth is twisted round: wretched singer, you know, attempting high notes generally outside his or her compass. The whole thing is revolting. That's television, so far as music is concerned.'

And, finally, on gramophone records: 'I have been very much helped by the invention of the gramophone, by listening to records, frequently records of other musicians. It's been of great use to me. Knowing what to avoid.'

In his biography of Delius, published in 1960, Beecham said of his eventual place in music: 'Opinions are bound to differ, and widely. For myself I cannot do other than regard him as the last great apostle in our time of romance, emotion and beauty in music.' This, it seems to me, is too pessimistic a verdict. There will be others. But that the fame of Frederick Delius will endure, I cannot doubt. It will not extend to the United States, or to the Latin countries, where his music is misunderstood—Beecham himself told me that, in America, they could only play him like Tchaikovsky, which was no good. It will rest, I think, not on the major works—not even on the *Mass of Life*—but on the shimmering tone poems which amount to no more (but no less) than rapturous improvisations in which he caught, as no other composer has ever done, the true lyric beauty of English poetry. It has been said of Delius that he was not a simple hedonistic dreamer at the sunset of romanticism, but a poet of the human heart as well as of the moods of nature, who interpreted the one in terms of the other; and who sang not of the unattainable past, but of the marvellous moment— emotional, sensuous, passionate, and, for that reason, somewhat formless and wholly subjective. This I believe to be true. Many of you here tonight will recall Thomas Beecham's playing of *In a Summer Garden* at the Festival, when the ravishing sound he produced reduced his Usher Hall audience to breathless and almost stricken silence. Let us end on that note.

THE MAUGHAM 'LEGEND'

I HAVE always enjoyed the bemused resentment of our professional intellectuals against the success of Mr. Somerset Maugham. Not long ago a distinguished Television Critic wrote: 'It is because Mr. Maugham lacks a compelling sense of the purpose of life that he remains, for me, an unimportant writer.'

I took him up on this point, in a letter to his extremely 'highbrow' newspaper. I asked him to explain, in a few crisp sentences, what compelling sense of the purpose of life animated the short stories of Maupassant and Chekhov, with whom Maugham might reasonably be compared; or the novels of Miss Austen, Thackeray, Balzac and Turgenev; or, indeed, the tragedies of Shakespeare. And added that it was conceivable that there might be no purpose in life. My letter remained unanswered—unless the contention that television must make up its mind whether its prodigious power is to be used to make people 'better' or 'worse' can be counted an answer.

Soon afterwards the *New Statesman* was at it again. The Diary, signed on this occasion by 'Beluncle', said that although Maugham was 'easily the most popular author in the world,' he was also an 'international myth.' It went on to say that he had led no causes, offered no ideals, and created no international scandal; and that, when his scenes were set abroad, they were out of date. He had, therefore, created nothing more than a 'legend'.

Back I came with a letter asking what causes, ideals or international scandals had been 'offered' by a host of writers to whom the designation great could, with general assent, be applied. Again no answer. The critics of Maugham are apt to give up, when pressed.

What, then, is the explanation of the so-called Maugham 'legend'? First, because, as 'Beluncle' himself grudgingly admitted, he is a story-teller of wide range and enormous skill. The British Empire, which was the background of his best stories, and of which he saw more than most of us, no longer exists. But the stories themselves are not out of date. On the contrary, the scenes remain, and also the characters, because they are true to life. If you visit Malaya, Borneo and Hong Kong, as I have done since the war, you can't escape him. At every turn he nudges your elbow, and reminds you of the tales he had to tell. In Singapore *The Letter*. In Malaya *The Book-bag*, a strange and wholly convincing story of an incestuous relationship. In Borneo *The Outstation* and *The Yellow Streak*. I slept in the house where the Resident, Mr. Warburton, had dressed for dinner every night, and meticulously laid out *The Times*, in the right order, to be read at breakfast six weeks later; and I gazed upon the yellow, sluggish river in which Maugham himself so nearly met his death at the hands of the Bore. In Hong-Kong *The Painted Veil*. Everywhere they told me that all the stories had a foundation in truth; and that, at first, they had been bitterly resented. But now, they said, they were proud to have provided the setting for some of the greatest short stories that had ever been written.

You may resent Maugham's final verdict—that, on balance, the English have left behind them a legacy of hatred. But, as with everything he writes, you feel the element of truth; and hesitate to contradict so shrewd and detached an observer.

He once told me that he didn't know why he happened, at the time, to be the most widely read author in the world; but that he suspected that it was because he was born with a dramatic instinct which made what he wrote readable. 'And then, of course,' he added, 'the simple way I write makes it a convenient way to learn English, with the result that for quite a long time boys and girls throughout the East have been learning our language by means of my stories. Though they read them for scholastic reasons, I am assured that they find this not only a task, but also a pleasure.'

It is indeed a pleasure. He takes you right out of yourself. Try him when you are ill, and see how well he does it. If he writes simple English, it can hardly be accounted a crime. He can also write passages of great lyric beauty—for example in *The Narrow Corner*. And, almost always, he holds your interest in a grip from which there is no escape.

Then there is his insight into human nature, often but not always in the raw. It may not cut as deep as that of Proust, but it is almost certainly keener than that of any other living writer. It is only when he deals with mankind, and not with individual characters, that he seems to me to go wrong. For example, at the end of *The Gentleman in the Parlour*, he makes one of his characters say, 'I'll give you my opinion of the human race in a nutshell, brother; their heart's in the right place, but their head's a thoroughly inefficient organ': and admits, in *The Summing Up*, that this is his own conclusion. Surely it is the other way round. They are as clever as monkeys, and as wicked as the Devil in which neither Maugham nor I believe. But he wrote this before the second world war; and, to use one of his favourite expressions, I have a notion that he has since changed his mind.

Finally, there is his own philosophy, which underlies all his work, and which goes far beyond the bridge table and the *savoir-faire* suggested by 'Beluncle'. A philosophy of toleration, sense and sensibility, which makes a growing appeal to millions who are sick to death of the 'smelly little orthodoxies' which George Orwell truly said were now contending for our souls.

As a schoolboy it was my fate to have to watch an entire generation not merely being decimated, but annihilated. This had its effect. By the time I had finished my own military training—I was demobilized on Armistice Day, 1918—I had come to the conclusion reached by Maugham in *Of Human Bondage*—that there is no reason for life, and that life has no meaning. I did not feel, like him, the exhilaration of a new freedom when 'the whole horrible structure, based not on the love of God but on the fear of Hell' tumbled down, for me, like a house of cards. But I read, with savage relish, Audubon's contribution, in the depths of the night, to Lowes Dickinson's *Modern Symposium*; Housman's *Last Poems*;

and A. J. Balfour's final verdict on the present position and future prospects of the human race in his *Foundations of Belief*, which belies the rest.[1]

I don't think I have altered my views much during the past forty years, except in one respect. For better or worse, we are here. Involuntarily, I admit. 'And that alone,' said Audubon, 'is enough to condemn the whole business.' Nevertheless, we might as well try to make it for better. As Lloyd George said, at the outset of his political career: 'I want to make life better, and kinder, and safer—now at this moment. Suffering is too close to me. Misery is too near and insistent. Injustice is too obvious and glaring. Danger is too present.'

But, if we are to make life better, we must face up to it, and live it. This is Maugham's creed. But it goes, also, for those who still believe in God, the Devil and Hell. It was, I think, Lin Yutang who remarked that it seemed odd that the problem of human happiness had been entirely neglected by Christian thinkers; and that the great question that bothered theological minds was not happiness but 'salvation'—a tragic word.

In *The Human Situation* Professor Dixon wrote, with irrefutable logic: 'The first and inescapable question for Christianity, as indeed for all men, is the simple question of acceptance or rejection of life, not as you would like it to be, but as it is…. Tell us, then, whether Christianity stands for living in the present world or against it, for participation or withdrawal, for action or quietism, for taking a share in the shaping of history, in its multifarious and dubious undertakings, a hand in the game, or refusing it. Throughout the history of the Church there has been a halting between two opinions, for co-operation and for withdrawal. It appears improbable that the future will permit the compromise.'

Maugham himself is for participation, and has little interest in the prospect of disembodied personal survival. He believes, as I do, that life itself is governed by blind chance; and that there is no valid explanation of the existence of evil beyond that given by Freud. The 'legend' is not difficult to comprehend if you judge him by his own standards—'The proper aim of the writer of

1. Printed as a postscript to this Essay.

fiction is not to instruct but to please. .... It is an abuse to use the novel as a pulpit or a platform.' He pleases. And he does not preach. What a relief!

POSTSCRIPT

'Man, so far as natural science by itself is able to teach us, is no longer the final cause of the Universe, the Heaven—descended heir of all the ages. His very existence is an accident, his story a brief and transitory episode in the life of one of the meanest of the planets. Of the combination of causes which first converted a dead organic compound into the living progenitors of humanity, science, indeed, as yet knows nothing. It is enough that from such beginnings famine, disease, and mutual slaughter, fit nurses of the future lords of creation, have gradually evolved, after infinite travail, a race with conscience enough to feel that it is vile, and intelligence enough to know that it is insignificant. We survey the past, and see that its history is of blood and tears, of helpless blundering, of wild revolt, of stupid acquiescence, of empty aspirations. We sound the future, and learn that after a period, long compared with the individual life, but short indeed with the divisions of time open to our investigation, the energies of our system will decay, the glory of the sun will be dimmed, and the earth, tideless and inert, will no longer tolerate the race which has for a moment disturbed its solitude. Man will go down into the pit, and all his thoughts will perish. The uneasy consciousness, which in this obscure comet has for a brief space broken the contented silence of the universe, will be at rest. Matter will know itself no longer. "Imperishable monuments" and "immortal deeds", death itself, and love stronger than death, will be as though they had never been. Nor will anything that is be better or be worse for all that the labour, genius, devotion and suffering of man have striven through countless generations to effect.'

It now looks as if this may happen sooner than Balfour thought.

ROBERT BURNS: THE POET AND THE MAN

At St. Andrews, January 1961

For the tenth—and last—time, I rise to propose the toast of the immortal memory of Robert Burns.

Burns was one of those rare phenomena to whom we give the name genius and who, like comets, make their fitful appearance upon the human scene. The son of a small and impoverished tenant farmer, he was born in an Ayrshire cottage which would be condemned by any modern sanitary inspector. In youth, a heavy silent lad without conspicuous ability or literary gifts, although an omnivorous reader; suddenly he breaks into the most exquisite song—as Rosebery said, like a nightingale in the brushwood—and goes on singing, with nightingale pauses, until his death at the age of thirty-seven. Explain this who can.

It is astonishing how much of his best work was produced in the early years, before his visit to Edinburgh. 'The Jolly Beggars', one of the most hilarious outbursts of untrammelled poetic genius that we know of, was written and forgotten before the Kilmarnock edition of his poems appeared—without it; and 'Holy Willie's Prayer', his greatest satiric poem, and one of the great satires of all time, was deliberately omitted. There is, however, enough in the Kilmarnock edition alone to secure for him an undisputed place on Parnassus.

For his own sake we might wish it had ended there; but we could not have afforded to lose him so soon. At Ellisland he proved that his creative power was as great as ever, but his work became more abstract; and so much wider that, more often than not, it reached universality.

Let me touch, to begin with, upon the Kirk satires, because I have been criticized in the past for saying that Burns's greatest single achievement was the emancipation of the Scots from the grim doctrines of Calvinism. I still believe it to be true. It is a fact that undiluted predestination was rejected by the General Assembly of the Church in 1720, sixty-five years before 'Holy Willie's Prayer' was written. But the works of Thomas Boston, that pillar of Auld Licht theology, were printed throughout the eighteenth century; and as late as 1762 a translation of Calvin's *Institutes* was published in Glasgow which, together with all taboos, traditions and emotions aroused, retained a firm grip on the West of Scotland.

What did they amount to? That, as a result of the Fall, man is utterly corrupt; and that this goes for every new-born baby. 'For,' to quote Calvin himself, 'although they have not yet produced the fruits of their own unrighteousness, they have the seed implanted in them. Nay, their whole nature is, as it were, a seed-bed of sin, and therefore cannot but be odious and abominable to God.... We have not the least hesitation to admit what Paul strenuously maintains, that all, without exception, are depraved and given over to wickedness.'

And the answer? Hell for ever, and for all of us except the predestinated Elect of God—by a happy coincidence the Auld Lichts themselves.

Charming, isn't it?

There are those who see in dogmatic Calvinism a certain splendour. For my part, I believe it to be the wickedest creed ever preached to human beings, by comparison with which Marxism positively glows with compassion, humanity and sunshine. Shaw's description in the preface to *Androcles and the Lion* deserves quotation:

'The Holy Ghost may be at work all round producing wonders of art and science, and strengthening men to endure all sorts of martyrdoms for the enlargement of knowledge, and the enrichment and intensification of life ("that ye may have life more abundantly"); but the apostles, as described in The Acts, take no part in the struggle except as persecutors and revilers. To this day, when their successors get the upper hand, as in Scotland and Ulster, heretics are ruthlessly persecuted; and such pleasures as money can purchase are suppressed so that its possessors are compelled to go on making money because there is nothing else to do. And the compensation for all this privation is partly an insane conceit of being the elect of God, with a reserved seat in heaven, and partly, since even the most infatuated idiot cannot spend his life admiring himself, the less innocent excitement of punishing other people for not admiring him, and the nosing out of the sins of the people who, being intelligent enough to be incapable of mere dull self-righteousness, and highly susceptible to the beauty and interest of the real workings of the Holy Ghost, try to live more rational and abundant lives. The abominable amusement of terrifying children with threats of hell is another of these diversions, and perhaps the vilest and most mischievous of them. The net result is that the imitators of the apostles, whether they are called Holy Willies or Stigginses in derision, or, in admiration, Puritans or Saints are, outside their own congregations, and to a considerable extent inside them, heartily detested. Now nobody detests Jesus, though many who have been tormented in their childhood in his name include him in their general loathing of everything connected with the word religion; while others, who know him only by misrepresentation as a sentimental pacifist and ascetic, include him in their general dislike of that type of character.'

There can be no doubt where Burns stood in the matter. In a reference to his boyhood and adolescence he wrote: 'Polemical divinity about this time was putting the country half-mad; and I, ambitious of shining in conversation parties on Sundays between sermons, funerals, etc., used in a few years more to puzzle Calvinism with so much heat and indiscretion that I raised a hue and cry of heresy against me which has not ceased to this hour.'[1]

The attack on the doctrine itself, and the effect of it, should not be underestimated:

1. To Moore, August 2, 1787.

'When from my mither's womb I fell,
Thou might hae plung'd me deep in hell
To gnash my gooms, and weep, and wail,
    In burning lakes,
Whare damnéd devils roar and yell,
    Chain'd to their stakes.'

'Yet I am here, a chosen sample,
To show Thy grace is great and ample:
I'm here a pillar o' Thy temple,
    Strong as a rock,
A guide, a buckler, and example
    To a' Thy flock.'

'Send ane to Heaven an' ten to Hell
    A' for Thy glory,
And no for onie guid or ill
    They've done before Thee.
I, wha' deserv'd most just damnation
    For broken laws
Sax thousand years 'ere my creation,
    Thro' Adam's cause!'

As for Robert Aiken:

'Lord, in Thy day o' vengeance try him!
Lord, visit him wha' did employ him!
And pass not in Thy mercy by them,
    Nor hear their pray'r,
But for Thy people's sake destroy them,
    An' dinna spare!'

But:

'Lord, remember me and mine
Wi' mercies temporal and divine,
That I for grace an' fear may shine
    Excell'd by name;
An' a' the glory shall be Thine—
    Amen, Amen!'

There never has been a more merciless assault upon hypocrisy. For this, of course, was an inevitable consequence of the attempted imposition of a dogmatic theology against which all human nature rebelled, giving rise to that dual personality—public virtue in continuous conflict with private vice—which for two centuries was an integral part of the Scottish character, and is not yet wholly eradicated. You get it in the story of the great Covenanter Thomas Weir, famed for his gift of prayer, who was found guilty at the age of seventy of adultery, incest and other 'horrible crimes', and died impenitent; in that of James Erskine and his friends who 'passed their time in alternate scenes of exercises of religion and debauchery, spending the days in prayer and pious meditation, and their nights in lewdness and revelling'; and, again, in the case of Burns's celebrated contemporary, Deacon Brodie. Only a Scotsman could have written the *Private Memoirs and Confessions of a Justified Sinner*, or *Dr. Jekyll and Mr. Hyde*.

No wonder that Burns went 'mad at their grimaces, their sighin', cantin', grace-proud faces, their three-mile prayers and hauf-mile graces, their raxin' conscience, whase greed, revenge, an' pride disgraces'; and finished them off with four words: 'Waur nor their nonsense.'

His own faith was expressed, with perfect simplicity, in the final stanza of the 'Address to the Unco Guid':

> 'Who made the heart, 'tis He alone
> Decidedly can try us:
> He knows each chord, its various tone,
> Each spring, its various bias:
> Then at the balance let's be mute,
> We never can adjust it;
> What's done we partly may compute,
> But know not what's resisted.'

and in a letter written to Robert Muir on March 7, 1788: 'If we lie down in the grave, the whole man a piece of broke machinery, to moulder with the clods of the valley—be it so; at least there is an end of pain, care, woes and wants: if that part of us called Mind does survive the apparent destruction of the man—away with old-wife prejudices and tales! Every age and every nation has had a different set of stories; and as the many are always weak, of consequence they have often, perhaps always been deceived: a man conscious of having acted an honest part among his fellow-creatures; even granting that he may have been the sport, at times, of passions and instincts; he goes to a great unknown Being who could have no other end in giving him existence but to make him happy [shades of my Rectorial Address!]; who gave him those passions and instincts, and well knows their force.'

I don't know how that strikes you. It's good enough for me. 'Four thousand volumes of metaphysics,' said Voltaire, 'will not teach us what the soul is.' And, despite the millions of words that have been written, and will be written, about the mystery of life and death, I sometimes wonder if there is anything that can usefully be added to this single paragraph.

'The Jolly Beggars' set the tone. There is something here, and in many later poems—for example 'Tam O'Shanter' and 'To a Louse'—beyond satire. Sympathy, and humour stretching out towards anarchy.

The descriptive power is always marvellous, as is the economy of words. Take the opening stanza of 'The Holy Fair':

'Upon a simmer Sunday morn,
    When Nature's face is fair,
I walkéd forth to view the corn,
    An' snuff the caller air.
The rising sun owre Galston muirs
    Wi' glorious light was glintin';
The hares were hirplin down the furrs,
    The lav'rocks they were chantin'
        Fu' sweet that day.'

The scene is etched to perfection by a hand that never falters.

I forbear to quote from the masterpiece. After what must have been careful research and prolonged reflection, 'Tam O'Shanter' was, according to Lockhart, composed in a single day. It is written in octosyllabic couplets—a medium seldom repeated. As a humorous narrative poem it ranks with *Don Juan* and, I think, above it.

His wife, Jean Armour, went to look for him towards evening, and found him near the river shouting the wondrous tale. 'I wish you had seen him,' she said later to a neighbour: 'He was in such ecstasy that the tears were happing down his cheeks.' It is not given to many to witness genius in the throes.

Then the sun began to go down; too soon, but what a sunset! It glowed on until the final visit to Jessie Lewars, who nursed him in his last illness, a few days before he died. She went to the piano and played over several times the tune of an old Scottish song beginning, 'The robin cam' to the wren's nest: and keekit in, and keekit in.' Burns sat down, and in a few minutes produced 'O wert thou in the cauld blast', which Felix Mendelssohn was one day to set to an even lovelier air. It was the last bright flicker of the guttering candle.

There are, I think, several basic reasons for the strange power that Burns continues to exercise over quite simple folk. To begin with, he is the most human, and the most natural, of all the poets. He came from the soil, he drew inspiration from it, and—with one brief and rather unfortunate interlude—he kept close to it all his life. He had no illusions about the technical difficulties of his craft, although he sometimes over-reached himself. 'The world may think slightingly,' he said, 'of the craft of song-writing if they please; but, as Job says, "O that mine adversary had written a book!"—Let them try.' In the main he stuck to recognized stanzas, and to his true course; and expressed himself in terms familiar enough to the only audience he cared to address.

John Drinkwater once defined the lyric as 'the product of the pure poetic energy, unassociated with other energies.' And it is in the songs which he set to the old Scottish melodies, refurbishing and recreating a national folklore which had been shattered and disintegrated by the Reformation and its aftermath, that Burns reached his greatest lyrical heights. To quote a memorable phrase of Harold Nicolson's, they do not often 'reel to the same drunken sense of beauty' as the odes of Keats or the lyrics of Tennyson at his uninhibited best; but sensibility, passion and vitality have seldom been more miraculously blended. 'There is certainly some connection between Love and Music and Poetry,' he wrote in

1783; 'I never had the least thought or inclination of turning poet till I once got heartily in love, and then rhyme and song were, in a manner, the spontaneous language of my heart.' By seizing the present, accepting the reality of a fleeting hour as the moment of truth, and treating it with an incomparable freshness of feeling, he gave expression to human emotions which are fundamental and unchanging; and that is why he lives in all our hearts today. I see him often, in my mind's eye, sitting brooding alone in a corner of the village hall as a young man, while the lads and lassies swung round, under oil lamps, to the gay tunes of the local fiddler:

'Yestreen, when to the trembling string
    The dance gaed through the lighted ha',
To thee my fancy took its wing—
    I sat, but neither heard nor saw;
Tho' this was fair, and that was braw,
    And yon the toast of a' the town,
I sigh'd, and said amang them a',
    "Ye are na Mary Morison".'

Here you get, in a single stanza, the compulsive and obsessive character of love.

Some of the songs are deeply moving:

'O pale, pale now those rosy lips
    I oft ha'e kissed sae fondly!
And closed for aye the sparkling glance
    That dwelt on me sae kindly!
And mouldering now in silent dust
    The heart that lo'ed me dearly!
But still within my bosom's core
    Shall live my Highland Mary.'

Others are gay and care-free:

'It was upon a Lammas night,
    When corn rigs are bonie,
Beneath the moon's unclouded light,
    I held awa to Annie;

> The time flew by, wi' tentless heed,
>   Till 'tween the late and early,
> Wi' sma' persuasion she agreed
>   To see me thro' the barley.
>
> Corn rigs, an' barley rigs,
>   An' corn rigs are bonie;
> I'll ne'er forget that happy night,
>   Among the rigs wi' Annie.'

Others again are shot through with romantic emotion, often amounting to anguish:

> 'Had we never lov'd sae kindly,
>   Had we never lov'd sae blindly,
> Never met—or never parted—
>   We had ne'er been broken-hearted.'

Listen to this:

> 'When I sleep I dream,
>   When I wauk I'm eerie,
> Sleep I can get nane
>   For thinkin' on my dearie.
>
> Lanely night comes on,
>   A' the lave are sleepin',
> I think on my bonie lad,
>   And I bleer my een wi' greetin'.'

And, even more desperate:

> 'Thou hast left me for ever, Jamie,
>   Thou hast left me ever!
> Thou hast left me ever, Jamie,
>   Thou hast left me ever!
> Aften hast thou vow'd that Death
>   Only should us sever;
> Now thou'st left thy lass for ay—
>   I maun see thee never, Jamie
>   I'll see thee never!

Thou hast me forsaken, Jamie,
  Thou hast me forsaken!
Thou hast me forsaken, Jamie,
  Thou hast me forsaken!
Thou canst love another jo,
  While my heart is breaking—
Soon my weary een I'll close,
  Never mair to waken, Jamie,
  Never mair to waken!'

This is vintage Burns. The repeated lines beat with hammer blows upon the heart. He understood women as few men have ever done.

But I should not like to end my song quotations on a note of sadness. Here is the other side of the medal—the happy, if poignant, ending:

'John Anderson my jo, John,
  We clamb the hill thegither,
And monie a cantie day, John,
  We've had wi' ane anither.
Now we maun totter down, John,
  And hand in hand we'll go,
And sleep thegither at the foot,
  John Anderson my jo.'

I must apologize for being unable to read this verse without tears. But I cheerfully conclude this part of my address with:

'To see her is to love her,
  And love but her for ever;
For Nature made her what she is,
  And never made anither.'

Burns was, in fact, the greatest song-writer Britain has ever produced. The directness of his assault, and the universality of his appeal, make it in no way derogatory to describe him as the Puccini of poetry. At the same time he shared with his illustrious compatriot, David Hume, a robust common sense which is never far afield. 'O wad some Pow'r the giftie gie us, to see oursels as others see us:' 'The best laid schemes o' Mice and Men gang aft agley:' 'Facts are chiels that winna ding, and downa be disputed.' When we come across these and other familiar quotations we feel that we are reading proverbs from antiquity translated into verse; and forget that the proverbs as well as the verse are his very own.

His influence on the great English poets who followed him was certainly profound. *Don Juan* owes much to him; and Wordsworth's classic simplicity derives in large measure from one who showed him, in early youth, 'how verse may build a princely throne on humble truth.' So it continues, right through to Housman.

> 'Fresh as the flower, whose modest worth
>   He sang, his genius glinted forth,
> Rose like a star that touching earth,
>   For so it seems,
> Doth glorify its humble birth
>   With matchless beams.'

Such was the judgment of Wordsworth. Compare it with Burns's own epitaph, in the same metre:

> 'Is there a man whose judgment clear,
> Can others teach the course to steer,
> Yet runs, himself, life's mad career,
>   Wild as the wave;
> Here pause—and, thro' the starting tear,
>   Survey this grave.
>
> The poor inhabitant below
> Was quick to learn and wise to know,
> And keenly felt the friendly glow,
>   And softer flame;
> But thoughtless follies laid him low,
>   And stain'd his name.'

'Perhaps the saddest lines in poetry,' commented J. M. Barrie in his Rectorial Address at St. Andrews, 'written by a man who could make things new for the gods themselves.'

It has been said of Burns that his prose equalled his verse, and that his conversation excelled both. A few years ago I re-read the letters in a new edition—appropriately enough in Dumfries. This was an exhilarating experience, not only because of their vigour and terseness of phrase, but because the poems emerge naturally from the text, which provides for them the best of settings.

Let me try to communicate some of my own excitement to you.

On March 11, 1791, he wrote from Ellisland to Alexander Cunningham as follows: 'I have this evening sketched out a song —intended to sing to a Strathspey reel of which I am very fond, "Ballendalloch's". It takes 3 stanzas of 4 lines each to go through the whole tune:

> "Sweet are the banks—the banks o' Doon
>   The spreading flowers are fair,
> And everything is blythe and glad
>   But I am fu' o' care.
> Thou'll break my heart, thou bonie bird,
>   That sings upon the bough;
> Thou minds me o' the happy days
>   When my fause love was true ..." '[1]

Then, on August 30, 1793, we get the following, to George Thomson: 'There is a tradition, which I have met with in many places in Scotland, that the old air, "*Hey tutti taitie*" was Robert Bruce's March at the Battle of Bannockburn—This thought, in my yesternight's evening walk, warmed me to a pitch of enthusiasm on the theme of Liberty and Independence, which I threw into a kind of Scots Ode, fitted to the air, that one might suppose to be the gallant Royal Scot's address to his heroic followers on that eventful morning:

---

1. A later version – 'That sings beside thy mate;
>   For sae I sat, and sae I sang,
>   And wist na o' my fate'
is quite as good, perhaps better.

> "Scots, wha hae wi' Wallace bled,
> Scots, wham Bruce has often led,
> Welcome to your gory bed—
> On to victorie." '

The poem is completed; and the letter ends, 'So may God ever defend the cause of Truth and Liberty, as he did that day!— Amen! R.B.'

Next month comes perhaps the most remarkable letter of all, again to Thomson: 'One more song and I have done. The air is but mediocre: but the following song, the old song of the olden times, and which has never been in print, nor even in manuscript, untill I took it down from an old man's singing, is enough to recommend any air.' Hardly an adequate description of the best-known song that has ever been written by mortal hand. As you read the opening line, 'Should auld acquaintance be forgot,' you can scarcely believe it. There it is, however, as part of the text, in the same bold clear script. And you get, also, the lovely verses that are seldom sung—a typical Burnsian *Recherche du temps perdu*:

> 'We twa hae run about the braes
>   And pu'd the gowans fine;
> But we've wander'd mony a weary foot,
>   Sin' auld lang syne.
>
> We twa hae paidl't i' the burn
>   Frae mornin' sun till dine:
> But seas between us braid hae roar'd
>   Sin' auld lang syne.'

'Tenderness, roughness—delicacy, coarseness—sentiment, sensuality, soaring and grovelling, dirt and deity—all mixed up in one compound of inspired clay!' This was Byron's comment after reading Burns's letters to Robert Cleghorn. It is a characteristic but inadequate verdict. However, the key word is there. Burns was 'inspired' by a daemon which drove him to write, and to act, precisely as he did. Pride and passion were, on his own admission, his great constituent elements; and his aim—'to sing the sentiments and manners he felt and saw in himself and his rustice compeers around him, to transcribe the various feelings—the loves, the griefs, the hopes, the fears—in his own breast.' This is what gives the sense of inevitability to so much of his work. His characters and dialogue are, like those of Shakespeare, level with life.

A word, in conclusion, about Burns the man. At first glance you are struck by the apparent contradiction of his ideas. But gradually, through all the varied moods to which he gave such vivid expression, an underlying unity makes itself felt. The unity born of a mystical love of Nature—'O Nature! a' thy shows and forms to feeling pensive hearts have charms'—and imposed by an unflinching intellectual honesty, an unquenchable thirst for independence, and hatred of cruelty and hypocrisy in any form. The truth is that the mind itself was integral. He saw life from many angles, and in many facets. But he never consciously deceived others, or himself.

It is the revelation of his own personality in all its aspects that constitutes Robert Burns's most signal service to humanity. He concealed nothing. What he thought, felt, and did, he hastened to avow. And he brooked no interference from the Establishment. Read him defiant:

> 'The Kirk and State may join and tell
> To do such things I mauna;
> The Kirk and State may gae to hell,
> And I'll gae to my Anna.'

Read him when he is tolerant, hopeful and wise—as in the 'Epistle to a Young Friend':

> 'The sacred lowe o' weel-plac'd love,
> Luxuriantly indulge it;
> But never tempt th' illicit rove,
> Tho' naething should divulge it;
> I waive the quantum of the sin,
> The hazard of concealing;
> But Och! it hardens a' within,
> And petrifies the feeling!'

Read him in an anarchical mood:

> 'A fig for those by law protected!
> Liberty's a glorious feast!
> Courts for cowards were erected,
> Churches built to please the priest.'

Read him in despair:

> 'God have mercy upon me! A poor, damned, incautious, duped
> unfortunate fool! The sport, the miserable victim of rebellious
> pride, hypochondriac imagination, agonizing sensibility and bed-
> lam passions! I wish that I were dead.'

Gradually the whole man emerges. And what a man!

His life, it seems to me, was from beginning to end an im-
passioned fight for liberty to live. To him the great sin against the
light was the maiming or destruction of individual human personality. Where did this land him? Inevitably, in rebellion. He wrote
—and reflected—against the background of the American Revolution, the French Revolution, an agrarian Revolution, and the
conflict between extremists and moderates within the Scottish
Church which has been aptly described by Professor Thomas
Crawford[1] as a specific and local extension of the general European movement known as 'the Enlightenment'. Apart from 'Tam
O'Shanter', which stands in a class by itself, tension underlies all
the masterpieces because the ideas which he valued, whether
ironically or positively expressed, were in continuous conflict with
forces that would destroy them—the pretensions of the 'unco
guid', the love of money for its own sake, the political power of
the landed aristocracy, and what he called 'the sober gin-horse
routine of existence'. He saw his own people being 'hauden doon'
by a ferocious theology and a political system of which he heartily
disapproved, and the authority for which he emphatically denied.

'A man's a man for a' that', is a clamant assertion of the right to
live, comparable with 'Man is born free, but is everywhere in
chains'. The subsequent impact of this poem upon the minds of
men is a good illustration of the power of human thought when

1. In his admirable Burns: A Study of the Poems and Songs.

ignited by emotion. It had almost as great an effect on the politics of the nineteenth century as Rousseau's *Social Contract* on those of the eighteenth.

That Burns 'sweetened an atmosphere bitter with Calvinism' is not to be denied. Today many of the repressions against which he rebelled have been removed. But we live again in an age of fear; and they have been replaced by other, and even more formidable menaces to the personality and freedom of the individual. Totalitarianism, materialism, virulent nationalism—to name only three —rear their ugly heads on every side. If Burns were still alive, you may be sure he would be in active revolt against them all. He would have led the revolution to free the human spirit from the tyranny of dogma, the tyranny of the machines, and the tyranny of the monolithic State. He would have been the ardent champion of a united Europe, as an essential prelude to the brotherhood of man.

To achieve his own independence Burns was never afraid of putting his head into the collar. His literary output is astonishing. He had a bad farm, but there is no evidence that he was a bad farmer. And as an exciseman he was, according to Findlater, his local supervisor, 'an active, faithful and zealous officer, who gives the most unremitting attention to the duties of his office.'

At the same time: 'I have often coveted the acquaintance of that part of mankind commonly known by the ordinary phrase of blackguards, sometimes farther than was consistent with the safety of my character; those who by thoughtless prodigality or headstrong passions have been driven to ruin; though disgraced by follies, nay sometimes "stained with guilt and crimson'd o'er with crimes", I have yet found among them, in not a few instances, some of the noblest virtues—Magnanimity, Generosity, disinterested Friendship, and even Modesty—in the highest perfection.' Isn't that splendid?

We approach, with dismay, the tragic end. Indeed it is not possible to contemplate the close of Robert Burns's life without feelings of intense emotion. 'Alas! my dear Thomson, I fear it will be some time 'ere I tune my lyre again! "By Babel streams", etc.—Almost ever since I wrote you last, I have only known existence by the pressure of the heavy hand of sickness; and have counted time by the repercussions of pain. Rheumatism, cold and fever have formed, to me, a terrible Trinity in Unity which makes me close my eyes in misery and open them without hope.' And the final *cri-de-coeur* to James Armour: 'Do, for Heaven's sake, send Mrs. Armour here immediately. My wife is hourly expecting to be put to bed. Good God! What a situation for her to be in, poor girl, without a friend! I returned from sea-bathing today, and my medical friends would almost persuade me that I am better; but I think and feel that my strength is so gone that the disorder will prove fatal to me.'

To sum up.

There was a dark side, upon which it is unnecessary to dwell. In an age of hard drinking, he drank—on occasion, and latterly, to his bitter regret. There are also one or two episodes which it is difficult to understand or excuse—for example an incident with his wife, Jean Armour, when she was pregnant, described not only with coarseness but with an unwonted brutality quite alien to his nature; and the lampooning of his old friend Maria Riddel. But in the latter case his pride, always on the alert, had been stung. And they made it up. A fortnight before he died she invited him to dinner. 'I was struck,' she wrote, in a subsequent letter to a friend, 'with his appearance on entering the room. The stamp of death was imprinted on his features. He seemed already touching the brink of eternity. His first salutation was: "Well, madam, have you any commands for the other world?" I replied that it seemed a doubtful case which of us should be there soonest, and that I hoped he would yet live to write my epitaph. He looked in my face with an air of great kindness and expressed his concern at seeing me look so ill, with his accustomed sensibility. We had a long and serious conversation about his present situation, and the approaching termination of all his earthly prospects. He spoke of his death without any of the ostentation of philosophy, but with firmness as well as feeling, as an event likely to happen very soon, and which gave him concern chiefly from leaving his four children so young and unprotected.... Passing from this subject, he shewed great concern about the care of his literary fame, and particularly the publication of his posthumous works. He said he was well aware that his death would occasion some noise, and that every scrap of his writing would be revived against him to the injury of his future reputation. ... The conversation was kept up with evenness and animation on his side. I had seldom seen his mind greater or more collected. There was frequently a considerable degree of vivacity in his sallies, and they would probably have had a greater share, had not the concern and dejection I could not disguise damped the spirit of pleasantry he seemed not unwilling to indulge.'

He did not die of drink, as is generally supposed. He was killed by his doctors; and is not alone in this fate. But when they tried to cure his aching heart, gnawing anxieties and rheumatic fever with port and sea-bathing, his race was run, his message delivered. The bright side overwhelms the dark. He achieved, in his lifetime, greater public recognition than Shakespeare; and there is no parallel to his subsequent fame. He revived the spirit of Scotland after a long night. His voice was heard through the Napoleonic wars into a more enlightened age, and beyond that to our own. It will never be stilled, for it spoke fundamental truths.

So let us leave him tonight—'the piercing eye, the thoughtful brow, the struggling heart.' The greatest Scotsman who has ever lived.

IN MEMORIAM

DUFF COOPER

I HAVE been asked by Diana to say a few words about Duff. It is an almost impossible task, but one that could not be refused. I cannot claim to have been one of his most intimate friends. They belonged to that remarkable generation which met the full impact of the first world war; and hardly one survived it.

This left a deep imprint on the mind of Duff Cooper, as indeed it did upon the minds of all of us who were old enough to see the heroes of our youth consigned to that terrible furnace. Duff passed with great gallantry through it, but the experience struck to the very depths of his soul. He neither forgot nor forgave.

There are only two things that I want to say about him today. The first is that, in an Age once described by the late Lord Baldwin as 'scorched and cynical', he was one of the comparatively few who felt deeply and passionately about public affairs. His sincerity was beyond dispute; and he was also fearless. This gave to his resignation speech that particular quality which will never be forgotten by those who heard it. In conversation he was a fine and intrepid talker, with a capacity for righteous fury which delighted his friends and dismayed only the pompous and the dull.

The second thing I want to mention was his gift, amounting almost to genius, for friendship. The late Charles Masterman gave to Arnold Bennett a great epitaph. When he was dying, he said to his wife: 'If you are in any difficulty or trouble—ever—go to Arnold. He's the man.' That was high praise, and it could be applied in equal measure to Duff. He was absolute for friendship; and at his best in the company of his friends. When he came into a room you felt a glow. You said to yourself: 'This is going to be stimulating and jolly'—and so, unfailingly, it was. Innumerable were the services which he rendered to his friends; and, in the main, unknown. They were not only given on the occasions of the major disasters of life. If any of them said a foolish thing, or wrote a foolish letter—and some of Duff's friends were sadly addicted to both—there was no trouble he would not take to extricate them. Whatever position he might have been holding, he always found time to go and see the man, or the men, or the committee involved, and soothe ruffled feelings and smooth over the difficulties. This cannot be said of everyone.

In his autobiography he referred more than once to autumn, his favourite period of the year.

> We will not weep that spring be past,
> And autumn shadows fall;
> These years shall be, although the last,
> The loveliest of all.

Thus he wrote in the dedication. The years were not vouchsafed, and this must be a matter for regret. But we should mourn, I think, nothing except our own loss. There is much to be thankful for. His marriage was a perfect thing. He wrote books that will live. He was a great Ambassador—one of the very greatest. His political career will be remembered for an act of signal courage when most others are forgotten. Last, but not least, in the setting provided for him by Diana with such loving care, he led a full and rounded life and enjoyed much happiness—more, perhaps, than is given to most of us. For all this he was grateful, and said so; and when the summons came he was ready to go.

(*1954*)

LEWIS NAMIER

FORTY years ago—all but one—I came across a ponderous
figure in the quadrangle of Balliol College, Oxford.
He stood his ground; for Lewis Namier was never one to
run after events or men. But he waved to me; and I walked over
to join him. When I reached his side he said: 'You have been
wasting your time by living a life of pure enjoyment. I am not
against that. But you have done no real work; and, if you want to
get your degree, it is too late for reading or writing.' He gave a
deep sigh, and then added: 'There is now only one hope. Talking.'
'To whom?' I asked. 'To me,' he answered. I consulted the President of my own College[1] about this, and he said: 'It is fortunate
for you that your grandfather, and I myself, were both at Balliol.
Go to Namier.' I went. It was by far the wisest thing I have ever
done in my life.

Lewis Namier was not only a great historian, with a miraculous
power of extracting the root of the matter from a mass of detail,
and avoiding the vague generalizations which too often did duty
before he revolutionized the writing of history. He was also a
great teacher, who could—for example—bring the whole sweep
of the French Revolution into the compass of a single hour of talk
which held you enthralled.

This is not the time, or the place, to attempt an assessment of
his work. But there are two aspects of his character upon which I
wish briefly to touch.

First, his moral courage.

Born the son of a Russian–Polish landowner, educated as a
cosmopolitan Polish gentleman and a Roman Catholic, he became

1. Sir Herbert Warren.

251

—by deliberate choice, and before he was twenty-one—a Jew, in the national but not the religious sense of the term; and a staunch British Imperialist. As such he fought, with passionate conviction, for the causes in which he most sincerely believed. The break-up of the Habsburg Empire. The destruction of Nazi Germany, and all it stood for. And the triumph of Zion. His selfless devotion to the Zionist cause, and the work he did for it, may well have been a loss to history. It was certainly a gain for Israel. And it is notable that all three causes succeeded.

Next, his insight—especially into the complex problems of Europe in the tumultuous and terrible years through which he, and we, have passed. His *Diplomatic Prelude* remains unsurpassed as a study of the origins of the second world war. He may not have possessed Macaulay's gift of sustained and sometimes inaccurate narrative. But everything he wrote was, as Alan Taylor has said, deeply personal. Every sentence reflected the working of a mind of impressive power; and one loaded with thought. The dazzling clarity and the gleaming scholarship were never absent. As a result, he helped to make everything he touched simpler, and easier for all of us to understand.

He had his prejudices. For example, he disliked economics; and whenever I mentioned the subject, as I often did, he used to say: 'Why do you talk to me about economics when you know I hate them?' Nevertheless, the comparison with Keynes stands. What the *General Theory* did for economics the *Structure of Politics* did for history. No historical or economic work will ever be the same again, after the things these two men wrought. And this can be said of no other scholars of our time. By any standards, his achievement was tremendous. And there he stands himself, four-square, in the line of the greatest British historians. When you think of his origins, and of his life, it makes you pause in awe.

Of the man himself I would say only this. He gave affection, and needed it. He found it not only in the love of his wife, and of a close circle of friends, but in the deep admiration of a host of pupils now scattered all over the world. In greater measure, perhaps, than he himself ever realized.

(*1960*)

CLEMENT DAVIES

I WAS proud when I was asked to pay a tribute today to Clement Davies; but to do any kind of justice to a man of his stature in the space of five minutes is extremely difficult. I well know how difficult it is, because I attempted it some time ago, in this very church, on the occasion of the Memorial Service to another old and close friend—Duff Cooper.

The political outlook of these two remarkable men differed greatly; but they had certain qualities in common which go far beyond, and above, politics. To name only four—Courage, Integrity, Sincerity, and a wonderful gift for friendship. Moreover, in the splintering crunch of the greatest crisis in our history they thought, and acted, in harmony.

It is about this crisis that I would now like to say a few words. The world does not yet know the part played by Clem Davies in the crucial events of May 1940. He was too modest to tell the story himself; but one day it will be told. I am not now concerned with the merits of the political argument. He became convinced that only a National Government, in which all parties would serve, could save this country; and, once that conviction laid hold of his mind, his path was guided by a sense of duty—and by that alone.

As a result, he was one of the architects—some may judge the principal architect—of the Government which first saved us from destruction, and then led us to victory.

I was very close to him at this time, because I was Secretary of an All-Party Committee of which he was Chairman; and for two or three critical days he found it convenient to do a good deal of his work in my flat. It was, in fact, this Committee that took the fateful decision to vote against the Chamberlain Government.

Clem Davies had all the qualities necessary for his self-imposed task. He possessed, to a marked degree, the confidence and friendship of the Labour leaders, notably Lord Attlee and the late Arthur Greenwood. Mr. Lloyd George was also his great friend. He was in some doubt about what to do; and it was Clem who went to his room and convinced him that it was his duty to come down to the Chamber, and make what Sir Winston Churchill subsequently described as "his last decisive intervention in the House of Commons".

What struck me most about his conduct throughout this crisis was his utter selflessness. He never thought of himself, he wanted nothing for himself, and took nothing. His only thoughts were for the future of our country, and of our civilization. And this is how it always was with him.

At a later stage he could have had Cabinet office. He refused it because he preferred to lead the Liberal Party, in which he passionately believed, through a dark hour. That he led it with dauntless courage, and no small measure of success, few would now deny.

It was causes that Clem Davies believed in, and for which he always fought. Never himself. One of these causes was a United Europe. But his mind vaulted beyond that. He saw, sooner than most, sooner indeed than many do today, that some kind of World Order or Government will have to be established on this earth before the end of the present century, if the human race is to survive. I have a notion that he regarded his work as President of the Parliamentary Association for World Government as the most important he had ever done.

Finally, to strike a purely personal and human note, he was one of the kindest men I have ever known. He suffered cruel personal misfortunes. With the sustained support of a devoted and wonderful wife, he faced them with a fortitude and courage at which one could only marvel. If others were in trouble they had only to go to him, and be sure of the friendly smile, the firm grip of the hand, and all the help it was in his power to give.

It is on this note that I would wish to end. He was a shining example of simple goodness in a world from which that particular virtue seemed—at the time he played his part on history's stage—to have departed. And this virtue, transcending all others, remained with him to the end of a life dedicated to the public service.

(*1962*)

'THE MATE'

A FEW weeks ago a familiar figure, in a curled billy-cock hat and a coat cut to a fashion that no longer exists, came up to me and said: 'I have got some bad news for you, Mate. I have decided that, if they give me a Memorial Service, you are to make the Address.'

Not unnaturally, I was pleased, because it betokened the friendship of a man whose regard I would rather have had than that of anyone else in the world. Nor was I apprehensive, because not for a long time had I seen him look so well, or in better spirits. Little did I realize that the hour of fulfilment would come so soon.

The career of Sir Jameson Adams was astonishing; and, indeed, unparalleled.

He joined the Merchant Navy in 1893, and the Royal Naval Reserve in 1895. He was one of the last to gain a Master Mariner's Certificate under sail. In 1907 the Captain of H.M.S. *Berwick* sent for him, and said:

'Look here, Adams, put on your frock-coat and sword tomorrow morning, I'm going to take you aboard the *Drake* to see Prince Louis. Arrangements have been made to give you a permanent commission in the Royal Navy with the requisite seniority, and your career is made.' He went down to the wardroom to celebrate; with—in his own words—'the greatest joy in the world'.

Minutes later a signal came from Shackleton, whom he had met only once, two years before, but had talked to for several hours, asking him to go as second-in-command of the *Nimrod* expedition to the Antarctic. Immediately he went up to the bridge and said to the Captain: 'Sir, I've changed my mind: this is my offer and I'm going to take it.'

For what reason? Little interest in the scientific side, or in the theory of meteorology. He didn't even believe that the records he was making could be of any consequence. 'I had an interest,' he said, 'in trying to see that England got where she should get—to the South Pole, and first.' They got within ninety miles.

And then: 'I always remember, on the worst part of the journey, when we were camping up for the night, having had a hell of a day, my book of records blew away, and Shackleton said to me: "You must go after it, Bill; no good going home without the records." So I had to turn to and skid down the crevasses and get my little log-book with all the records in. He appreciated it very much.' I should think he did!

Bill Adams was by nature something of a hero-worshipper; but he gave it, wholeheartedly, to two men alone.

First, to Shackleton. After the return of the *Nimrod* expedition they drifted apart. It was inevitable. Adams went to establish the Labour Exchanges in the north-east of England. Shackleton was lionized by Edwardian society and wanted to make money, and —as Sir Jameson said—'went off lecturing all over the place'. This was no good for 'The Mate', who hated the limelight and avoided it all his life. But the final verdict, given almost half a century later, stands. Shackleton was, in his eyes, 'the greatest leader that ever came on God's earth, bar none.'

Second, to Admiral Sir Horace Hood. He was his Flag-Lieutenant when he commanded the Dover Patrol at the beginning of the first world war; and Sir Jameson was rightly convinced that a great injustice had been done to his Chief when he was relieved of his command in 1915. It was, indeed, the only subject on which I ever heard him speak with bitterness.

Amends were later made to Admiral Hood by the Admiralty, when he was appointed to the command of a Battle-Cruiser Squadron. By this time Sir Jameson had been recalled to do a special job at the Ministry of Munitions; and went on from that to the Naval Siege guns off the Flanders coast, where he won the D.S.O. and the Croix de Guerre.

So it turned out that he escaped death, by a narrow margin, on two occasions. If Shackleton had delayed his decision to turn back by one more hour, they could not have got back. Hood led the Battle Fleet into action at Jutland. If 'The Mate' had still been with him, as he would have wished, he would have gone down in the *Invincible*, standing by the side of his beloved Admiral.

The rest of the story can, and must, be recounted briefly. After the war he returned to the Ministry of Labour, as controller of the north-eastern division. He cared, passionately, about the ravages of sustained mass unemployment; and, above all, its effect upon the young generation. He concentrated his energies upon the promotion of emigration to the Colonies, and the Boys Club Movement. His success, achieved by sheer energy and force of personality, was never in doubt. The Duke of Windsor once told me that no one made him work harder, as Prince of Wales, than Sir Jameson Adams; and that was saying a lot.

In 1935 he was appointed Secretary to King George's Jubilee Trust; and this was yet another success story. I need hardly say that the second world war found him back with the Royal Navy, in Contraband Control, first at Aden, later in Gibraltar.

We come, now, to the last phase of his almost incredible life. As Honorary Appeals Secretary to the King Edward VII Hospital —or, as I prefer to call it, Sister Agnes's—he raised a sum of money which must have amounted to something in the neighbourhood of half a million pounds. It is today a living, and permanent, memorial to him, and to his life's work.

'I am not a bad beggar,' he once said—he might just as easily have used another, and not dissimilar word. It was an understatement. I wonder if any man has ever raised so much money for charitable purposes, by his own unaided efforts; and taken nothing—but nothing—for himself. You and I know how exhausting it is to visit patients in hospital, even when they are our best friends. He did it every day; bringing hope, comfort, and cheer to all.

I vividly remember his saying to me, about four or five years ago, when I was ill—and felt it: 'You don't look very well, Mate. I think you'd better come back to "the Dump" for a bit. We'll do our best to stop you killing yourself. And if we fail'—this with a twinkle in his eye—'the box is always ready.' From that moment I never looked back.

Loving and lovable; courageous and kind; trenchant and humorous; rough and tender; pirate and saint; a life of selfless devotion to the service of others; and, underlying it all, a heart of pure gold. You can hardly beat that.

We therefore do well to pay tribute to the memory of this extraordinary man, who had no enemies, and countless friends.

(*1962*)

CHAIM WEIZMANN

I AM very conscious that I stand today, as I have always stood with Chaim, in the presence of greatness of a kind which I have never encountered in any other human being; and that there is not much that I can say. His spirit broods over this place, and over this land; making silence more becoming than chatter. It was the same when he was alive. I am not by nature modest or retiring. Usually I talk a great deal, and think that I talk rather well—more sense than the others. With Chaim it was different. When I was with him I never wanted to talk. I just wanted to listen.

All I really want to do, at this moment, is to stand beside his grave and think. For at no period in the world's history has the distilled wisdom that was his most priceless possession been more urgently required. If I am here, talking, it is simply because he was, to me, a wonderful friend, in good times and in bad. A friend whom I both venerated and loved.

The eyes, at times, were tragic, as well they might be. But it would be a great mistake to regard Chaim Weizmann as a tragic figure. He saw life with the perspective that a rich and pervading, if somewhat sardonic, sense of humour alone can bring. The secret of his overwhelming charm lay in the fact that he was, at heart, an amused and amusing man. Once, when he was attending an international conference of Jews in Switzerland, in an atmosphere charged with emotion, and at which he thought a lot of nonsense was being talked, he turned to a great friend of his, of mine, and of Israel, and said: 'This is when all my latent anti-semitism rises to the surface!'

The State of Israel is the product of what we are still—but only just—able to call the conscience of Western civilization. Weizmann pricked it into life; and kept it alive for thirty years. Scientist, philosopher, statesman—he was all of these; and not one of them could be separated from another. It followed, inevitably, that when he came to deal with the harsh realities of politics he was a pragmatist and a gradualist. That is why he accepted, in place of the original Balfour Declaration which was clear and specific, a Declaration which could mean nothing—or everything. 'It is one of the "ifs" of history,' he subsequently wrote, 'whether we should have been intransigent, and stood by our guns. ... Or would the Government have become wearied of these internal Jewish divisions, and dropped the whole matter? Our judgment was to accept, to press for ratification.'

History must surely judge that, in the light of events, he was right. The Western world, under the leadership of the Great Power which had conquered Palestine, was willing to listen to him, and to be convinced by him, in 1917. Confronted by a violent conflict between the Jewish assimilationists and the Zionists, it would not, I think, have listened for long. Within three years the Russian revolution became a reality, and the tide of Arab nationalism had been set in motion by the Wilsonian doctrine of 'self-determination'. If Weizmann had not persuaded the British Government to make the Balfour Declaration at that particular moment of time, and then to accept the Mandate and create a British Protectorate in Palestine, the Zionist Movement would almost certainly have been crushed between these two forces.

As it was, although he did not foresee the outcome with any precision—it was not of his making, and not what he most desired —he knew that if he could get the Jewish Agency rightly constituted the problem of the Homeland versus the State would be solved by events; and that the Zionist cause would ultimately prevail.

He did it with only weeks to spare. The verdict of Richard Crossman cannot be challenged. 'Without the personality of Weizmann there would have been no Balfour Declaration and no Mandate. ... The supreme justification of Weizmann as a Jewish statesman is that the spell he cast gave the Yishuv just enough time. When it failed, his own people had grown up to the point where they were strong enough to disown him as pro-British, and accept as leaders men fitted not to charm the British but to get rid of them.'

Weizmann had one final and signal service to render to Israel. If the war of independence was to be won it was essential to secure a majority decision of two-thirds in favour of partition at the United Nations. I happened to be in New York at the time. I saw him there; and can testify that, on more than one occasion, his personal influence at Lake Success was decisive.

After that it was time for him to hand over the reins of political power to David Ben-Gurion; and to give, as President, the immense prestige of his name and world-wide fame to the State which his vision and sagacity had done so much to create. The miracle had been achieved. The memorial is here, at Rehovoth. And it is not unworthy of him.

What of the future? I know only that the children of Israel are back again; and that, in the last resort, you must fight or swim. And, as Ben-Gurion once said to me: 'We are not going to swim.' I hope and pray and believe that it will never come to that. But I am not, like Chaim, a prophet, a mystic, or a dreamer of dreams that come true. All I can do is to quote his last words to Meyer Weisgal, and beg of you to heed them: 'I have loyal friends, more than I deserve. Tell them not to permit the destruction of the thing we have laboured to build. We Jews can do something very good, something which can be an honour to us all and to mankind. But we mustn't spoil it. We are an impetuous people, and we spoil and sometimes destroy what has taken generations to build up.'

Let me take my leave with a verse from the psalm which all of us sing: 'Behold, he that keepeth Israel shall neither slumber nor sleep.'

November 1960.

SELECT BIBLIOGRAPHY

Amery, L. S. *Thoughts on the Constitution*, Oxford University Press (1947).

Beecham, Sir Thomas. *Frederick Delius*, Hutchinson (London, 1960).

Cardus, Neville. *Sir Thomas Beecham: A Memoir*, Collins (London, 1961).

Carr, E. H. *Conditions of Peace*, Macmillan (London, 1942).

Churchill, Winston. *The World Crisis*, 6 vols., Thornton Butterworth (London, 1923-31).

- *The Second World War*, 6 vols, Cassell (London, 1948-54).

Crawford, Thomas. *Burns: A Study of the Poems and Songs*, Oliver & Boyd (Edinburgh, 1960).

Crossman, Richard. *The Charm of Politics*, Hamish Hamilton (London, 1958).

Dalton, Lord, memoirs in 3 vols., *Call Back Yesterday, The Fateful Years*, and *High Tide and After*, Muller (London, 1953-62).

Dixon, W. Macneile. *The Human Situation: The Gifford Lectures delivered in the University of Glasgow, 1935-37*, E. Arnold (London, 1937).

Drucker, Peter. *The Future of Industrial Man*, Heinemann (London, 1943).

Fenby, Eric. *Delius as I Knew Him*, Quality Press (London, 1949).

Halifax, Lord. *Fulness of Days*, Collins (London, 1957).

Humphreys, Sir Travers, Foreword to *The Trials of Oscar Wilde* (ed. H. Montgomery Hyde) in *Notable British Trials* series, Hodge (London, 1948).

Keynes, J. M. *The Economic Consequences of the Peace*, Macmillan (London, 1919).

- *Essays in Persuasion*, Macmillan (London, 1931).

- *Essays in Biography*, Macmillan (London, 1933).

Luthy, Herbert. *The State of France*, trans. from German: Secker & Warburg (London, 1955).

MacLaughlan, D. (editor). *Defence in the Cold War*, Royal Institute of International Affairs (London, 1950).

Macleod, Iain. *Neville Chamberlain*, Muller (London, 1961).

Mantoux, E. *The Carthaginian Peace*, Oxford University Press (1933).

Millin, S. G. *General Smuts*, Faber (London, 1936).

Namier, Sir Lewis. *The Structure of Politics at the Accession of George III*, Macmillan (London, 1957).

Snow, Sir Charles. *Science and Government*, Oxford University Press (1961).

Steen, Marguerite. *A Pride of Terrys*, Longman (London, 1962).

Walker, Kenneth. *The Physiology of Sex*, Penguin Books, Pelican Books No. 71 (London, 1940).

Ward, Barbara. *The West at Bay*, Allen & Unwin (London, 1948).

Westwood, Gordon. *Society and the Homosexual*, Gollancz (London, 1952).

Wrench, Sir Evelyn. *Geoffrey Dawson and Our Times*, Hutchinson (London, 1955).

Young, G. M. *Stanley Baldwin*, Hart-Davis (London, 1952).